GCSE English

Complete Revision and Practice

Contents

Contents

Published by Coordination Group Publications Ltd.

Editor:
Chrissy Williams

Contributors:
Adrian Burke, Taissa Csáky, Chris Dennett, Margaret Giordmaine, Dominic Hall, Kerry Kolbe, Abigail Lear, Jill Lessiter, Tim Major,
Becky May, Katherine Reed, Tim Scott, Rachel Selway, Julie Schofield, Audrey Sullivan, Claire Thompson, Sharon Watson,
Erika Welham, Lynn Weston.

With thanks to Rosamund Miles and Anne Thomas for the proofreading.

AQA (NEAB) / AQA examination questions are reproduced by permission of the Assessment and Qualifications Alliance.

Edexcel (London Qualifications Ltd) examination questions are reproduced by permission of London Qualifications Ltd.

OCR examination questions are reproduced by permission of OCR.

Please note that AQA questions from pre-2003 papers are from legacy syllabuses and not from the current specification.
CGP has carefully selected the questions contained in the practice exam to cover subject areas which are still relevant to the
current specification. As such the exam provides a good test of your knowledge of the syllabus areas you need to
understand to get a good grade in the real thing.

ISBN 1 84146 372 8
Website: www.cgpbooks.co.uk
Printed by Elanders Hindson, Newcastle upon Tyne.
Clipart source: CorelDRAW

What You Have To Do

The course is split into three parts.

1 — The Exams

This is the 'meat' of the exams:

| **LITERATURE ESSAYS** | Answer questions about the <u>poetry</u>, <u>prose</u> or <u>drama</u> that you've been studying in class. They could cover characters, style, tone, themes etc. |

| **EXPLAINING ESSAY** | <u>Explain</u> or <u>describe</u> something to the reader, or <u>inform</u> them about something. |

| **ARGUING ESSAY** | <u>Argue</u> a particular point and <u>persuade</u> readers to agree with a point of view, or <u>advise</u> readers about something. It needs strong persuasive writing skills. |

| **DIFFERENT CULTURES** | Write about poems or short stories by writers from outside the UK. |

| **RESPONDING TO UNSEEN TEXTS** | <u>Read</u> a piece of text in the exam (often a magazine or newspaper article) and then answer questions in <u>response</u> to it. |

2 — Coursework

There shouldn't be any sweaty-palm moments here.

| **LITERATURE ESSAYS** | Same as above — write essays about the <u>texts</u> you've studied in class. This time, though, you'll have lots more time to think about it and make it extra brilliant. One of them will have to be about a Shakespeare play. |

| **ANALYSING ESSAY** | <u>Analyse</u> and <u>comment</u> on something, or <u>review</u> something. (Some exam boards do this part in an exam essay rather than in coursework — check with your teacher.) |

| **ORIGINAL WRITING** | Write <u>creative</u>, <u>imaginative</u> and <u>entertaining</u> stories about whatever takes your fancy really (although usually within some kind of guidelines). Sometimes you're asked to write in a certain style, e.g. for a newspaper. |

3 — Listening and Speaking

This part might not feel like an exam — but it's just as important to do well in it.

| **SPEAKING AND LISTENING EXERCISE** |

Communicate ideas by speaking. This could be tested through a <u>drama-based</u> activity, a <u>group</u> activity (e.g. a debate), an <u>individual presentation</u> or a combination of the three.

Stick with this revision guide, and your exams will be just fine

Talking about exams isn't the nicest way to start a book, but it's good to know exactly what's coming. It's going to get nicer — just go through the book page by page.

Planning

You've got to make a plan for every single essay you ever write, whether it's for coursework or the exams. That's a plan on paper — not in your head. There are no shortcuts with planning.

Decide What to Say *Before* You Start

You have to have a good think about what you're going to write about <u>before</u> you start — otherwise your ideas won't follow a clear structure and you'll lose marks.

Good writing <u>makes a point</u>. It doesn't just ramble on about nothing.

Whatever kind of essay you're writing, make sure you've got <u>enough ideas</u> to keep you writing till your time's up — without having to waffle. Waffle won't get you any marks at all.

Write Your Points Down On Paper

1) Jot down a <u>plan</u> of the points you want to make before you start writing.

2) That way you won't get to the end and realise you've <u>forgotten</u> something.

3) Don't bother writing your plan in proper sentences — it's a waste of time.

4) In the exams spend <u>5 MINUTES</u> planning every essay.

Q. Write an article for a newspaper about an issue that's important to you. Explain why you think the issue is important.

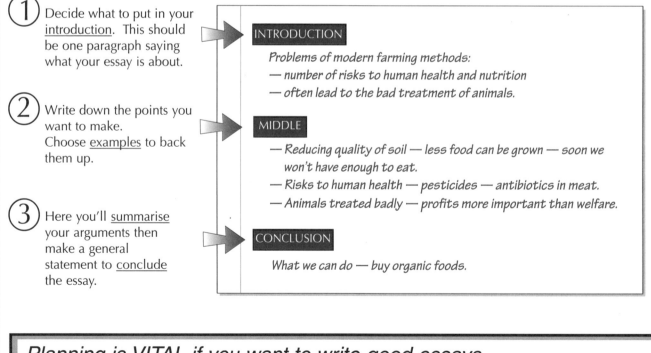

① Decide what to put in your <u>introduction</u>. This should be one paragraph saying what your essay is about.

INTRODUCTION

Problems of modern farming methods:
— number of risks to human health and nutrition
— often lead to the bad treatment of animals.

② Write down the points you want to make. Choose <u>examples</u> to back them up.

MIDDLE

— Reducing quality of soil — less food can be grown — soon we won't have enough to eat.
— Risks to human health — pesticides — antibiotics in meat.
— Animals treated badly — profits more important than welfare.

③ Here you'll <u>summarise</u> your arguments then make a general statement to <u>conclude</u> the essay.

CONCLUSION

What we can do — buy organic foods.

Planning is VITAL if you want to write good essays
Once you've done a plan, you're ready to start writing your essay. Planning gets the tricky thinking out of the way, so you can make the best use of your actual writing time.

Starting Your Essay

You need to write a clear and punchy introduction to your essay — no waffle allowed.

Start With a Good Introduction

In your introduction you must introduce the <u>overall point</u> that your essay is making — and do it clearly.

The introduction gives a <u>brief answer</u> to the question.
The rest of the essay <u>expands</u> on your answer and gives <u>evidence</u> for it.

Q. Why do you think Harper Lee chose Scout as the narrator in *To Kill A Mockingbird*?

It's fine to make a <u>personal statement</u> in the introduction. Just don't keep using "I" all the way through the essay (see P. 6).

It makes it easier to answer the question if you use <u>similar wording</u> to that of the original question.

<u>I believe</u> that <u>Harper Lee chose Scout as the narrator in *To Kill A Mockingbird*</u> <u>because her youthful innocence provides a contrasting backdrop against which the story's themes of prejudice and hate can unfold</u>.

You've said what you think and <u>clearly answered the question</u>. The rest of the essay can now back this up with examples from the text.

Grab the Reader's Attention at the Start

There are three ways to make the introduction grab the examiner's attention:

Q. Is testing beauty products on animals justified? Write an essay giving your opinion.

1) Use <u>strong, emotive language</u> to get your opinion across, especially in persuasive essays.

   Testing beauty products on animals is an <u>unforgivable</u> and unjustifiable <u>evil</u> in this so-called age of technology. It is a <u>bitter reminder</u> of the human race's <u>obsession</u> with vanity.

2) Say something <u>controversial</u>. You'll only lose marks if you can't back it up.

   Use forceful language in your statement as long as you back it up.

   Testing beauty products on animals is <u>too often written off as being unjustified</u>. In the developed world, we expect a certain standard of living and, <u>without animal testing, our lives would be significantly less easy</u>.

3) Start with a <u>short, quirky statement</u> for immediate impact.

   <u>Animals do not use beauty products</u>. With this in mind, it seems unjustified that they should suffer for the continued development of such products.

A good introduction will really impress an examiner

Examiners have to mark lots of papers. If you can make yours stand out from the start, they'll <u>want</u> to give you marks for making their job less dull. It's worth trying to make it really good.

Paragraphs

It is easy to forget to start new paragraphs in an exam,
but you must use them properly if you want to get a C or above.

Paragraphs Make Your Writing Clearer

1) A <u>paragraph</u> is a group of sentences. These sentences are about the same thing, or follow on from each other.

2) All of the sentences in a paragraph are <u>related</u> to each other.

3) You need to start a new paragraph every time <u>something new</u> has happened.

> ...before he went home.
> The street was quiet and very dark. Alex walked on tiptoes, trying to make as little noise as possible. He kept wondering what might be lurking around the next corner.
> Suddenly Alex heard a noise. He stopped dead and stood still, trying to work out who else was there.

The <u>ideas</u> in this paragraph are all about Alex walking down the street. When something new happens, you start a <u>new paragraph</u>.

Start a New Paragraph Every Time Something Changes

Each Time a New Person Speaks

"I'll find him," muttered Donald. "He won't get away this time."

"What makes you so sure?" asked Mickey.

"What's going on, guys?" A figure stepped out of the darkness. It was Her.

Someone new is <u>speaking</u> so you need to change paragraph.

When You Start Writing About a Different Time

The first paragraph is about <u>five o'clock</u>.

This one's gone forward to a <u>different time</u>.

By five o'clock, Edwin was angry. Shirley was late again, and the flower he'd bought was starting to droop.

Six o'clock came, and still she didn't appear. Enough was enough. Stuffing his flower into a rubbish bin, Edwin went home.

Three years before, Edwin had been stood up. He had never seen or heard from the girl again, and he didn't fancy going through another emotional crisis.

Here's one about the <u>past</u>.

When You Start Writing About a New Place

This paragraph is about the playing fields.

The playing fields were quiet and peaceful. There was no one around except Pete. He listened to the song of the distant birds and sighed happily.

Further down the valley, a huge cloud of dust rose into the summer sky, as the storm gained in power and advanced towards a blissfully unaware Pete.

Here's a new paragraph because this is happening <u>somewhere else</u>.

When You Talk About a New Person

This paragraph is about Liam.

Liam sat on the side of the stage. He couldn't believe it. His guitar was broken, and without it he wouldn't be able to play at the school concert.

Then he saw Keith. Keith was a skinny, ill-looking boy who always got picked on. He was carrying an enormous guitar case.

Time for a new paragraph — there's a <u>new person</u>.

Learn when you need to start new paragraphs

Remember, start a new paragraph whenever you change the person speaking, the people, the place or the time. You've got to do it to keep the examiners happy.

Paragraphs

Knowing when to use paragraphs will only get you so far.
To get an A*, A or B you've got to make your paragraphs flow on from each other.

Each Paragraph Needs a **Clear Topic**

Make only <u>one point</u> in each paragraph. You'll lose marks if the examiner can't follow your argument.

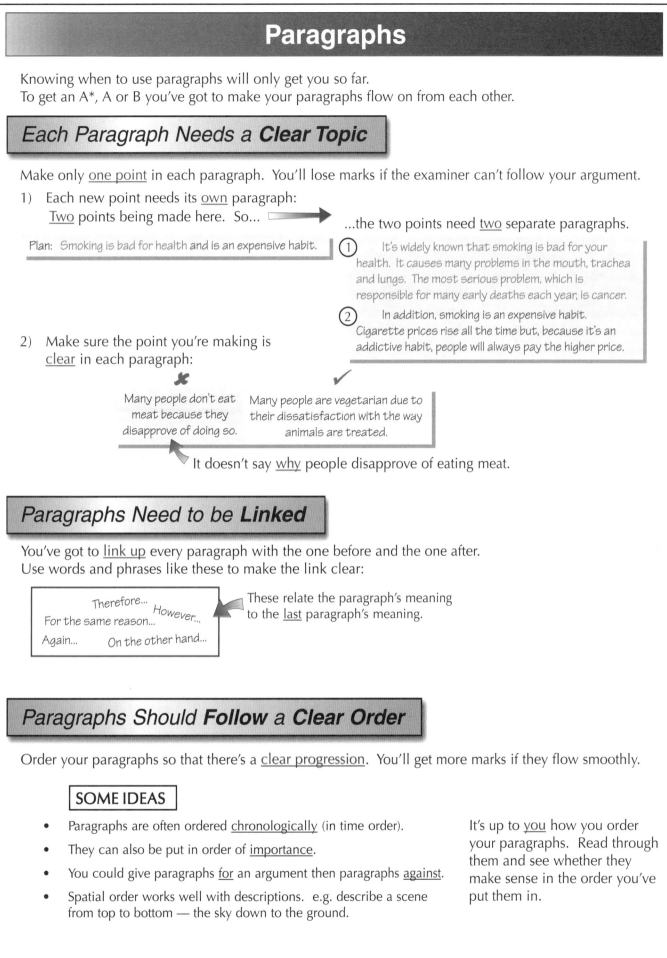

1) Each new point needs its <u>own</u> paragraph:
   <u>Two</u> points being made here. So... →   ...the two points need <u>two</u> separate paragraphs.

Plan: Smoking is bad for health and is an expensive habit.

① It's widely known that smoking is bad for your health. It causes many problems in the mouth, trachea and lungs. The most serious problem, which is responsible for many early deaths each year, is cancer.

② In addition, smoking is an expensive habit. Cigarette prices rise all the time but, because it's an addictive habit, people will always pay the higher price.

2) Make sure the point you're making is <u>clear</u> in each paragraph:

✗ Many people don't eat meat because they disapprove of doing so.

✓ Many people are vegetarian due to their dissatisfaction with the way animals are treated.

It doesn't say <u>why</u> people disapprove of eating meat.

Paragraphs Need to be **Linked**

You've got to <u>link up</u> every paragraph with the one before and the one after.
Use words and phrases like these to make the link clear:

Therefore... However...
For the same reason...
Again... On the other hand...

These relate the paragraph's meaning to the <u>last</u> paragraph's meaning.

Paragraphs Should **Follow** a **Clear Order**

Order your paragraphs so that there's a <u>clear progression</u>. You'll get more marks if they flow smoothly.

SOME IDEAS

- Paragraphs are often ordered <u>chronologically</u> (in time order).
- They can also be put in order of <u>importance</u>.
- You could give paragraphs <u>for</u> an argument then paragraphs <u>against</u>.
- Spatial order works well with descriptions. e.g. describe a scene from top to bottom — the sky down to the ground.

It's up to <u>you</u> how you order your paragraphs. Read through them and see whether they make sense in the order you've put them in.

Paragraphs — just do it
Paragraphs give structure to your essay and break it into separate points so it's easier for the examiner to read — which is great. I can't emphasise enough how important it is to use them.

Formal and Informal Language

In general essays, you'll get more marks if you use formal language. You have to use it if you want to get more than a D. BUT you need to know when to use informal language too.

Write in *Formal Language*

Using formal language means doing certain things:

1) Be accurate and <u>concise</u>. Don't be chatty — that means no slang:

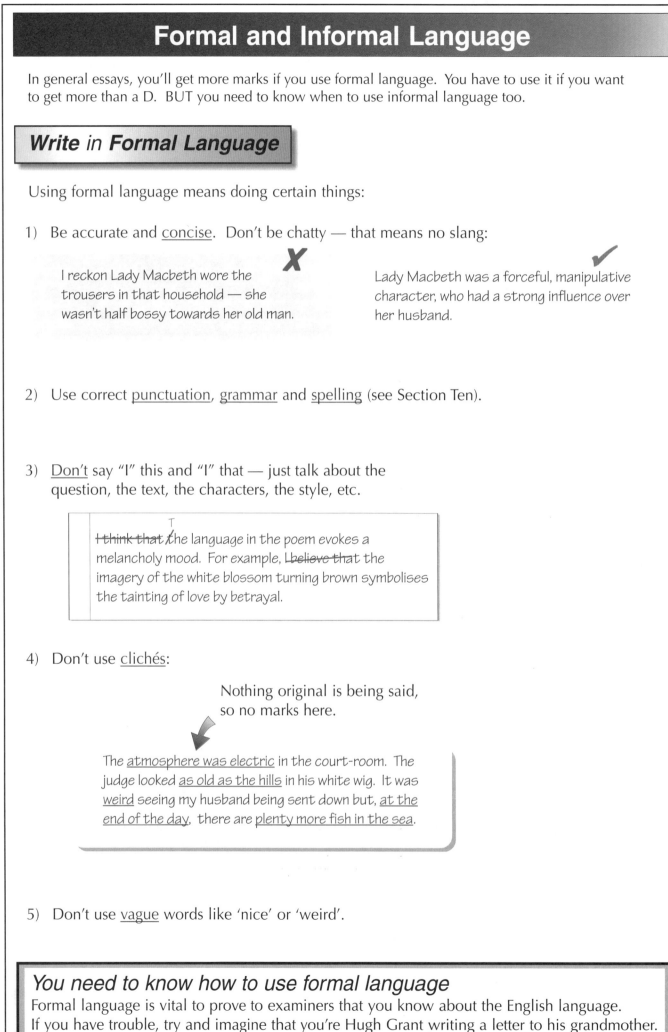

> I reckon Lady Macbeth wore the trousers in that household — she wasn't half bossy towards her old man.

✗

> Lady Macbeth was a forceful, manipulative character, who had a strong influence over her husband.

✔

2) Use correct <u>punctuation</u>, <u>grammar</u> and <u>spelling</u> (see Section Ten).

3) <u>Don't</u> say "I" this and "I" that — just talk about the question, the text, the characters, the style, etc.

> ~~I think that~~ ᵀhe language in the poem evokes a melancholy mood. For example, ~~I believe that~~ the imagery of the white blossom turning brown symbolises the tainting of love by betrayal.

4) Don't use <u>clichés</u>:

Nothing original is being said, so no marks here.

> The <u>atmosphere was electric</u> in the court-room. The judge looked <u>as old as the hills</u> in his white wig. It was <u>weird</u> seeing my husband being sent down but, <u>at the end of the day</u>, there are <u>plenty more fish in the sea</u>.

5) Don't use <u>vague</u> words like 'nice' or 'weird'.

You need to know how to use formal language

Formal language is vital to prove to examiners that you know about the English language. If you have trouble, try and imagine that you're Hugh Grant writing a letter to his grandmother.

Formal and Informal Language

Only Use *Informal Language* When It *Suits The Task*

1) Use formal language for all <u>general</u> essays. BUT — sometimes you'll be asked to write in a certain style, e.g. for a tabloid newspaper. Here you're being tested on how well you <u>adapt</u> your style to suit your audience — and formal language won't always be appropriate:

> Q. Write an article for a tabloid **OR** broadsheet newspaper about government plans to impose road tolls.

TABLOID

> The government has come up with yet another 'foolproof' plan to get cars off the roads — but it means that drivers had better start saving their pennies.
> People are fuming at the new plans to make drivers pay road tolls. Do politicians really think such an unpopular scheme will work?

Need to adapt the language by being less formal.

BROADSHEET

> Following lengthy discussions, the government has disclosed plans for a new solution to the problem of overcrowded roads in Britain: the construction of toll-roads. The proposals have proved unpopular with many road users, who doubt its potential for success.

Formal language is OK here.

2) In <u>original writing</u> you're expected to write in a more creative way — i.e. NOT in formal language. You'll be marked on how well you create moods and feelings with your words.

The words create an eerie mood.

> The wind screamed through the trees, whipping branches into a frenzy and scattering leaves into the air in a manic, whirling dance.

> The gale-force wind caused branches to move considerably and leaves to fall to the ground.

Formal language just doesn't have the same mood-creating effect.

Informal language is fine — only if you use it AT THE RIGHT TIME

Be aware of what things are written in formal language, and what kinds of things are written in informal language. Think about the language for everything you read — it's great practice.

Giving Evidence and Quoting

You MUST give evidence for what you say and you have to quote your sources of evidence.

Give an **Example** Every Time You Make a **Point**

If you <u>don't</u> give examples for what you write, the examiners can't tell if you know what you're talking about. They're not going to give you marks for something which could just be completely made up.

> The woman was cruel to her dog.

This answer <u>doesn't</u> give any reasons...

...but this answer gives <u>examples</u> to justify the point it makes. That's a lot better.

> The woman was cruel to her dog. She kept him chained up in the sun all day, with very little food and no water.

Not giving examples to back up your points is the road to <u>losing</u> a lot of marks.

Use the 4 Rules for **Quoting**

<u>Quoting</u> means using someone else's words to back up your arguments.
Put <u>quotation marks</u> (" ") round quotes to separate other people's words from your words.

1) Use <u>exactly</u> the same words and punctuation as the person you're quoting used.

2) Always keep the same <u>meaning</u> — e.g. you couldn't quote *"she approved of the idea"* if the original was *"she pretended that she approved of the idea."*

3) Always say <u>where</u> you got the quote from. This means putting who said the quote and when they said it in brackets after it: *"Vegetarians are healthier than meat-eaters" (The Vegetarian Society, 2002).*

4) You don't need quotation marks if you <u>rephrase</u> someone else's words:

Jan says, "**Reading greatly improves vocabulary.**"

Direct quote ➤

Jan claims a good way to improve vocabulary is through reading.

➤ Rephrased words

Writing Must *Flow* Around *Quotes*

✗ Doesn't make much sense

> A representative said, "Encouraging children to explore drama is our top priority." The board has agreed to finance the drama workshops.

✔ Ideas flow much better

> The board has agreed to finance the drama workshops. A representative said, "Encouraging children to explore drama is our top priority."

Insert <u>short</u> quotes into your paragraphs (as in the example above). BUT — <u>long</u> quotes need their own paragraph. They don't need quotation marks but they do still need to be cited:

> ...blah blah blah blah blah blah blah:
>
> Quote quote quote quote quote quote quote quote quote quote quote quote quote quote.
> (Spencer 2001, 2)
>
> Blah blah blah blah blah blah blah blah blah blah blah blah blah...

Leave a line above and below the quote.

"Use quotes — they're great" (CGP, 9th April 1604)
You'll definitely improve your grade if you make sure you put loads of good examples and quotes in your answers. It proves that you're making a strong, authoritative argument.

Concluding and Checking

You've got to conclude your essay and check it over — but it shouldn't be a last-minute rushed job. You'll pick up lots more marks by doing it thoroughly and carefully.

Bring Together the Key Points In Your Conclusion

1) Start a new paragraph by going back to the original question.

2) Restate the main points of your essay briefly. This makes it clear how you've answered the question. Don't go on and on, though. Be focused.

> For many, there is no disputing the fact that backpacking is by far the best way to travel round different countries. It gives you the flexibility and freedom to travel wherever you please, and it's great for meeting interesting fellow travellers along the way. It is also the cheapest form of travelling and allows those who would otherwise be unable to afford it to visit far-flung countries . It's good to know that, in a world where money and luxuries seem to rule, people still find the 'back to basics' lifestyle appealing.

3) Once you've summed up, write a final sentence to conclude.

Check Over Your Essay When You've Finished

1) Leave time at the end to read through your essay. Check that it makes sense, that you haven't got any facts wrong, and that it says what you want it to say.

> Macbeth
> (Mcbath)

2) Check the grammar, spelling and punctuation. If you find a mistake, put brackets round it, cross it out neatly with two lines through it and write the correction above.

3) If you've written something which isn't clear, put an asterisk (*) at the end of the sentence. Put another asterisk in the margin beside the sentence, and write what you mean in the margin.

> *He had him killed. | Macbeth wasn't nice to Banquo.*

4) If you realise you should have started a new paragraph, put "//" to show where it starts.

> while Tony's swan glided smoothly into position. //Shortly before dawn, the lake

Don't Panic If You Realise You've Gone Wrong

If you realise you've forgotten something obvious, write a note about it at the bottom of the final page, to tell the examiner. You'll get marks for noticing your mistake.

Never cross out your whole essay if you realise it's wrong. Don't panic, just continue the essay, explaining to the examiner why it's wrong. If there's time, tell them what the real answer is.

Don't give up if you're running out of time: even with only five minutes left, there's still time to pick up extra marks.

Check your work, re-check it, then check it again

Examiners will be far more strict when marking coursework essays, because there's no excuse not to check them really carefully. Read them over and over again until there are no mistakes.

Warm-up Questions and Short Tasks

These warm-up questions should ease you gently in and make sure you've got the basics straight. If there's anything you've forgotten, go back through the section to check what you need to know. This section covers the essential skills you'll need for doing English answers well, so make sure you go through every single one of these warm-up questions.

Warm-up Questions

1) Re-write the following statements using formal English. (Note the writing style.)

   a) <u>Persuasive</u> — Well, I reckon it's flipping obvious; only an idiot thinks school uniform is a good thing. For a start kids hate it so it just causes aggro.

   b) <u>Informative</u> — Make sure your kids turn up with the proper kit: none of these scruffy jeans and trainers. Let the side down, they do.

   c) <u>Discursive</u> — I can see both sides. On one hand uniform is dead expensive, but then, so is trendy gear.

2) Match each sentence with a style of writing from the box below. All statements are about fire.

   a) 'I stumbled, terrified, fleeing the inferno behind...'

   b) 'The third reason why smoke is more dangerous than the actual fire is...'

   c) 'Steve Knight, 37, witnessed the blaze...'

   d) 'The percentage damage caused by the smoke is greater than the damage caused by the fire which indicates...'

   e) 'Another way to reduce the risks of having a fire at home is to install and regularly test smoke alarms...'

   Style of writing:

Advice
Newspaper report
Creative writing
Analytical writing
Persuasive writing

3) Un-jumble the words to show when you should begin a new paragraph in creative writing. (i.e. when any of the following things change.)

   a) miet

   b) htaerccar

   c) etgistn

   d) kpaeers

4) Write the opening of a story where you use all four types of paragraphing (as you answered for Q3).

Warm-up Questions and Short Tasks

5) Imagine you are writing a persuasive essay about the dangers of teenagers listening to pop music, based on the following quote:

"Loud music can give you hearing problems, rap lyrics encourage violence and pop idols are negative role models. And all pop music seems to be the same style so teenagers have a very limited experience."

Write topic sentences to show how you would split your essay into paragraphs.

6) Think of counter arguments for the points in Q5 above. Write topic sentences for a discursive essay about the benefits and dangers of pop music to teenagers.

7) Read the following extract:

'Why study English?

 English is essential for communication as it equips you with life skills, but, much more than that, it has the power to develop both mind and character. On a practical level, it gives you the skills essential for everyday life, whether letter writing or reading a report. Doing well at English can improve your life chances after school and enable you to obtain a good job.
 English also instils confidence, especially through speaking and listening activities where you get used to thinking laterally, arguing your opinion and listening sensitively.
 English is much more than just practical skills though, it also deals with the essence of life. Issues are explored, varying perspective analysed, different cultures observed and much, much more. It is the gateway to other worlds.'

   a)   Find two different quotations to show that English broadens the mind.
   b)   Find one quotation to show that English is of use every day.
   c)   Rephrase one statement about the benefits of speaking and listening activities.

8) Does the writer of the passage above think that English is essential for all aspects of life? Using two quotations, show the writer's point of view. Remember to work your quotations into your answers so that they flow.

9) Match the following ways to organise writing to a possible essay:

In order of importance	"account of an event"
For and against alternated	"creative writing"
Sequential	"discursive writing"
Flashback	"instructional writing"
Chronological	"persuasive writing"

10) Rewrite the following sentence, correcting all the spelling and grammatical errors:

"Kieron never realised how much his life would changed after selling his his comic book script. Now people every where would read his comics. He was starting to believe that he could accomplish anything.

Revision Summary

Every now and then throughout this book, you'll find pages like this one. They may look a bit dull, but they're really important, so <u>DON'T SKIP THEM</u>. You've read the section, and you've done the warm-up questions, but you need to do these ones too to see how much you know. There are no answers to look up for these, so you'd better be certain you know exactly what the answers are from the section — you can look up the bits you didn't know. Check them, and do the <u>whole lot again</u> until you get 100% correct. GO.

1) Write down every type of essay you have to do for English GCSE.

2) What's the difference between an 'arguing' essay and an 'explaining' essay?

3) Explain what 'speaking and listening' exercises are.

4) Why is planning your essays a good idea?

5) Should your plan be written in proper sentences? Why?

6) How long (roughly) should you spend planning an essay?

7) Complete this sentence — "A good plan needs an introduction, a middle bit and a ....".

8) What should a good introduction do?

9) Should the question you're answering play a part in your introduction?

10) Why should you try to grab the reader's attention right at the start of your essay?

11) Why should you write your essays using paragraphs?

12) Say why your ideas need to flow clearly from paragraph to paragraph.

13) Write a definition of what 'formal' writing is.

14) Rewrite the following sentence so that it is formal and grammatically correct — "theres no way lady macbeth was a really nice woman cos she was well bossy with her fella"

15) "Duncan was as <u>dead as the dodo</u>" — what's wrong with the second half of this sentence and why?

16) Explain why there is no single writing style you can practise for your 'original writing' essays.

17) Why do you need to give evidence for the points you make in your essays?

18) Why do you need to say where you got your quotes from?

19) Do you need to use quotation marks when you paraphrase someone else's words?

20) What should a good conclusion do for your reader?

21) Explain why it's a good idea to leave yourself time at the end of the exam to check through your essay.

22) What's the best thing to do if you realise that the essay you've written (in an exam) has failed to answer the question?

23) Explain why you need to spend more time checking and polishing your coursework essays than your exam essays.

Answering Literature Questions

There are different <u>types</u> of literature questions and you need to know how to answer <u>all</u> of them.

Step 1 — Work Out *What the Questions Are About*

1) You have to <u>answer the question properly</u> to get a decent grade.

2) The first thing to do is work out what the question is about.

3) The two subjects that come up time and again are the <u>writer's message</u> and the <u>characters</u>:

This one's about the WRITER'S MESSAGE. ➡

> In *The Three Little Pigs* the Wolf dies at the end. What do you think the writer is trying to say about the behaviour of the three pigs?

The 'message' is the moral, or just an opinion the writer's got about what they're writing about. There's more about this on Page 19.

This one's about one of the CHARACTERS. ➡

> How does the writer bring out different traits of the Wolf?

More about character questions on Pages 15 to 17.

4) For the 'different cultures and traditions' question in the English exam, you'll also have to write about the writer's <u>background</u>, and how it links with the poem or story. (See P. 20)

> Compare *The Enormous Turnip* with *The Enormous Beetroot* showing how the writers reveal their ideas and feelings about the cultures in which they have set their stories.

5) Once you know what the questions are about, you're ready to <u>choose</u> between them.

Step 2 — *Choose* the Question That's *Best For You*

1) You always get a <u>choice</u> with literature questions.
2) There's usually a choice of two questions on each book.
3) For questions on stuff from the Anthology you could get a choice of three questions.
4) <u>Obviously</u> you want to choose a question that you can answer really well, but in the panic of the first few minutes of the exam, it's easy to make a bad choice.
5) Don't panic. Take a deep breath, and then choose:

> * A question which gives you lots of IDEAS on what to write about.
>
> * A question which is on material you're FAMILIAR with.
>   (i.e. you've read the book, the poems or the stories)
>
> * A question which you definitely UNDERSTAND.

6) If you're doing <u>coursework</u> this isn't as relevant. Just make sure you understand the question before you stay up all night writing your essay.

Use your brain to choose the right question

It's simple — just PICK THE EASIEST ONE. Lots of people go wrong by picking the most interesting one, then finding out it's very hard once they start writing. Don't fall into that trap.

Answering Literature Questions

Step 3 — Break the Question Into Bullet Points

1) You can't just give a one-sentence answer to literature questions.

Does Little Red Riding Hood change at all in the course of the story?
Write about **two** episodes, one at the beginning of the story and one at the end, showing how she changes or stays the same.

2) You have to go into detail and make lots of separate points.

3) If you're doing Foundation, the exam paper helps you by breaking the question into bullet points:

Write about:
• what she says and does
• her attitudes and feelings
• how the writer shows you how she changes or stays the same.

Figure out the first 2 things and it'll help you work out the answer.

4) If you're doing Higher, you'll have to break the question into bullet points yourself. Ask your teacher for a stack of old literature Foundation papers so you can practise.

5) Scribble a plan based on the bullet points.

• BEGINNING - picking flowers, no hurry to get to Grandma's; END - she tricks wolf
• BEGINNING - feels confident and secure; END - cross with herself, more confident
• BEGINNING - "drifted along", compares her to butterfly; END - looks the wolf in the eye, "now she knew what to do"

Choose things that can be compared to show how she changes.

Step 4 — Write a General Answer Then Follow the Plan

You can make your introduction pretty short — just make sure it gives a quick answer to the question so the examiner has a rough idea of what you're going to say.

There are several episodes in the story which show how Little Red Riding Hood changes — in particular the flower-picking in the forest glade, and the escape from Grandmother's house. They show how Little Red Riding Hood starts off naive, but learns from her experience.

The rest of your essay should back up what you say in the introduction.

1) Keep your essay clear by dealing with the bullet points in order.

2) Don't chop and change between different ideas. Deal with one at a time and use a separate paragraph for each one.

Step 5 — Don't Forget the Conclusion

Run through all your points briefly in your conclusion and sum up. Make sure your summing-up answers the original question.

At the start of the story Little Red Riding Hood doesn't have a care in the world. By the end she has been through a terrifying experience. The writer shows that she has learnt from her experience and become more wary and cautious.

Break the question up
If there's not enough in your plan, there won't be enough in your essay. Simple as that. Get the planning right and not only will the essay be easier to write, it'll be a better essay.

Writing About Characters

This character stuff seems obvious — but it's not. So make sure you read everything on this page.

Find Bits Where the Writer **Describes** the Characters

1) The writer will <u>deliberately</u> describe characters in a way
that tells you what he or she wants you to think about them.

2) You need to find these descriptions of how they look or act.

> | BASE DETAILS — SIEGFRIED SASSOON |
> | --- |
>
> *The majors are described as "scarlet"
> and "fierce, bald, and short of breath".
> It makes them sound like grumpy old men,
> not soldiers.*

Find Evidence For What They're Like In **What They Do**

It's the same whether you're writing about a book, a play, or a poem
— look at what people do, then write down <u>what that says about them</u>.

> | OF MICE AND MEN — JOHN STEINBECK |
> | --- |
>
> *Lennie can't help hurting the puppies
> when he strokes them — he isn't in
> control of his own strength.*

> | KING LEAR — SHAKESPEARE |
> | --- |
>
> *There can be no doubt about Regan
> and Goneril's cruelty, after they
> turned against their father in Act 2.*

Work Out the Reasons **Why Characters Do Things**

When you're writing about what a
character does, always say <u>why</u> they do it.

1) Some characters are motivated by things like...

2) Some characters want things so badly it leads them to <u>manipulate</u> others.

3) Some characters want to be <u>liked</u>.

4) Some characters do things for <u>revenge</u>
or to prove they have <u>power</u> over another character.

Working out what characters are like is VITAL to your essays
They really are vital. Does their character make you really believe in the plot and what's going on?
Authors often make characters very complex, and you need to have lots ready to say about them.

Writing About Characters

Look At the Way Characters **Speak**

1) The way characters, including the narrator, <u>speak</u> tells you a lot about them.

2) This is true for poetry, plays and prose.

"Oh, you're one of those little men who reads the gas meters? How hilarious..." ← arrogant and rude

"So, erm, do you think it would be alright, I mean if you didn't mind, could you possibly... pass the salt please, Dad?" ← painfully shy

These things should be going through your head <u>whenever</u> you've got a characters question. You <u>can't fail</u> to pick up marks if you talk about them.

Look At How the Characters **Treat Other People**

You can tell a lot about the <u>main characters</u> by watching how they get on with others. It can reveal sides to their character that they keep <u>hidden</u> from the other main characters.

> Everyone loved Jack. His family, his friends, and everyone who knew him thought he was warm and caring.
> Jack was getting into a cab, when a homeless man shuffled up and asked him for change. Jack spat into the man's face, saying, "Don't ever speak to me again, old man, or you'll be sorry."

Although people believe Jack is warm and caring, in reality he is rude and mean.

The way to prove what you know is to quote the bit that says so

Evidence is no good whatsoever if you don't use it. Describe your character in as much detail as you can. Use all your bits of evidence — and plenty of quotes to back up everything you say.

Writing About Characters

Stories Tell You What Characters Think

1) Novels and short stories give <u>descriptions</u> of characters' thoughts and behaviour — the voice telling the story fills you in on <u>what characters are thinking</u>.

2) Pinpoint those bits, quote them, and say how they help answer the question.

> Sarah was disgusted by Jamie's behaviour at the bar and refused to speak to him.

Sarah has a very low opinion of the way Jamie behaves at the bar, which suggests that at this point in the book, she still hasn't forgiven him for causing the car crash.

3) Books with a <u>third person</u> narrator (who isn't one of the characters) let you in on the secret thoughts of <u>all</u> the characters.

> Jennie didn't want to tell anyone that she was ill. Of all her friends, no one suspected except Caitlin, and Caitlin didn't feel comfortable talking to anyone about it. If Caitlin had known how upset Jennie was, she would have helped.

The narrator = the person telling the story.

First Person Narrators Can't Always Be Trusted

1) <u>Books</u> that are written in the <u>first person</u> — so the story's told by one of the characters — give you a picture of that character all the way through. You get a first hand description of exactly what the character <u>sees</u>, <u>says</u> and <u>thinks</u>.

2) Find bits where they <u>tell you</u> what they're like, or give away what they're like by their attitudes.

> I've never been a nice person.

3) Don't take what they say for granted though — you're only getting one side of the story.

> That evening I went to a dinner party. If there's one thing I can't stand it's a group of people enjoying themselves. It makes me sick.

> All the other people there were so boring. No one had anything interesting to say to me, and there wasn't a single one there that wasn't a fool.

The narrator feels that he is superior to the other guests. However, the fact that no one else has anything "interesting" to say to him suggests they don't really think that much of him.

Narrators can be tricky

Just have a look and see what's there in the text — you'll find something to write about. Before you get carried away, remember to think about WHO is telling you things, and whether or not you can trust them.

Warm-up Questions

It may seem like warm-up questions have very little to do with the kinds of questions you'll have to answer in the exam, but you're wrong. They test you on essential knowledge that you <u>will need</u> in order to get a decent mark, so make sure you don't go on until you can answer all of them.

Warm-up Questions

1) Which two subjects are literature questions most likely to be on? Pick two:
   a)   the writer's life story
   b)   the writer's message
   c)   the writer's style
   d)   the characters.

2) Say whether each of these is good advice or bad advice:
   a)   Always do the first question on the exam paper.
   b)   Always do a question on a book you haven't read.
   c)   Always do a question which gives you lots of ideas
          on what to write about.
   d)   Always do a question on a book you know really well,
          even if you don't understand what the question's asking for.

3) Describe one good way of writing an essay plan.

4) Should your introduction be:
   a)   Short, giving a basic idea of what you're going to say in your essay?
   b)   Long and detailed so you don't have to write as much in the essay?

5) How many ideas should you cover in each paragraph of your essay?

6) What should you say in your conclusion?

7) Go back to pages 13 and 14 and draw a flow chart of the five steps for tackling a literature question. Then memorise it. Then draw it from memory.

8) Copy out the following description and underline everything in it which tells you what Jason is like:
   Jason groaned and rolled over on the grey and greasy sheets. He reached out a thick, hairy hand and grabbed the alarm clock. He battered it against the floorboards five times before he realised that it wasn't the alarm clock ringing but the phone. He picked it up and barked, "What the hell do you want?" then slammed the receiver down and collapsed back onto his pillow. He sighed deeply. The phone began to ring again. Without looking, Jason reached down for the cord and wrenched it out of the wall.

9) Write a paragraph explaining what Jason is like, using evidence from above.

10) Write down at least three things that could motivate a character.

11) Write down a definition for each of these words:
   a)   motivate
   b)   manipulate
   c)   revenge

12) What's a third person narrator? Which characters' thoughts and feelings can they describe?

13) What's a first person narrator? Which characters' thoughts and feelings can they describe?

14) Should you believe everything a first person narrator says?

The Writer's Message

This page is about learning how to spot the author's message and how to write about it.

Message Questions Can Be Hard To Spot

1) Questions about the message can be worded in all sorts of different ways:

> When the Woodcutter kills the Wolf what is the writer trying to show?

> Why do you think the Woodcutter is important?

> What does *The Three Little Pigs* have to say about architecture?

2) They're all asking the same thing:

> *What does the writer think? Write about all the bits of the text that give it away.*

3) Work out what the message of the text is, then write about all the bits which helped you work it out.

Work Out the Message of Your Set Texts Before the Exams

Obviously if you work out the message of your set texts before the exams you'll have a lot less to worry about on the day. If you haven't read the texts yet, this is a great way to get a quick overview:

This is what you could do for The Grapes of Wrath by John Steinbeck.

┌─ **story** ─┐
The Joad family lose their Oklahoma farm to a big corporation. They travel to California to find work as fruit pickers. The journey is tough, and life gets even tougher when they reach California.

┌─ **characters** ─┐
Characters who stick with the family do OK. Anyone who goes off on their own has a tough time. Characters in powerful positions like police and landowners are described in a negative way.

┌─ **tone** ─┐
Life back in Oklahoma is remembered with affection. In the camps in California, life is mostly sad and difficult.

┌─ **title** ─┐
"The grapes of wrath" is a big hint that Steinbeck is angry about the events he describes in his book.

Once you've looked at all that, put it all together to work out what the message is. I'd say it's something like...

> *The Great Depression had a terrible effect on the lives of ordinary people.*

...or

> *It's important for people to help each other, however tough life gets.*

The notes you've made about the story, the character, the tone and the title are the evidence you need to back up the points you make in your essay.

The message — it's one of the reasons why writers write

Bold claims need backing up, otherwise you're just ranting. I've said it before and I'll say it again — you need to get evidence from the text and quote it in your answer, so read the book properly.

Different Cultures and Traditions

"Different Cultures" questions <u>aren't that different</u> from any others. There's just some <u>extra bits</u> to learn.

There Are **Two Big Things** to Write About

There are <u>two</u> main types of "Different Cultures and Traditions" question:

<u>How</u> the poems or stories are written

Write about the same stuff as you would in any literature essay, but look out for these things too:

1) Unfamiliar words from other languages or dialects.
2) Words spelt so they sound like an accent or dialect.
3) The <u>form</u> of poems. It's a lot more varied in the "Different Cultures" poems than in the other ones you have to study.

The main <u>thoughts and feelings</u>

1) Feelings about <u>differences between cultures</u> come up all the time. It could be someone who's moved to a different country feeling out of place, or the contrast between rich and poor in one country.
2) A lot of the material for "Different Cultures and Traditions" is more <u>political</u> than anything you'll study by British writers. Look for views on equality and democracy.

Even if the question seems to ask <u>mainly</u> about the way things are written, DON'T ignore the thoughts and feelings. The same goes for questions about the thoughts and feelings — DON'T ignore the way it's all written. If you totally ignore one thing, and only write about the other, you <u>won't get</u> a C or above.

The Examiners Just Want a Bit of **Understanding**

For the thoughts and feelings bit you have to show 'empathy' with the writers' ideas and feelings. That doesn't mean you have to <u>agree</u> with what they say — it just means you have to <u>show you understand</u> the writers' points of view. You also have to 'explore' the ideas in the work for a higher mark. That means <u>go into detail</u> and <u>be specific</u>.

So don't just say: *She is unhappy because she misses speaking her own language.*

Say: *English is not the poet's mother tongue. Speaking English all the time makes her feel as though she is physically damaged.*

Much better — shows you understand <u>why</u> she's unhappy, and exactly how she feels.

It Pays to **Know About** the Writers

The best <u>revision</u> you can do is read the Anthology. After that find out a bit about each of the writers, and note down how that links with their work. Don't <u>just</u> make notes. LEARN THEM.

1) Where the writer's from.
2) Where the writer lives now.
3) How the poem or story fits in with the writer's life story.

GRACE NICHOLS, <u>*Island Man*</u>

1) Born in Guyana (Caribbean).
2) Has lived in the UK since 1977.
3) Sympathises with others living far from what is familiar.

You don't have to go on and on about this stuff in your essay. Just make sure you know it — it'll help you come up with ideas about what to say, and avoid saying anything <u>embarrassingly wrong</u>.

If you know the work well, you can write much better essays

You must READ the Anthology. You usually have to compare, (P. 24) so if you haven't read them, you're a bit stuck. But if you've revised properly, you could go up a whole grade.

The Writer's Techniques

You have to show that you understand the writer's style, so get on and learn this page properly.

Writing Style Affects The Way You Feel

The style of a text is a combination of features like these:

words you hear every day	lots of fancy comparisons
unusual, difficult words	no fancy comparisons

short, simple sentences	lots of action
long, complicated sentences	lots of description

The style influences the way you feel about characters, ideas and events.
Show the examiners you understand how the writer manages to affect the way you feel.

If you're saying a character is on the verge of insanity, show how the style backs it up.

The writer makes the character speak in a very confused way.

MAC: I'm late - late - late, better late than never Mother said to me. I'm never late - never been better. So late, so late...

If you're saying you think the writer is disgusted by greed, show how the style backs it up.

The writer shows how he or she feels through a descriptive bit.

All around me the round, red faces of the customers shone with sweat and wine. I stared at them with grim fascination. A woman sitting alone in the corner raised a dripping slice of steak to her lips. Cream and blood ran down her chin and she laughed as the little terrier sitting in her lap licked it away.

The author will always try to manipulate the reader
Don't always believe what the author tells you to believe.
You should always question an author's motives for letting us know something.

The Writer's Techniques

Pay Attention to Settings

Writers just love using <u>settings</u> to mess with the way you feel about what's happening.

> The candlelight cast huge, shifting shadows on the mossy walls. The wind howled down the chimney, throwing sparks around the room.
>
> "Dinner is served," the butler announced. The Count took my arm and led me to the dining room.

Creepy.

> The candlelight cast soft shadows around the room. I stretched out lazily in the armchair by the fire.
>
> "Dinner is served," the butler announced. The Count took my arm and led me to the dining room.

That sounds a bit more enjoyable.

Look At the Order of Events

1) Stories aren't always told <u>in order</u>.
   Writers mess around with the order to keep you interested.

2) <u>Flashbacks</u> are a favourite trick. What happens is that the story's going along nicely in the <u>present</u>, and suddenly the scene <u>shifts</u> to the <u>week before</u>, or <u>some years before</u>.

3) <u>Foreshadowing</u> gives clues about what will happen <u>later on</u> in the story.

<u>Example of Foreshadowing</u>

> At the start of <u>Macbeth</u> the Witches predict what will happen to Macbeth.

> Everything they predict comes true — though not always in the way Macbeth expects.

Don't get carried away with the present — always ask why

There are always reasons for what happens, and they're often buried in the past. The authors like to tease the reader, so we often don't find out why things happen the way they do until the very end.

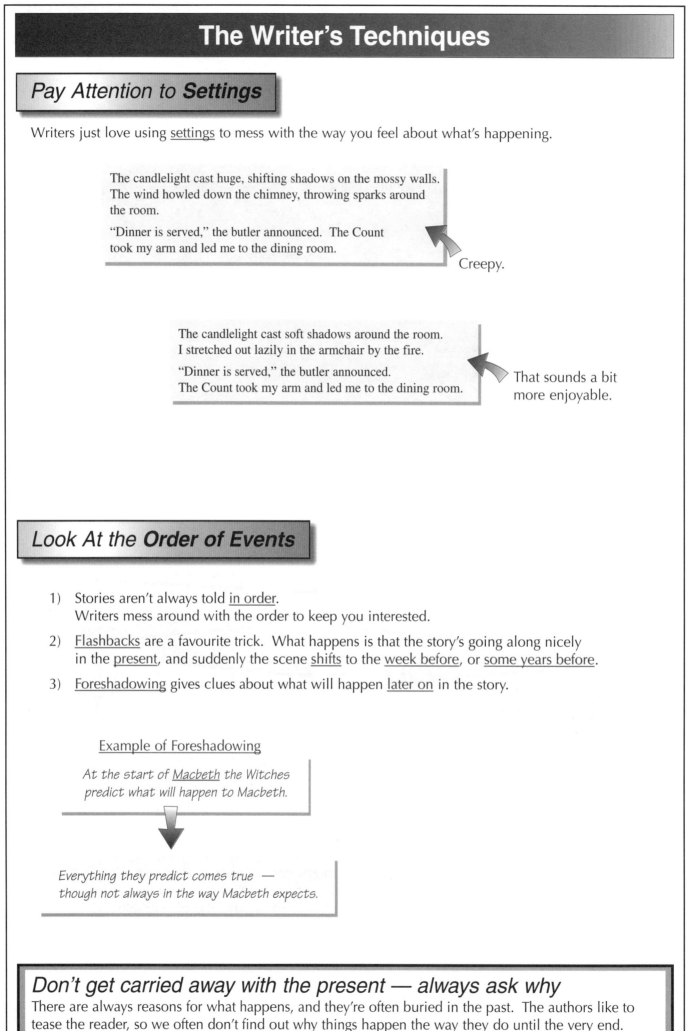

Useful Literature Words

Use These Words — AND GET THEM RIGHT

There's a lot to learn here — but these words are really useful.
Don't just learn how to spell them. Learn what they <u>really mean</u>.

simile

Don't get these two mixed up.

A simile <u>compares</u> one thing to another. Similes often use the words 'like' and 'as'.

> His socks stank <u>**like a dead dog**</u>.

> His dog was as mean <u>**as an old bandito**</u>.

metaphor

Metaphors describe <u>one thing</u> as if it <u>were another</u>. Metaphors <u>never</u> use 'like' or 'as'.

> My car <u>**is a heap of old rubbish**</u>.

> But, soft, what light through yonder window breaks? It is the east, and Juliet <u>**is the sun**</u>.

imagery

If you're not sure whether you're writing about a metaphor or a simile then just call it 'imagery' — it's the general term for comparisons like metaphors and similes.

symbolism

Making an <u>object</u> stand for an emotion or idea.

> Harry's pigeons flew high above the dismal suburban gardens.

If Harry wanted to leave home, the pigeons could be a <u>symbol</u> of freedom.

allegory

A story where <u>characters</u> and <u>settings</u> can stand for something else.

> The Crucible by Arthur Miller describes a witch-hunt in a small town in 17th-century America.

> Really it's about a period in the 1950s when the US government started accusing artists and film-makers of being Communists.

ambiguity

Words or events have <u>more than one</u> possible meaning. If you notice something that could be interpreted in two or three different ways then say so — that's A and A* material.

irony

The words say <u>one thing</u>, but the writer means <u>something else</u>. Say Carter is awful at football, and has played badly in a game. The author writes:

> Carter really excelled himself this time.

He's being ironic — he actually means "Carter played even worse than usual."

WARNING — if you use these words and get them wrong you'll end up looking a bit pretentious, and a bit stupid. If you can see a writer's used some clever technique but you're not sure what to call it, then just <u>describe it in your own words</u>.

You HAVE to know what ALL of these words mean

These tricky words WILL get you marks. Not one of them is too hard to get your head round. You absolutely HAVE TO LEARN THEM. No excuses. Just get learning them all NOW.

Comparing

One last page on Literature Essays and it'll all be over.

Comparing = Finding **Similarities** and **Differences**

You have to look at two or more things <u>together</u>.

Compare these two poems. You should consider:
- *the language used*
- *the ideas they contain*
- *how the poem is presented*

> This example is about two poems, but you could be asked to compare any of your texts — including media texts...

You've got to describe the <u>similarities</u> and <u>differences</u> between the poems for <u>each</u> of these points.

Compare Both Things in **Every Paragraph**

The whole point of these questions is that you write about both things <u>together</u>. It's about <u>MAKING LINKS</u> between them. If you tackle each point in the question in turn, it's like having your own ready-made essay plan.

(1) – *the language used*

You need to say whether the language is <u>similar</u> or <u>different</u> in the two poems, along with examples to prove your point.

The language used in 'The Laboratory' is very simple, almost as if the narrator were in a hurry to tell his story without paying attention to his wording. The language used in 'Ulysses' is far more complex and doesn't rhyme.

(2) – *the ideas they contain*

You need to look at the ideas in both poems. You're trying to <u>make links</u> between ideas that are <u>similar</u> and ideas that are <u>different</u>.

Ulysses is a noble but weary warrior — he seems proud when he says he has "drunk delight of battle with my peers". In contrast, the main character in 'The Laboratory' is bitter towards the woman he is trying to poison — he says "He is with her... they laugh, laugh at me".

(3) – *how the poem is presented*

You have to write about the <u>structure</u> of the two poems for this bit of the question — say why they are <u>similar</u> or <u>different</u>.

'The Laboratory' features very short sentences and verses, which has the effect of conveying the excitement of the narrator. The verses in 'Ulysses' are much longer, which makes the poem feel less frantic.

You could be asked to compare other things too...

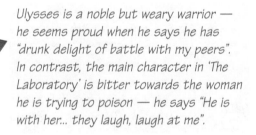

imagery message setting structure characters

...so if you think about these things <u>before</u> the exam, you'll be sorted.

You will need to make the effort to do a GOOD comparison

It might not come to you very easily, but it's not *that* hard. At least you often get to choose which stories or poems to compare — that's brilliant because you can pick the ones with lots you can write about.

Warm-up Questions

Doing these warm-up questions will soon tell you whether you've got the basic facts straight or not. If not, you'll really struggle, so take the time to go back over the bits you don't know.

Warm-up Questions

1) What is a writer's message?

2) Write down the four things that you could make notes on to help you work out the message of your set texts.

3) What do you have to do to show **empathy** with the author? Pick one:
   a)   show you agree with everything the writer says,
   b)   show you understand the writer's point of view, <u>or</u>
   c)   show that you have your own point of view and that there's no way you're changing what you think?

4) Is learning a few basic facts about the authors in the anthology:
   a)   pointless,
   b)   OK if you're stuck on a desert island with no one to talk to and nothing to do except read the anthology,
   c)   an excellent idea if you want to show that you know what you're talking about?

5) Read this paragraph:
   The soldier looked over the sandbags. He saw a shape moving. He cocked his rifle. The shadow stopped. The soldier paused. Click. Bang. The shadow fell.
   Say which of these options is the best description of the writer's style and explain why:
   a)   using lots of unusual, difficult words,
   b)   packing in lots of description,
   c)   short, simple sentences?

6) Describe how you think the writer wants to make you feel in each of these paragraphs:
   a)   *The curtain snapped in a sudden gust of wind. Outside an owl screeched. She put her hand to her throat and listened. Somewhere a tap was dripping and one by one the candles blew out.*
   b)   *The cake making went well. Well, it began well. Then the butter fell on the floor and cook slipped on it. The flour was full of ants and the oven wouldn't work properly. Luckily the fire station was only round the corner.*

7) Match each of these words with its correct definition below:
   a)   flashback   b)   foreshadowing
   * this point in the story provides hints about what will happen later
   * the story is in the present and then the scene shifts back to the past

8) A simile compares one thing to another. True or false?

9) Find the metaphor in the passage below and explain what makes it a metaphor.
   The boys sat down at the table and started on the plate of pies. Gravy splattered their chins. Crumbs were scattered over the table. "You pigs!" screamed Tabitha.

10) Match these literature words up with their meanings:
   symbolism   where words or events have more than one meaning
   allegory   where characters, settings and events can stand for something else
   ambiguity   where the writer says the opposite of what is really meant
   irony   making an object stand for an idea

Revision Summary

There's <u>literally</u> just one page left till this section is over. Keep going — these questions are a pretty good measure of what you've taken in. You know what kind of questions are going to come up. And you know the five-step guide to writing your answer will make it all a whole lot easier. True, there are all those annoying technical bits to learn — but just think how good it'll feel to know exactly what you're on about in that exam.

1) What two subjects are most likely to come up in your literature exam questions?

2) What's the extra topic you'll have to write about for the 'different cultures and traditions' question?

3) Write down the five steps you should follow to answer an essay question well. Give a short explanation of each step.

4) What should you put in a good conclusion?

5) Explain four things you could talk about when you're writing about characters.

6) What is a third person narrator?

7) What is a first person narrator? Why can't you take what they say for granted?

8) Message questions can be hard to spot — but what is the one thing that they'll all essentially be asking you?

9) Give four areas you could look at if you were working out the message of a set text before an exam.

10) You're writing about different cultures and traditions. What are the two big things you should talk about? Write a quick paragraph explaining each one.

11) What is empathy?

12) What would it pay to know about each of the authors in the anthology?

13) List any four features of writing style.

14) Explain how the style of a text can influence the person reading it.

15) Explain what authors use settings for.

16) What are flashbacks?

17) What is foreshadowing?

18) Write a short explanation for each of these technical words:
    i) simile
    ii) metaphor
    iii) imagery
    iv) symbolism
    v) allegory
    vi) ambiguity
    vii) irony

19) Explain what you have to do when comparing two texts.

20) What should you make sure you do in every paragraph of a comparison essay?

21) You're preparing for the exam. List five things you could compare in texts beforehand.

What The Examiner Wants

Basically, the examiner wants to know that you've understood the play. It's as simple as that.

Show You've **Understood** the Play

1) The examiner wants to know you understand the order everything happens in. This is quite simple — you just have to avoid making stupid mistakes like "Juliet kills herself in Act 1".

2) The examiner wants to know you're familiar with all the characters, not just the main ones. So, it'll look really good if you refer to some minor characters in your answer.

   You've also got to know stuff about the characters — who's related to whom, what are they like, how they behave, etc... If you get people mixed up, you'll lose marks.

3) You need to quote little bits of text every now and then, to back up your points and prove you've understood the play.

Explain the **Major Issues** the Play Deals With

Plays are about more than just the plot — they deal with wider issues.
Look out for these 3 things in any play — you'll boost your grade if you mention them:

1 Social Issues — 'Death of a Salesman' deals with the American Dream of the self-made man.

2 Moral Issues — 'An Inspector Calls' deals with what drives people to suicide.

3 Philosophical Issues — Lots of Shakespeare's plays ask questions about what love actually is, not just how people act when they're in it.

Show You Know that Plays Should be **Watched** not **Read**

You need to show that you realise plays are meant to be performed, not read silently.
The examiner wants to know you've thought about the impact a play would have on an audience.
You can do this easily by throwing in the odd line a bit like this —

This would look particularly spectacular when performed on stage because of the...

This is a visual joke that an audience would find very amusing because...

Come Up With Some **Ideas** of Your Own

1) Examiners love it if you can come up with something original.

2) If something occurs to you but you're not sure if it's right, try and stick it in anyway.

3) As long as you can back it up with a QUOTE from the text, you'll be fine.

Stop playing around — and get this learnt

Remember that plays are meant to be acted, not read in your head. So if you're struggling, put on your best thespian's voice and read it aloud — that way the characters will be clearer.

What The Examiner Wants

You always have to write about these things in drama essays — whether it's in exams or coursework.

Go back to P.27 and remind yourself what to look out for.

Write About the Style

1) The person marking wants you to go into <u>detail</u> about the language.

2) Say <u>which</u> effects you think they're trying to create.
e.g. suspense, humour, anger, etc...

3) Mention any <u>imagery</u> — there's plenty in drama.
e.g. Playwrights use a lot of <u>personification</u>.
This is when an object, or something in nature,
is given human characteristics. It can bring the
landscape to life, and make the mood more intense.

...Shall I believe
That unsubstantial Death is amorous,
And that the lean abhorred monster keeps
Thee here in dark to be his paramour?

Romeo and Juliet Act 5 Scene 3

4) Mention any <u>repetition</u> — anything repeated is important.

Show You Understand the *Significance* of the Play

Almost all plays have something to say about <u>society</u> at the time they were written in
— even light-hearted comedies and histories that were set in different periods.

WAR
What's the point?
Is it a good thing?

JUSTICE
What makes a good ruler?
Can a ruler be just?

ORDER
Can we maintain order?
Is chaos inevitable?

LOVE
What is love?
Is it always a good thing?

FATE
Do we control our own lives?

You need to think very carefully about which of these <u>themes</u> comes up,
and what the playwright might have been trying to say.

Show You Appreciate *Stagecraft*

'Stagecraft' means the writer's skill at writing for the stage.
Appreciating it means asking yourself a few key questions —

1) How would this scene look on stage? 2) How would the audience react? 3) Is it effective?

The final act of Romeo and Juliet features above average 'stagecraft':

Romeo fights Paris in the tomb while the audience, knowing that
Friar Lawrence is on his way, hope he'll arrive and avert this tragedy.
But he arrives too late. These events happen in a very short space of
time and the tension is incredible. Even though we know from the start
of the play that they'll both die, we still hope that they won't.

Stagecraft is relevant to ANY play you write about
This is all worth learning for sure, as it's relevant for any play you end up studying.
So learn the headings and mention them in any drama essay. Even ones about Shakespeare.

Reading Plays

Plays Can Be **Serious** or **Funny**

Tragedy
1) Tragedies are the most <u>serious</u> kind of play and are about <u>big topics</u> — e.g. religion, love, death, war.
2) Tragedies are meant to be really moving and often have a moral message.
3) A tragedy tells the story of the downfall of the central character due to a character flaw.
4) Tragedies are sometimes set in an <u>imaginary</u> or <u>past</u> world. The characters are often kings and queens or even gods and goddesses.

Comedy
1) Comedies are supposed to be lighthearted and make you <u>laugh</u>.
2) Events and characters are based on things that happen <u>in real life</u>, but are much more silly and exaggerated.
3) Comedies sometimes have a moral too — such as good triumphing over evil.

> ⚡ Don't forget History Plays ⚡
>
> They're any kind of play based on real historical events — very popular with Shakespeare.

Dialogue is One Character Talking to **Another**

Write about dialogue to show how characters react.
It looks like this on the page...

LORD CRUMB:	Where exactly is the pizza?
VERNON:	In the basement, my Lord.
LORD CRUMB:	Very good, Vernon.

If two or more people talk to each other it's called <u>dialogue</u>.
If one person speaks for a long time it's called a <u>monologue</u>.
If one character stage-whispers to the audience, but other characters <u>can't hear</u>, it's called an <u>aside</u>.

> VERNON: (aside) *Well, it's not there yet, but it will be in 10 minutes.*

It's easy to spot because it says "<u>aside</u>" after the character's name.

A **Soliloquy** is Thinking **Out Loud**

A soliloquy only involves <u>one character</u> (like a monologue). The character doesn't talk <u>to</u> anyone — they're just thinking out loud. <u>Only the audience</u> can hear what they're saying — other characters <u>can't hear a thing</u>.

Stage Directions Give More **Detail** About the Story

You can write about <u>stage directions</u>. They tell you lots about how the playwright wanted the play to look.

| **STAGE DESIGNS** *scenery, lighting, special effects* | A cluttered attic room: stuffed bear, upright piano, pot plants. Moonlight filters through a dirty window. | The room is dirty and cluttered, so it sounds as if it's not well looked after. |

| **ACTION** | Unseen by Lord Crumb, Vernon slides the pizza into an envelope and conceals it beneath a cushion on the couch. |

| **DIALOGUE** *little details about how the actors say their lines* | LORD CRUMB: *I was wondering...*
 VERNON: (interrupts) RUN!!! |

Never forget — plays are meant to be PERFORMED, not read

You need to know how plays are different from books and poems to write about them properly. That may sound obvious but you'll lose lots of marks if you ignore the fact that the text is a <u>play</u>.

Language in Shakespeare Texts

Shakespeare's language can seem a bit daunting — but don't be afraid.
Examiners are impressed if you use the right words, so even a little goes a long way.

Show You're Aware of How **Old** (and Weird) It All Is

1) Shakespeare's plays are about <u>400 years old</u>, so it's not surprising the language is a bit strange.

2) The sense of <u>humour</u> was different too — lots of the jokes are <u>puns</u> (words with double meanings).

3) They also thought the idea of <u>girls dressing up as boys</u> was funny (basically because all the actors in Shakespeare's time were men, so you ended up with boys dressed as women dressed as boys).

4) <u>Mention the different sense of humour</u> to show that you're aware of when the play was written.

Be **Specific** When You Write About **Language**

Shakespeare wrote in a mixture of poetry and prose. You can write about whether people are posh or not, and are serious or joking around — just by looking at the <u>form</u> they speak in.

Poetic Verse is the Most **Dramatic** — and It **Rhymes**

1) Poetic verse is definitely the most dramatic one of the lot.

2) You can spot it easily because it has 10 or 11 syllables in each line and it <u>rhymes</u>.

3) It sounds more <u>impressive</u> than the rest of the text, and is used especially by the posh characters and at the beginnings and ends of scenes.

> *From forth the fatal loins of these two foes*
> *A pair of star-cross'd lovers take their life,*
> *Whose misadventur'd piteous overthrows*
> *Doth with their death bury their parents' strife.*
>
> *Romeo and Juliet* The Prologue

Blank Verse **Doesn't Rhyme**

1) This is just like poetic verse, only harder to spot because it <u>doesn't rhyme</u> (but still has 10 or 11 syllables).

2) It sounds <u>grander</u> than plain old prose, but any of the characters can speak in it.

3) The <u>majority</u> of the lines are written in it.

> *If music be the food of love, play on;*
> *Twelfth Night*

> *Wilt thou be gone? It is not yet near day:*
> *Romeo and Juliet*

Prose Can Be Spoken By **Anyone**

 The rest is written in normal prose, like this paragraph. Prose is mainly for <u>minor</u> characters, although anyone can talk in prose.

It's for <u>general chatting</u>, larking about or bits that just move the plot along, and aren't particularly meaningful.

> *FESTE: Vent my folly! I am afraid this great lubber,*
> *the world, will prove a cockney. I prithee*
> *now, ungird thy strangeness and tell me*
> *what I shall vent to my lady.*
>
> *Twelfth Night* Act 4 Scene 1

Words, words, words

If you can just get all these terms out quickly and efficiently (and in the right places, obviously) — the examiner will know you've understood it all. It'll mean that you get more good marks too.

Warm-up Questions

When writing about a play, you have to do more than just write about the story and the characters. You have to show that you've understood the main issues and the message the author is trying to present. You also have to remember that the play was written to be performed and be able to write about the effects of the dramatic methods and language used. Here are some warm-up questions to see if you have remembered all the terms used in this section. Make sure you know the answers to all these, and then you'll be able to move on and have a stab at the practice essay questions.

Warm-up Questions

1) What should you do in your essays to prove to the examiner that you know the play? Write down all the 'true' options:
   a) get the facts straight about the story
   b) only write about the main characters
   c) quote whole scenes off by heart
   d) quote relevant snippets to prove each point you make.

2) How would writing about minor characters improve your marks?

3) Write down the names of all the plays you're doing for GCSE.
   For each one write down whether it's about:
   a) social issues
   b) moral issues
   c) philosophical issues
   d) some other type of issues — try and define what they are.

4) Which of these sentences would show the examiner that you're thinking about the play being performed, not just read? Explain why.
   a) In this scene the language fills the audience with tension.
   b) In this scene the language is very tense.

5) Write a definition for each of the following words:
   a) stagecraft
   b) tragedy
   c) comedy
   d) dialogue
   e) soliloquy
   f) imagery

6) What kind of imagery is being used here?

   "Tomorrow, and tomorrow, and tomorrow,
   Creeps in this petty pace from day to day,
   To the last syllable of recorded time..."
   (Macbeth, Act 5, Scene 5)

7) Why do playwrights put in stage directions?

8) In a Shakespeare play, what's the difference between poetic verse and blank verse?

9) Match the following different types of writing to the situations where they're usually used in Shakespeare plays. (There's more than one answer to some of these.)
   poetic   when it's a funny bit
   blank   when a posh character's talking
   prose   at the beginning of a scene
                   when it's not a very important bit
                   at the end of a scene
                   most of the time

Worked Exam Answer

Sometimes it's hard to see how to answer exam questions. This worked example will really set you on the right track — then you'll be able to tackle some exam essay questions.

Worked Exam Question

1. The Inspector's 'fire and blood' speech at the end of 'An Inspector Calls' contains the key message of the play and issues a warning to those 'in a position of responsibility' who refuse to accept responsibility for others. Which members of the Birling family accept responsibility at the end of the play?

Essay plan:

Important to keep the introduction brief.

1   briefly introduce the argument

2   comment on the effect the Inspector has on the audience and the other characters

3   show which characters haven't accepted responsibility and explain why

4   show which characters have accepted responsibility and say why

5   conclude by referring back to the question and summing up argument

Important to show you have kept the question in focus.

Essay:

This speech warns the Birlings, 'in a position of responsibility', to accept responsibility for others or face dire consequences. Not everyone learns the Inspector's lesson by the end of the play.

It's important to refer back to the question.

The Inspector is described as having a 'powerful presence'. He has a 'disconcerting habit of looking hard' at each character, making it impossible for them to avoid his questions. He also knows things an 'ordinary' inspector would not know indicating he may not be a 'normal' policeman.

It's important to analyse dramatic details like these — they can tell you just as much as the actual dialogue can.

Show ideas and themes — in this case, that Inspector Goole is not a normal policeman.

Worked Exam Answer

The older Birlings fail to accept responsibility. Birling's a typical <u>Edwardian</u> self-made businessman who believes his only responsibility is to make money. When he thinks the Inspector was 'a piece of bluff,' he's relieved. He forgets that sacking Eva began the chain of events leading to her death.

It's good to show you're aware of the social / historical setting.

Mrs Birling's also stereotypical. She abuses her position to reject Eva's appeal to the Brumley Women's Charity Organisation and, unwittingly, <u>condemns</u> her own grandchild to death. She prefers not to help a girl 'of that class'. She proudly tells the others she was 'the only one' not to give in to the Inspector.

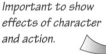

Important to show effects of character and action.

Gerald's also unchanged and is instrumental in presenting the case for the Inspector being a fake. He is the one who feels that 'everything's all right, now'.

The character most changed is Sheila. She is <u>first presented as being vain and spoilt</u>; as shown in the Milward's incident. She recognises the Inspector's intentions very early on, 'you talk as if we were responsible'. She warns her mother that the Inspector will break down her resistance and is accused of doing the Inpector's work.

Important to show how characters change — say what they were like before.

Eric changes from being reckless to becoming aware of his responsibility. The audience sees this when explanations are given for believing the Inspector was a fake. When <u>Gerald suggests there may have been 'four or five' girls involved</u>, Eric replies, 'that doesn't matter to me. The one I knew is dead'.

Important to explore layers of meaning.

Only the younger members of the Birling family accept any responsibility at the end of the play. As the Inspector says, '<u>we have more effect on the young</u>'.

Always a good idea to finish on a quote that backs up your point nicely.

Exam Questions

<u>You are allowed to use the text to write your essay.</u>

Q1   'An Inspector Calls' by J B Priestley.
      Who do you consider to be most responsible for the death of Eva Smith?

Q2   'Twelfth Night' by William Shakespeare.
      Explore the different forms of disguise and deception that feature in 'Twelfth Night'.

Q3   'Romeo and Juliet' by William Shakespeare.
      How far is Friar Lawrence responsible for the deaths of Romeo and Juliet?

Q4   'Macbeth' by William Shakespeare.
      Discuss whether you think Macbeth is a tragic hero or a tyrant.

Q5   N.B. If you are not studying any of these plays, you can write about the main character
      in a play that you *are* studying, and say whether you consider them to be a hero or a
      villain, and why. Use the comments in the answer to Q5 to help you work out if your
      essay's any good or not.

What The Examiner Wants

Some questions are phrased in a difficult way, but actually loads of them are quite similar. If you know what you're doing, it's easy to earn yourself lots of marks.

Break Down *Questions* Into *Parts*

When you're working out what to write about, underline the key words in the question so that they <u>stand out</u>.

Here's the <u>instruction</u>.

This is the <u>topic</u>.

<u>*Choose 3 poems*</u> *which show feelings about <u>relationships</u>.*

Write about the <u>similarities and differences</u> among the texts by comparing:

- *the feeling in the texts about relationships*
- <u>*how the writers convey these feelings*</u> *to the reader.*

The red bits are all telling you <u>what to write about</u>.

You have to follow the <u>instructions</u> in order to get a good grade. If it says "write about 3 poems", then just writing an answer about 2 of them will lose you marks.

Write About The Same *3 Things* In Every *Poetry Essay*

1. *The topic specified by the question*
2. *Language*
3. *How the writer wants you to feel*

e.g. experience, misunderstanding, strength and weaknesses, attitudes, feelings, time, place, thoughts about writing, and so on...

These are all things that will get you points if you write about them.

You'll *Always* Have to Write About *Language*

Sometimes questions are obvious — *How does Simon Armitage use language to create particular effects?*

Other times, the question will still <u>want you</u> to write about language, but it'll be worded differently —

These all want you to write about the poet's use of language.

Write about how the poets convey (or "show") these feelings to the reader.

Write about the unusual ways in which these ideas are presented.

Write about the ways in which this idea is expressed.

When you are asked to comment on something "<u>interesting</u>", this normally means language too.

There are 3 basic things to write about — never forget language

Once you've understood the question, it's easy to start planning your essay. But read the question through a few times, just to make sure you're not charging off in the wrong direction.

What The Examiner Wants

There are ways to make poetry easier. Put some of these ideas into your poetry essay, and watch your marks go up.

Always Stick To the Facts

1) Keep on referring to the text in order to back up your argument.

2) Quote a few words at a time, to strengthen your points.

> He implies she was unfaithful by saying she was "Too easily impressed". instead of He thinks she was unfaithful.

3) Make positive statements, not wishy-washy ones — this will make you sound convincing.

> 'Digging' is a poem about writing poetry. instead of 'Digging' would seem to be a poem about writing poetry.

Comparing Different Poems Will Get You Better Marks

In comparing questions the examiner wants to see that you can find similarities and differences between poems.

> ...leaves and branches
> Can raise a tragic chorus in a gale
> Heaney 'Storm on the Island'

> O let them be left, wildness and wet;
> Long live the weeds and the wilderness yet.
> Hopkins 'Inversnaid'

Both of these poems deal with understanding nature. You could say something like...

> While Heaney hears beauty in a big, terrifying storm, Hopkins says that the very wildness of nature is what we should admire and preserve.

DON'T just write about one poem then the other.

You Must Show You Appreciate What the Poet is Doing

To get the top marks you have to empathise with the poet.

> Empathy — *understanding another person's feelings*

So write about how the poet feels and how they want to make you feel.

Be Imaginative

1) A lot of poems deal in hidden meanings and only hint at what they might really be about.

2) This can be irritating, but as far as the exam goes, it's brilliant.

3) It means there are no right or wrong answers, and that any reasonable idea will get you marks.

4) There's only one rule — **you must back up your idea with a quote from the text.**

5) The more creative you are, the better. As long as it's not made up, you will get more marks.

Poems are like suitcases — you need to unpack them

With poetry, you have to look past the obvious things and search for hidden meanings.
Read each poem at least 3 times, and scribble down any flashes of inspiration you have.

Style and Structure in Poetry

Look at the poem 'as a whole' first. Different structures and styles are chosen for different kinds of poem, and it's worth writing about what you notice...

Learn the Different **Types** of Poem

There are different types or <u>forms</u> of poems.
Writing about the right form when you spot one WILL get you extra marks.

Ballads

They have a <u>regular rhythm</u> and are usually in <u>four-line verses</u>. They usually tell an epic or dramatic story.(e.g. 'The Rime of the Ancient Mariner') and often have a <u>chorus</u> (e.g. Irish folk songs).

Elegies

An elegy is written for someone who has <u>died</u>, and is usually quite a slow, thoughtful poem.

Free Verse

When poems are written in free verse, it means they have lines of <u>irregular length</u> that <u>do not have to rhyme</u> (though some do anyway).

So if the poem is in free verse, you can say: "So-and-so wrote it like this because it's more like the way people talk".

Some poets think it's more like the way people talk, while other poets think it's an excuse to be lazy.

Sonnets

Sonnets are usually <u>14 lines</u> long, with a <u>regular rhyme</u> scheme. Popular with Shakespeare himself, and many other traditional writers.

You should be able to recognise these four types of poem

Some poems have structures that are easy to write about (e.g. sonnets). But you can write about <u>any</u> poem's structure, even if it's to make the point that it doesn't have a regular one.

Style and Structure in Poetry

Learn How to Describe the **Structure**

You've got no excuses for not knowing these words — they're really easy, and they make you sound ten times more convincing if you use them.

> A <u>stanza</u> is the proper word for a verse.
>
> A <u>couplet</u> is a two-line stanza.
>
> A <u>triplet</u> is a three-line stanza.
>
> A <u>quatrain</u> is a four-line stanza (traditionally the most popular).

Work Out the **Voice** of the Poem

Examiners will be very impressed if you spot the <u>type of narrator</u>, and say how it makes you <u>feel</u>. You can spot a <u>first-person narrator</u> pretty easily. They're the ones that use "I" and "me". Most poetry is written in the first person. It can have these effects:

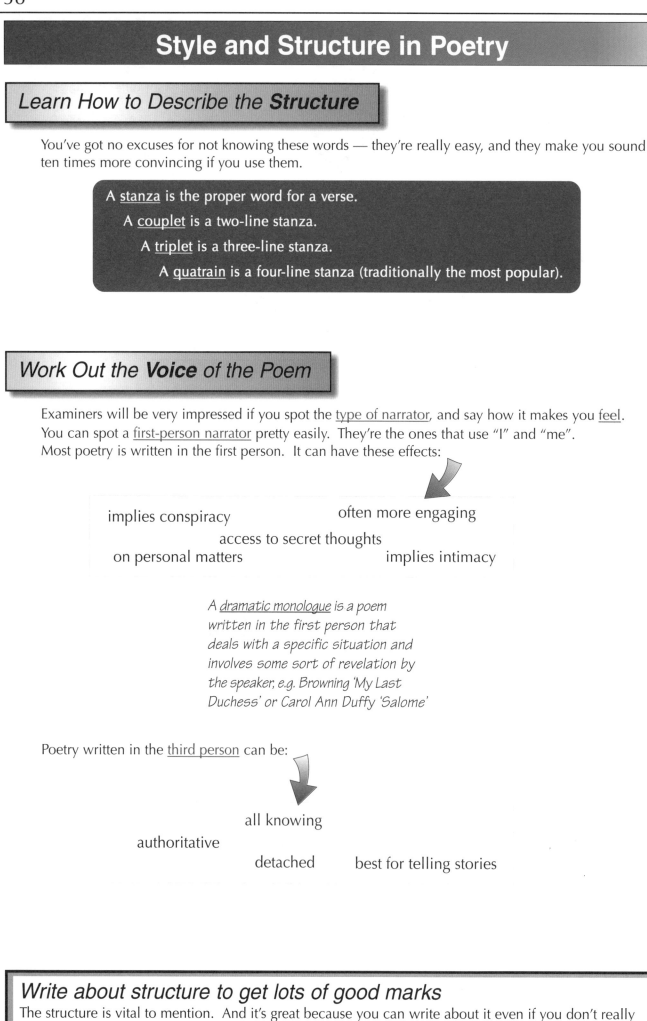

implies conspiracy   often more engaging

access to secret thoughts

on personal matters   implies intimacy

A <u>dramatic monologue</u> is a poem written in the first person that deals with a specific situation and involves some sort of revelation by the speaker, e.g. Browning 'My Last Duchess' or Carol Ann Duffy 'Salome'

Poetry written in the <u>third person</u> can be:

all knowing

authoritative

detached   best for telling stories

Write about structure to get lots of good marks

The structure is vital to mention. And it's great because you can write about it even if you don't really understand what the actual poem is going on about. So get cracking and learn it all properly.

Words To Use When Writing About Poetry

Technical terms are where it's at when it comes to writing about poetry.
It'll impress the examiner and get you better marks — but only if you use the terms properly.

Using the **Right Technical Words** Will Get You Marks

Don't use these words if you're unsure what they mean,
but you've really got no excuses for not knowing them by now...

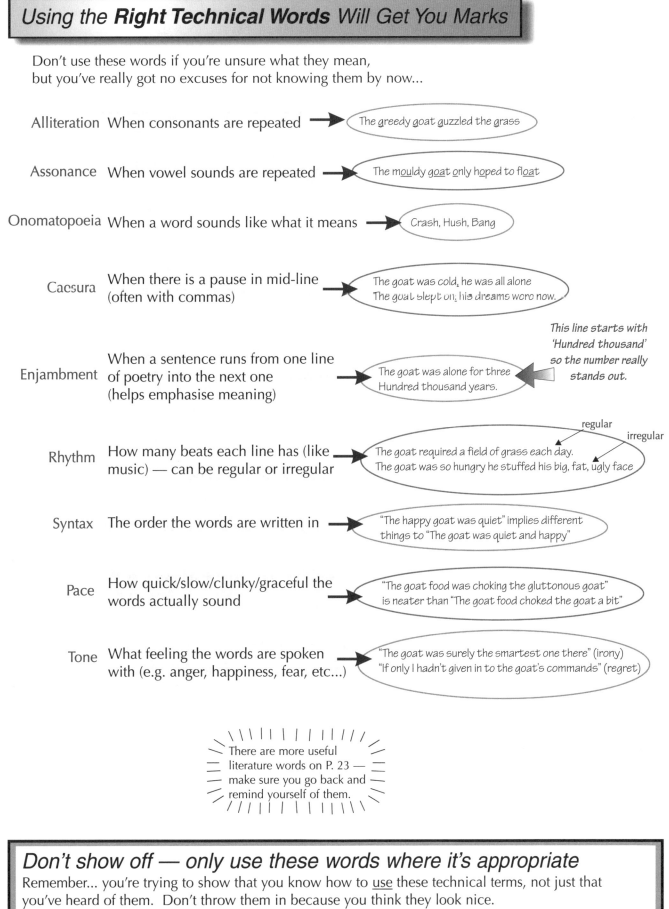

Alliteration When consonants are repeated → *The greedy goat guzzled the grass*

Assonance When vowel sounds are repeated → *The mouldy goat only hoped to float*

Onomatopoeia When a word sounds like what it means → *Crash, Hush, Bang*

Caesura When there is a pause in mid-line (often with commas) → *The goat was cold, he was all alone / The goat slept on, his dreams were now.*

Enjambment When a sentence runs from one line of poetry into the next one (helps emphasise meaning) → *The goat was alone for three Hundred thousand years.*

This line starts with 'Hundred thousand' so the number really stands out.

Rhythm How many beats each line has (like music) — can be regular or irregular → *The goat required a field of grass each day. / The goat was so hungry he stuffed his big, fat, ugly face*

regular   irregular

Syntax The order the words are written in → *"The happy goat was quiet" implies different things to "The goat was quiet and happy"*

Pace How quick/slow/clunky/graceful the words actually sound → *"The goat food was choking the gluttonous goat" is neater than "The goat food choked the goat a bit"*

Tone What feeling the words are spoken with (e.g. anger, happiness, fear, etc...) → *"The goat was surely the smartest one there" (irony) / "If only I hadn't given in to the goat's commands" (regret)*

There are more useful literature words on P. 23 — make sure you go back and remind yourself of them.

Don't show off — only use these words where it's appropriate

Remember... you're trying to show that you know how to <u>use</u> these technical terms, not just that you've heard of them. Don't throw them in because you think they look nice.

Warm-up Questions

People often find poetry quite tricky to cope with, especially if they have to decipher a brand new poem for the first time. Remember though — almost all poetry exam questions will want you to talk about the language used in the poem. If you learn all of the terms used in this section off by heart, then you should have lots of impressive things to talk about in the exam, even if you're not quite sure what the poem *actually* means. Go through these quick questions, and look up any answers you're not sure of. Keep on going over it until you don't have to look any of the answers up — then you'll know you've got enough information to sound knowledgeable in the exam.

Warm-up Questions

1) Why should you use positive statements (instead of wishy-washy ones) when writing about a poem?

2) What is an elegy?

3) What is free verse?

4) What is a stanza?

5) What is the proper term for each of the following:
   a) two-line stanza
   b) three-line stanza
   c) four-line stanza

6) What is a dramatic monologue?

7) Write down two words that describe a third person narrator.

8) Define a "caesura" and give an example.

9) Define "enjambment" and give an example.

10) Why should you underline the key words in a poetry question?

11) What are the three main things you should write about in any poetry essay?

12) What should you include in your essay in order to strengthen your point?

13) What is wrong with the statement 'My Last Duchess would seem to be a bitter poem.'?

14) What is the examiner looking for in a comparing question?

15) You should always write about one poem and then the next poem in your answer. True or false?

16) Define 'empathy'.

17) Why is it a good thing that poems often have hidden meanings?

18) How many times should you read a poem before you attempt to write about it?

19) What is a sonnet and who is very famous for writing them?

20) What is traditionally the most popular length stanza in poetry?

21) Give two characteristics of poetry that has a first person narrator.

22) Define 'alliteration' and give an example.

23) Define 'onomatopoeia' and give an example.

24) What is meant by the word 'tone' when referring to poetry? Give an example.

25) What is it important to remember when you are using technical terms about poetry?

Worked Exam Answer

Poetry essays can be difficult to get the hang of. There are a few practice exam questions at the end of this section for you to have a go at, but first here's an essay question shown with a sample answer, and a few helpful hints to keep in mind for your own answers. It's worth taking the time to read through the whole thing.

Worked Exam Question

1.   'Havisham' by Carol Ann Duffy is a poem where strong dislike for another person is shown. What is the reason for dislike in the poem and how does the poet convey this dislike?

Essay plan:

1)   Introduction – include first part of the question, give some background to the poem and explain who is disliked. Use the language of the question.

2)   Main body – look closely at language and analyse HOW the poet conveys dislike. Remember to quote to support the points. Find some quotes that show dislike and use them to structure the essay. Make a solid point for each quote.

3)   Language and structure – use technical vocabulary and show how and why it is being used by the poet. Refer back to the question to ensure that the essay stays focused.

4)   Sum up key points in short, concise conclusion.

Essay:

Use technical vocabulary.

'Havisham' by Carol Ann Duffy is a dramatic monologue, written from the perspective of the fictional character Miss Havisham from Dickens' novel 'Great Expectations'. In the novel, Miss Havisham was famously jilted at the altar, so in the poem, strong dislike is shown for the man who did this to her.

Use the language of the question.

Explain quotes.

From the first line of the poem it is clear that the narrator has strong but confused feelings about her ex-fiancé. She refers to him as 'Beloved sweetheart bastard'. Her words combine loving feelings shown by 'sweetheart' with feelings of hatred shown through the use of the harsh, colloquial expletive 'bastard'. The poet's use of an oxymoron shows that the narrator is quite confused. However, as the poem progresses, her feelings for this man become stronger

 Use quotes that fit into the body of your essay, so the poet's words flow easily into your argument.

Remember to empathise with the poet.

Worked Exam Answer

and more negative. She refers to her own appearance and blames the jilting bridegroom for her becoming older. She refers to the veins on her hands, saying:

"ropes on the back of my hands I could strangle with."

Use technical vocabulary.

This shows that the narrator dislikes this man so strongly that she wishes she could strangle him. In the second <u>stanza</u> she says:

"Spinster. I stink and remember."

Keep referring back to the question.

The alliteration in the hard 's' sound creates an image of a woman spitting the words out in disgust. She has become a spinster because she was left at the altar and has never remarried. This implies that she never recovered from the experience, as does the fact that she now sits in her wedding dress and 'stinks and remembers', which would explain her <u>violent dislike</u> for this man.

Halfway through the poem the narrator asks the question 'who did this to me?' The tone of this question is very accusing and it is clear from the rest of the poem that she already knows the answer, as do we, since she has already informed us that there is 'not a day since then I haven't wished him dead." Such violent images are frequent throughout the poem and in the final stanza she says:

"...a red balloon bursting

in my face. Bang. I stabbed at a wedding cake."

Include reference to imagery (if appropriate).

<u>Such images are very violent</u> and again show feelings of anger and dislike for the man who has done this to her. The onomatopoeic 'bang' almost seems like a gun shot and reinforces the sense of strong dislike, whilst the reference to the wedding cake again reminds the reader who she blames for her unhappiness. In the final, moving line, however, she breaks down in tears:

"Don't think it's only the heart that b-b-b-breaks."

Although throughout the poem it is clear that the narrator hates her ex-fiancé for what he has done to her, here, as with the opening line she seems confused once again because her dislike is mingled with feelings of love.

Relate conclusion to introduction. This will make your whole essay hang together better.

Exam Questions

<u>You are allowed to use the text to write your essay.</u>

Q1   'Education for Leisure' and 'Havisham' by Carol Ann Duffy are regarded
by many people as disturbing poems. Do you find the poems disturbing?
Give reasons for your answer, referring to language, tone and structure.

Q2   In 'My Last Duchess' by Robert Browning, what techniques does the poet
use in order to convey a negative impression of the Duke to the reader?

Q3   "Simon Armitage's poem 'Those bastards in their mansions...' is a poem about
the antagonism between the upper and lower classes."
What evidence is there in the poem to support this statement, and to what extent
do you agree with this suggestion?

Q4   'Ozymandias' by Percy Bysshe Shelley is a poem with a very clear moral.
What do you think this moral is, and how is it conveyed by the poet through
language, imagery and tone?

(N.B. If you have not studied 'Ozymandias', then choose any poem from your anthology
that you think has a clear moral you could write about for this essay. You can use the
answers table for Q4 to work out if your essay's any good or not.)

What The Examiner Wants

This page is simple. It's about things you can do to <u>impress</u> the examiner in your essays.

Write a Bit About **When** it was **Written**

1)   You must show you know <u>when</u> the text was written and published, and what significance this has.

2)   Some books are set in the same period they were written in.
     Other books are set in a <u>different</u> period from the one they were <u>published</u> in.

3)   This means the author can write about present day issues without criticising anyone openly.

> *George Orwell wrote Animal Farm in 1945. It tells the story of a group of pigs who take over a farm. It's not actually about pigs though — it's an allegory about events which took place around that time in Communist Russia.*

Show You **Understand** the **Issues** Being Dealt With

Show the examiner that there are <u>wider issues</u> being raised by the text, and comment on them.

Texts can have <u>social</u> implications.

> *Robin Hood is concerned with poverty.*

They can have <u>historical</u> implications.

> Different versions of *Robin Hood* have
> different interpretations of the role
> the royals played at that time.

They can have moral or <u>philosophical</u> implications.

> *Robin Hood basically condones theft and mugging.*

Show the examiner you mean business
The examiner will want to know that you've learnt about where the author was coming from. So show them you know about the author's background, and the context of the novel or story you're reading.

What The Examiner Wants

Write in Detail

Most questions ask you to comment on how a writer has <u>shown</u> the reader things.

> Personality of a character

> Experiences of characters

> Attitudes of characters

> Conflicts between characters

> Message and meaning of the text as a whole

You have to answer in detail — Write about how Dickens shows us the changes in Scrooge's character.

Chapter 23 comes after chapter 22 but before chapter 24. This would be a bad answer. It's too general.

Scrooge's return to reality needs to be urgent and vivid. Dickens precedes it with the scene where Scrooge foresees his own funeral, making sure that the return to life has a great impact, as it is shown just after death. This is much better.

Try to Be Original

If something occurs to you while you're reading the text (about language, a character, <u>anything</u>), then say it in your essay — even (and especially) if you've never been taught it.

> **Remember — you need a quote to back it up.**
> **It must be relevant to the question you're answering.**

Any <u>reasonable</u> observation will impress the examiner and get you better marks. The main thing is to <u>read</u> the question carefully, so you don't go off at a tangent.

Questions About the Message Can Look Scary

Don't get scared by questions that ask about the overall message of the text. As long as you cover your back with <u>quotes</u> and <u>details</u> from the text, you'll be just fine. This is the kind of question you might get:

Here's the <u>topic</u> you need to write about.

What do you think are the main <u>reasons for the change from friendship to violence</u> in *Lord of the Flies*, and <u>what is the writer trying to show by this change</u>?

This is the <u>message</u> bit.

In questions about the message, you <u>always</u> need to write about <u>what the writer is trying to say</u>.

Golding suggests in Lord of the Flies that all of us are capable of degenerating into violence when cut off from society. We can tell this because...

Originality gets marks — but you have to back it up

Maybe it's a bit mean to tell you to "be original". Being original is hard, but even the odd thought here and there will help you impress an examiner. Don't panic about it. Just do it.

What The Examiner Wants

Some Questions Talk About a **Specific** Chunk of **Text**

Some questions will quote a page or so of one of your set texts and ask you to respond to it. These can be easier to answer, as you've got the text in front of you to quote from, and also because you'll recognise it from the book.
BUT — just because the text is right there, it doesn't mean you're allowed to be lazy.

Above all, answer these 3 questions:

> What is the extract's relevance to the rest of the text?
> Why is it important?
> What implications does it have for the text as a whole?

You Might Have to Write About **Style**

Some questions will ask you specifically about the writing style.

Your answer will be about the usual style things (e.g. language, imagery, style, tone). Remember — don't talk about these things impersonally, as if they just happen by accident.

> Let the examiner know that you understand it's all done by the writer on purpose.
> — that the story doesn't just write itself. It really is the key to better marks.

The symbolism in this section highlights... ✗

The writer uses symbolism in this section in order to highlight... ✓

Steer clear if you don't recognise WHERE the text comes from

If you don't recognise exactly which bit of the novel or story the chunk of text in the question comes from, then avoid it. You'll just end up proving to the examiner that you don't know what you're talking about.

Some Tips About the Writer

Here's a tip — don't trust narrators. Too many end up being untruthful.

You Need to Ask Yourself **Questions** About the **Writing**

Some questions ask you to think about how the writer <u>communicates</u> with the reader.

How Does the Writer Put the Text Together?

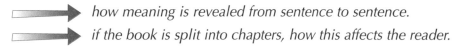

Paragraph structure → how meaning is revealed from sentence to sentence.

Book structure → if the book is split into chapters, how this affects the reader.

With language → implications and what is left unsaid.

Through the narrator → how the story is told.

With imagery → how emotions and scenes are built up.

Why Does the Writer Choose One Way Over Another?

It's what writing is all about — finding the best way to tell your story.
There's no right or wrong way — it's just about finding what's <u>appropriate</u>.

Irvine Welsh wrote *Trainspotting* in Scottish dialect, as this was appropriate to the book's main characters.

Kurt Vonnegut wrote *Cat's Cradle* in very short sections. This is appropriate to the way the facts are uncovered slowly and in pieces by the main character.

Show You Understand **How** the **Writer Does It**

1) The examiner wants to know that you understand that short stories and novels have been <u>thought up</u>, <u>manipulated</u> and <u>written</u> by the writer.

2) You can show that you are aware of this in a very simple way — by referring to the writer.

In "Your Shoes", the author Michèle Roberts shows us only the mother's side of the story. This means our understanding of what happened isn't complete.

The **Narrator** is **NOT** The **Writer**

1) It can be tempting to think that the voice telling the story is the voice of the actual writer.

2) BUT — this is totally wrong. You must remember that the narrator is <u>created</u> by the writer in order to tell the story.

3) They know as much or as little as the <u>writer</u> wants them to know.

4) So, make sure you refer to the writer, to show you understand how books are put together — something like "The <u>writer uses the narrator</u>..." NOT "The <u>narrator says</u>...".

Repeat after me: the narrator is not the writer

The examiners want to know that you understand that stories are made up by a real human being. Make sure you stick the odd "The writer says..." or "The writer uses the narrator..." into your essay.

Questions About Characters

Character Questions Are the Examiner's *Favourite*

Questions about characters are the most <u>popular</u>.

It's pretty obvious why, really — characters act out the story, and <u>shape the plot</u>.

Their actions and experiences are what stories are all about — they come into everything.

You need to be able to write about them <u>confidently</u> if you want to get good marks.

Make Sure You **Prepare** For Character Questions

Make <u>revision notes</u> on these things for the texts you're studying — then you'll be sorted for any exam question on characters. Not all of these will apply to all stories — pick the ones that fit best.

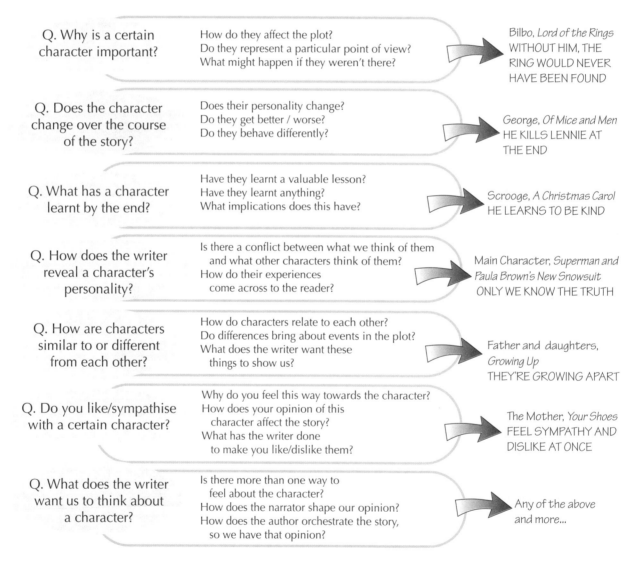

Q. Why is a certain character important?

How do they affect the plot?
Do they represent a particular point of view?
What might happen if they weren't there?

Bilbo, *Lord of the Rings*
WITHOUT HIM, THE RING WOULD NEVER HAVE BEEN FOUND

Q. Does the character change over the course of the story?

Does their personality change?
Do they get better / worse?
Do they behave differently?

George, *Of Mice and Men*
HE KILLS LENNIE AT THE END

Q. What has a character learnt by the end?

Have they learnt a valuable lesson?
Have they learnt anything?
What implications does this have?

Scrooge, *A Christmas Carol*
HE LEARNS TO BE KIND

Q. How does the writer reveal a character's personality?

Is there a conflict between what we think of them and what other characters think of them?
How do their experiences come across to the reader?

Main Character, *Superman and Paula Brown's New Snowsuit*
ONLY WE KNOW THE TRUTH

Q. How are characters similar to or different from each other?

How do characters relate to each other?
Do differences bring about events in the plot?
What does the writer want these things to show us?

Father and daughters, *Growing Up*
THEY'RE GROWING APART

Q. Do you like/sympathise with a certain character?

Why do you feel this way towards the character?
How does your opinion of this character affect the story?
What has the writer done to make you like/dislike them?

The Mother, *Your Shoes*
FEEL SYMPATHY AND DISLIKE AT ONCE

Q. What does the writer want us to think about a character?

Is there more than one way to feel about the character?
How does the narrator shape our opinion?
How does the author orchestrate the story, so we have that opinion?

Any of the above and more...

This ISN'T so you can pre-plan essays — that's ridiculous. You can't tell what the questions will be. It's just so that you've prepared the background, and have the best possible chance.

Don't pre-plan SPECIFIC essays — just learn your stuff

It's not that hard to gather together some information about particular characters. If you do, it means you'll have a much better chance of getting to the heart of an exam question quickly and efficiently.

Warm-up Questions

Take a deep breath and go through these warm-up questions one by one.
If you don't know the answers to these basics, there's no way you'll cope with the exam questions.

Warm-up Questions

1) When you're writing about a book, why bother mentioning the times when it was written?

2) Some stories are set in the past, the future or an imaginary world even though they deal with current issues. Why would a writer want to do that?

3) Write down the names of all the novels and short stories you're studying for GCSE. Next to each one, say whether it deals with social, historical or philosophical issues. If it's not about any of these, say what it is about.

4) If you have a random flash of inspiration about the book as you're writing your essay, should you:
   a) Ignore it. New ideas are dangerous and subversive.
   b) Stick it in the essay — the examiner will be pleased to see that you can think for yourself.
   c) Send your idea to the Patent Office in London.

5) Fill in the gaps in this sentence with words from the box:
   Quoting to _____ your points is _____ in any English Literature essay.

stupid	back up	irrelevant	vital	undermine

6) If they ask you to write about an extract from a book in the exam, should you:
   a) just write about the part of the book that's quoted and ignore the rest of the book
   b) mention a couple of things that happen towards the end of the book so the examiner will think you've read the whole thing
   c) write about how this extract fits in with the rest of the book, and why it's important.

7) Which of these sentences would the examiners prefer to see in a GCSE essay?
   a) "The chapters are given prime numbers instead of being numbered normally."
   b) "The writer heads the chapters with prime numbers instead of numbering them normally."
   Explain your choice.

8) Are the writer and the narrator the same person:
   a) in a novel written in the <u>third person</u>?
   b) in a novel written in the <u>first person</u>?

9) Write down five questions you could ask yourself about the main characters in your set books, so you're ready for any character questions they could throw at you in the exam.

10) Say what you think about the character of Rhi in the following extract, and say why:

    "Rhi's really happy about moving to her new school. She talks about it all the time!" said Rhi's mum to Mrs. Jenkins. Mrs. Jenkins smiled at the pair of them. Rhi gave no sign of having seen her, and kept staring blankly out of the window.

Worked Exam Answer

This worked essay question is exactly the type of essay you might have to write in your exam, or in your coursework. Go through it very carefully to get an idea of what makes a good essay answer.

Worked Exam Question

1. Discuss how Susan Hill effectively uses 'territory', or places, to highlight the difference between Hooper and Kingshaw in 'I'm the King of the Castle'.

Essay plan:

Important to highlight knowledge of author's purpose.

1. Comment on the title of the book and how it refers to 'territorial' rights

2. Examine the importance of Warings

3. Comment on the significance of the Hang Wood episode to both characters

4. Mention Leydell Castle and the farm

5. Return to the <u>importance</u> of territory and how it is used to highlight the difference between the two characters

Important to show the examiner you have focused on the question.

Essay:

The book takes its title from the old-fashioned children's game, 'I'm the King of the Castle'. In this game there are 'safe' and 'unsafe' places to be. The game is about the importance of territory and power.
In the book, different places reveal important things about the two central characters.

Important to show insight into theme.

Warings is Hooper's home and his 'territory.' He is proud of it: 'the idea that it was his pleased him,' although it is dark and ugly. He is determined to prevent Kingshaw from invading his space: he warns him his presence is unwelcome when he drops the note saying, 'I didn't want you to come here'. Kingshaw experiences conflict and fear inside Warings, especially when locked inside the red room with its cases of butterflies and moths, which remind him of death: something which obsesses and terrifies him. Warings is oppressive and <u>Kingshaw feels trapped and unsafe. He has no defence against Hooper's bullying</u> while inside this house. This is confirmed when Hooper invades his bedroom and leaves the dead crow. There is no escape from Hooper's tyranny at Warings.

Important to show critical response to characters.

Worked Exam Answer

During the Hang Wood episode the reader sees another side of Kingshaw and Hooper. Kingshaw feels comfortable and in control when away from Warings: the wood is a safe haven. Conversely, Hooper feels uncomfortable and unsafe in natural surroundings and away from the safety of 'his' house. <u>Kingshaw is able to take control during the storm: when he saves Hooper's life this places him in the position of victor.</u> Hooper has to rely on Kingshaw for his safety. For a time there appears to be a truce and the reader, and Kingshaw, thinks that the relationship will change for the better. However, when they return to Warings, Hooper regains control: he is back in his own 'territory' and is 'king' once again. Hooper will once again be 'thinking of things to do to' Kingshaw.

Important to show writer's purpose.

<u>We see that Kingshaw is in control in 'outside' settings.</u> We can see this when he visits Leydell Castle and justifiably 'bullies' Hooper. We also see this when he visits the farm: Kingshaw finds this 'normal', reassuring and a relief from the oppression he experiences at Warings, especially with the developing relationship between his mother and Mr Hooper and the prospect of a future of persecution at the hands of Hooper. The knowledge that neither his mother nor Mr Hooper believe him makes the situation unbearable. This makes him depressingly aware of the unfairness of adults: Hooper is believed and he is distrusted. The last straw is the plan to send him to Hooper's school.

Important to show insight into meaning.

Kingshaw seeks death in Hang Wood: a natural setting for him to choose and a symbol of rebirth. Kingshaw feels the situation is hopeless and seeks relief in death. Kingshaw chooses death by water, returning from the hostile world to the one element, water, that he always loved.

Hooper feels in control and empowered when inside Warings. Kingshaw is only in control when he is outside Warings. When they 'trespass' on each other's territory they are powerless.

Important to refer back to the set question.

Hooper's preferred <u>territory</u> represents death and symbolises his evil nature. <u>Kingshaw's preferred territory represents rebirth and symbolises his goodness.</u> <u>Hooper's evil dominates and results in Kingshaw's death.</u> <u>Hooper has won the game.</u>

Important to show insight into writer's intended purpose.

Exam Questions

You are allowed to use the text to write your essay.

Q1 'To Kill a Mockingbird' by Harper Lee.
Compare and contrast the characters of Atticus Finch and Robert Ewell.

Q2 'Lord of the Flies' by William Golding.
Show how the sense of order on the island deteriorates over the course of the novel.

Q3 'Of Mice and Men' by John Steinbeck.
Consider the theme of loneliness in the novel 'Of Mice and Men.'
How does it affect the friendships and relationships in the novel?

Q4 'A Kestrel for a Knave' by Barry Hines.
In Section 2 of the novel Billy tells his 'tall story': in what ways does this reinforce the themes of the novel and what does it reveal about Billy's life?

N.B. If you aren't studying any of these texts, don't worry — the practice exam paper at the end of the book has an even larger number of texts to choose from.

Revision Summary

Well, that's another big chunk under your belt. If you can remember the big areas you have to include when you do each kind of essay, that's a good start. But you do have to go into a bit of depth and detail to score the good marks. Go through these questions and make sure you know your stuff.

Drama

1) You're writing about a play. Give four examples of things you can do to impress the examiner.

2) Explain three major issues that a play might deal with.

3) Explain the difference between a tragedy and a comedy.

4) What is dialogue?
      a) A character speaking their thoughts aloud
      b) One character talking to another

5) What are stage directions? What is the point of giving them?

6) What does personification mean?

7) What is stagecraft? What things should you talk about to show that you appreciate it?

8) How old are Shakespeare's plays? Explain two things about them that are old-fashioned.

9) What's the difference between poetic verse and blank verse?

Poetry

1) What three areas should you write about in every poetry essay?

2) Explain two ways of making your argument convincing.

3) How do you show you appreciate what a poet is trying to do (and get the top marks)?

4) Describe the four different forms of poem.

5) What is: a) a stanza?   b) a couplet?   c) a triplet?   d) a quatrain?

6) Explain three effects that a poem with a first-person narrator can put across.

7) List the nine different technical terms that you can use to talk about poetry.
   Write a line to explain what each one means.

Stories and Novels

1) When writing about a text, what four things should you do to thrill the examiner?

2) How does an author put a text together? Name the five things they use.

3) Who is the narrator?
      a) The author
      b) Someone created by the author

4) Write down five questions you could ask about characters to prepare yourself for the exam.

5) What are the two vital things you should include when writing about the message of a text?

6) What three questions should you ask when you're faced with a specific chunk of text?

7) What should you make clear when talking about the writing style?

Structure Your Essay

You know you're right — you just have to persuade everyone else you're right.
You need a good argument and lots of evidence or no one's going to believe you.

Keep your Essay Structured

To get a good grade your essay needs to be: COHERENT: *easy to follow, consistent, smooth-flowing*
LOGICAL: *well-reasoned, realistic*
PERSUASIVE: *convinces readers*

To achieve this you need a clear structure.

1) Work out a plan — decide on your main points, then spend about five minutes
using them to form a plan like the one below. A plan will help organise your
thinking into paragraphs. You need to write in paragraphs to get grade C or above.

2) Don't keep repeating the same idea — organise your essay
into 3 or 4 key ideas and use your plan to put them in order.

3) Fill in the gaps — once you've got a plan you can see where to fit in bits
of evidence, facts, opinions, etc. and where you need more ammunition.

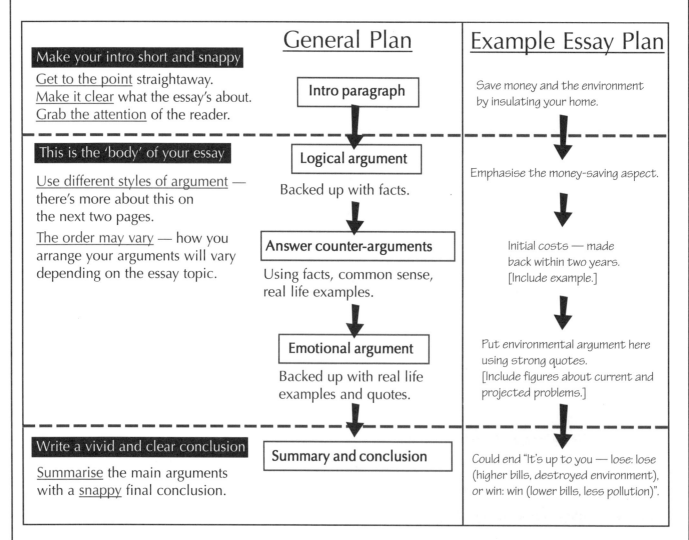

General Plan

Make your intro short and snappy

Get to the point straightaway.
Make it clear what the essay's about.
Grab the attention of the reader.

Intro paragraph

This is the 'body' of your essay

Use different styles of argument —
there's more about this on
the next two pages.
The order may vary — how you
arrange your arguments will vary
depending on the essay topic.

Logical argument

Backed up with facts.

Answer counter-arguments

Using facts, common sense,
real life examples.

Emotional argument

Backed up with real life
examples and quotes.

Write a vivid and clear conclusion

Summarise the main arguments
with a snappy final conclusion.

Summary and conclusion

Example Essay Plan

Save money and the environment
by insulating your home.

Emphasise the money-saving aspect.

Initial costs — made
back within two years.
[Include example.]

Put environmental argument here
using strong quotes.
[Include figures about current and
projected problems.]

Could end "It's up to you — lose: lose
(higher bills, destroyed environment),
or win: win (lower bills, less pollution)".

Structure is all-important

Plan what to write and write what you planned so there's no way that your essay can stray off the point.
The examiner won't be spending hours reading your essays — you need to be clear and precise.

Setting Up Your Argument

Use these tricks to make your essay persuasive — logic, emotion, analogy and ethical beliefs.

Use **Logical Reasoning**

You won't begin to impress the examiners unless your argument is logical.

1)   Show the reader that your argument provides the only logical position.

2)   Use definite language (e.g. 'will', 'all', 'definitely') rather than vague language (e.g. 'might', 'some', 'possibly') — it makes you sound more confident.

3)   Check your reasoning. If it's flawed, your argument fails.

If you want our farm animals to be treated humanely and raised organically, becoming vegetarian isn't the answer. Choosing to eat meat from organic and humane farms will promote this kind of farming and put pressure on stores to stock more of these brands...

Definite language and a logical argument makes this point convincing.

Add **Emotion** to the Logic to Build your Argument

Logic is crucial, but it's not enough on its own.

1)   A passionate belief makes people sit up and take note.

2)   Use striking language to show how you feel.

3)   Don't rely on emotion alone. Always base your argument in logic and emphasise it with emotion.

There is no time left for mulling things over. If we don't act now our river ecosystem will be destroyed. It will be nothing more than polluted sludge, littered with the rotting carcasses of an ecosystem that took thousands of years to establish...

This emotional language makes you feel guilty about destroying the environment.

Use **Analogies** if they Fit

1)   Use analogies if the idea is complex. They help readers to grasp the basic argument using simple ideas.

2)   They provide a powerful and memorable image.

3)   Don't try to squeeze your idea into an analogy. Only use an analogy if it's useful to explain your point.

These new statistics just conceal the problems without solving them. It's like trying to ignore a river by building a dam. The water, like the problems, will just build and build...

This analogy helps the reader understand the buildup of problems.

Include **Ethical Beliefs**

1)   Ethical beliefs are commonly held beliefs about things that are right and wrong, e.g. 'poverty is bad' and 'freedom of speech is good'.

2)   Use them to give your argument an ethical perspective.

Giving aid to poor nations is not enough. In many cases debt is crippling their economies, keeping 80% of the population below the poverty line. We should also cancel all their debts.

You don't actually need to say 'poverty is wrong'. People already know that.

If you want to persuade, you've got to know the tricks

Tug at people's heartstrings and they'll be putty in your hands. It's the oldest trick in the book. But don't get carried away — the moment you stop being realistic, that's when you lose them.

Supporting Your Argument

You get <u>marked</u> on <u>how well</u> you've <u>backed up</u> your argument. And now that you know that, there's <u>no excuse</u> for not researching your essays — especially in your coursework.

Use Facts **Carefully**

1) Don't get bogged down in <u>complicated statistics</u>.

2) Use <u>simple</u>, easy-to-understand facts.

3) Keep figures to a minimum — but make sure you <u>don't</u> alter what they mean.

> Using the Keyword method, word retrieval increased by 16% with a mean improvement of 36 words (and a standard deviation of 8).

Confusing — too much detail.

> 36 more words were recalled on average when the Keyword method was used. ✓

This is a good statistic, because it's easy to understand.

Use **Opinions** from **Experts**

1) Use expert opinion to give <u>backing</u> to your arguments.

2) Say <u>who</u> they are and <u>how</u> they're related to your argument.

3) You can include opinion as <u>quotes</u> (see example below) or <u>part of the text</u> (see example above).

Use **Relevant Quotations**

1) Use good quotes to provide <u>sound bites</u> that stick in people's minds.

2) Don't just stick in a quote for the sake of it: make sure it's <u>relevant</u>.

3) Keep it short. <u>Don't</u> include long extracts.

4) Use <u>quotation marks</u> and also say <u>who</u> you're quoting — otherwise you won't get the marks for using the quotation.

5) <u>Never</u> make up quotes, or alter existing ones. It's the same as lying.

> Chief Medical Officer Robert Thial agrees, saying, "I've investigated each method of execution and they all cause unnecessary pain and suffering".

Use **Real-life Examples**

1) Your argument should sound as though it's true in <u>real-life</u> terms, not groundless theory.

2) Give real-life examples to provide your argument with cold, hard <u>reality</u>.

3) Choose examples that fit your argument as <u>closely</u> as possible. If the connection is weak, don't use it.

> ✓ After initial reservations a skate park was built within the main park. Youth crime has since dropped. This was a direct result of the park, according to local police sergeant Rose Leven.

> ✗ The creation of a rose garden in the park has increased visitor numbers. This may have contributed to a reduction in youth crime in the local area.

Pick your evidence carefully

Facts, examples, opinions and quotes all <u>add punch</u> to your argument — but don't overdo it. <u>Good rule of thumb</u>: use one <u>well chosen</u> piece of evidence for <u>each part</u> of the argument.

Persuasive Writing Tools

To get an <u>A grade</u> your essay <u>really</u> has to be persuasive — here are <u>four more handy tips</u> to help you.

Keep Your Writing **Polite** and **Non-aggressive**

1) Being polite is very important when you're writing about people with the <u>opposite opinion</u> to yours.

2) You should criticise their <u>opinions</u> only. Don't criticise them personally — you'll lose marks for being rude.

3) If it sounds like a <u>personal attack</u> it will make you sound angry, and it won't help you persuade anyone.

A lot of people think school uniforms make everyone equal. They are wrong...

It is often said that school uniforms make everyone equal. This isn't true...

Make Your **Positive** Points **Personal**

You need to make the readers feel that you're all on the <u>same side</u>.

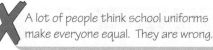 <u>We</u> all believe that individuality is important.

The "<u>we</u>" makes it sound as if your readers <u>agree</u> with you already.

You can also use "<u>you</u>" to talk <u>directly</u> to your readers, especially if you're trying to persuade them to do something. as if you're trying to persuade them personally.

Giving blood saves lives. As a compassionate person, do <u>you</u> really need to read further before <u>you</u> take action?

Use **Rhetorical Questions** To Make Your Points

1) A <u>rhetorical question</u> is a question that requires no answer — the answer should be obvious from the text. It's used for effect.

Is this sort of thing acceptable in our society?

2) It's a brilliant trick that writers and politicians use all the time — and the <u>examiners</u> will be looking out for it too. Leaving the readers to put the answer together themselves is a great way of making them <u>agree with you</u>.

Can anyone tell me why road builders are <u>ruining the countryside</u>?

Use language like "ruining the countryside" to <u>emphasise</u> your opinion.

Keep Your Writing Punchy with **Magic Threes**

It's one of the <u>easiest</u> and most useful tricks for <u>emphasising</u> your points.

Instead of just using one describing-word in a sentence, use <u>three</u>.

The development of a European single policy is an expensive, time-consuming, and unworkable nightmare.

This sounds <u>much better</u> than "A European single policy is expensive and unworkable". It's a trick you'll hear <u>politicians</u> using in speeches — it <u>stresses</u> the points you're making.

Can I write rhetorical questions?

What a fantastic page. <u>Four ways</u> of making your writing really punchy. And on top of that, anyone reading it will be <u>convinced</u> that what you're saying is <u>completely true</u>.

Think About Your Readers

Put Yourself in the *Reader's Shoes*

1) Any piece of writing is designed to be <u>read</u> by someone — so you should <u>suit</u> your writing to the reader.

2) That means trying to <u>second-guess</u> what a reader's reactions might be.

Identify Readers' **Concerns** and **Address** *Them*

Think about <u>concerns</u> the reader might have, and then:

1) Make their concerns sound like <u>understandable reactions</u>.

2) Let them know that you've <u>thought</u> about these concerns.

3) <u>Tell them</u> how your argument addresses the concerns.

A concern that many residents may have is the question of litter after the concert. Cleaning up quickly is of the utmost importance to us. To do this there will be a twenty-strong team working quietly through the night to clear it by 6:00am the next day.

Imagine **Counter-Arguments** and Argue **Against** Them

A good way of persuading people is to imagine how they would argue against you, and answer their points. Imagine you're writing to persuade the RSPCA to let you work for them...

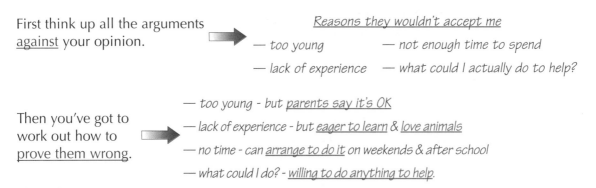

First think up all the arguments <u>against</u> your opinion.

Reasons they wouldn't accept me

— *too young*   — *not enough time to spend*

— *lack of experience*   — *what could I actually do to help?*

Then you've got to work out how to <u>prove them wrong</u>.

— *too young - but <u>parents say it's OK</u>*

— *lack of experience - but <u>eager to learn</u> & <u>love animals</u>*

— *no time - can <u>arrange to do it</u> on weekends & after school*

— *what could I do? - <u>willing to do anything to help</u>.*

Challenge **Biases** and **Expectations**

1) Your first paragraph is <u>crucial</u> — you've got to keep them reading — it needs <u>impact</u> and interesting ideas that make them want to keep reading.

2) <u>Don't</u> disguise your argument and don't say things you disagree with. If you do, your argument will sound <u>weak</u> and you'll sound as if you don't believe in what you're saying.

3) <u>Challenge expectations</u> — come at the issue from a different <u>point of view</u> from the one they expect.

Second-guessing what the reader will think is vital

<u>Remember</u> — <u>think</u> like your reader and you'll always be <u>one step ahead</u> of them.
Which means they'll be <u>easier</u> to <u>bend to your will</u>. It's what all authors think — well, usually.

Analyse, Review and Comment

"Analyse, Review and Comment" — it's a bit more clinical than an arguing essay (like a report). So leave out the <u>emotional</u> stuff.

You Still Have to be **Convincing**

1) 'Analyse' and 'review' might sound like vague words. But they're not.

2) They still mean you have to be <u>clear</u>, <u>logical</u> and <u>precise</u>.

3) The examiner wants you to sound as though you know what you're talking about.

4) You have to write <u>convincingly</u>.

> Q1.   Analyse the merits and disadvantages of wearing uniforms to school.

<u>Analyse</u> — break the subject down into pieces and look at each one individually.

> *Merits — sense of identity, easy for others to identify, smartness.*
>
> *Disadvantages — restricting, less individuality,   (etc... go into detail on all these points).*

<u>Review</u> — bring them all together again, with an overview of the whole topic.

> *School staff tend to feel the merits, while pupils are the ones who live with the disadvantages.*

<u>Comment</u> — Make a balanced comment on the arguments you've discussed in your essay.

> *Ultimately it should be recognised that not all teachers think pupils should wear uniforms, and not all pupils hate wearing them.*

Make Your Writing More **Detached**

1) You're still trying to show readers <u>why</u> they agree with you — but now you have to sound <u>detached</u>.

2) It needs to read more like a <u>clinical report</u> than a persuasive essay.

3) That doesn't mean it has to be boring — it just means <u>you can't take sides</u>.

Make Sure You Plan **All Sides** of the Argument

You're presenting a report on <u>all the different sides</u> of an argument.

The whole point is to make it all as <u>concise</u> and orderly as possible.

Planning an analysis essay needs <u>bullet points</u>.

For Congestion Charge:	Against Congestion Charge:
• good for health	• inconvenience
• good for environment	• cost
• safer	• causing congestion elsewhere
• less noise	• poor public transport

Make sure you have a strong argument
The main thing is to be logical. Don't use emotional pleas unless they're relevant. You'll just sound like an idiot if all you say is "oh go on, please agree with me". You need sound arguments.

Making Your Analysis Sound Good

Here are the tricks for sounding authoritative and impartial. They're easy to learn — and once you've got it, you can set about making people believe pretty much anything. Politicians do it all the time.

Never Use "I" or "You"

1) While the first person ("I...") is useful for making fiction sound believable, it's useless for trying to make your own real opinions sound credible.

2) Using "I" sounds like it's just your personal, unimportant opinion.

3) Using the third person (normally "It") sounds more detached, professional and authoritative.

I have noticed that the temperature of swimming pool water has been rising for the last 3 months. ← bad

The temperature of swimming pool water has been rising over the last 3 months. ← good

Keep it Simple

1) On no account get carried away in an analysis essay.

2) They're not the same as arguing essays — they have to be detached and impartial.

3) Don't use analogies and emotional pleas. They won't sound believable.

4) Just write your points simply and clearly. e.g. 'Vegetarians are not universally respected' NOT 'Vegetarians get laughed at in butchers' shops on a daily basis'.

Your Essay Could Be About the Pros and Cons

Structuring your essay around good and bad points of the topic keeps it focused.

This is the analysis part of the essay.

Essay plan

Intro — about vegetarians

Pros and cons of vegetarianism

Review — good: idealistic points; bad: practical points

Comment — should ask whether you would rather be idealistic or practical

There are 2 different ways of writing about pros and cons:

Make 3 points IN FAVOUR of something... ... then make 3 points AGAINST it.

or:

Analyse good and bad together, putting your points coherently, in a logical order.

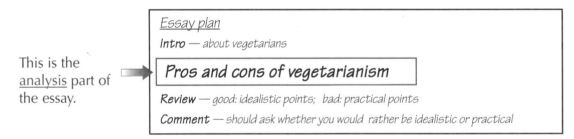

Good — *moral, personal, good for environment*
Bad — *unhealthy, inconvenient, anti-social*

It doesn't really matter which approach you use, just make it sound clear and professional.

Point 1 — *it's moral, but can be unhealthy*
Point 2 — *it's a strong personal choice, but it can be inconvenient for shopping and eating out*
Point 3 — *it's good for the environment but some people see it as being anti-social*

Keep focused when writing your essays — don't lose your thread

It's a shame when someone's got a great argument that starts off making you think "hang on, they might be onto something" — then they spoil it by going off on one and losing the thread of the whole thing.

Finishing Your Essay

Finish off with a <u>clear conclusion</u> and then <u>check</u> your work.

End With a *Clear Conclusion*

Start by <u>summing up</u> all the <u>key</u> points.

> To sum up, banning cars on the road during school hours is not practical. There are too many businesses and homes nearby. Reducing the speed limit is a good idea, as long as it is properly enforced. This could definitely be helped by putting in speed bumps as a form of traffic control.
>
> Even though traffic all around the town would be affected, the second and third plans are worth putting into practice. They could save a child's life.

Based on the <u>whole</u> report, say what <u>you think</u> should be done and <u>why</u>.

Leave Enough *Time* For a Proper Ending

This may sound stupid, but in an exam situation it's surprisingly easy to <u>run out</u> of time. You've <u>got to leave</u> enough time to <u>finish</u> your essay properly — with a <u>clear ending</u>.

Give yourself **at least five minutes** to write a **conclusion** for your essay.

Look Over the Essay — 3 *Final Checks*

Leave at least <u>five minutes</u>, at the end, for checking your work.

Check your ARGUMENT / ADVICE   clear, no waffle, well-structured, all points covered

Check your ENGLISH   spelling, punctuation, paragraphs, style, language

Check the DETAILS   accurate quotes, accurate figures

Every argument needs a conclusion
I know, you've heard this all before. I'm only going on so much about the conclusion because it's important — it's the bit they're left remembering. You <u>must</u> always leave room for a good ending.

Warm-up Questions

There's only one way to do well in the exam — learn the basics then practise lots of exam questions to see what it'll be like on the big day. We couldn't have made that easier for you — so do it.

Warm-up Questions

1) Should you use logical reasoning in an 'arguing and analysing' essay?

2) Define 'ethical belief' and give an example.

3) What is an analogy and why are analogies effective?

4) Define 'rhetorical question' and give an example.

5) Define 'emotional language' and give an example.

6) Why is it better to use simple facts rather than complicated ones?

7) Why is it better to use real-life facts than fictitious ones?

8) How can using 'we' help to persuade an audience to a particular point of view?

9) Why is it useful to include the opinion of an expert in an arguing and analysing essay?

10) How might you show that you have thought about your readers in your essay?

11) Which of the following should an 'analyse, review and comment' essay be like?

    a) detached

    b) emotional

    c) biased

12) List 2 tricks to make your analysis sound authoritative and impartial.

13) Explain why you should use the third person 'it' in an analysis rather than the first person 'I'.

14) Turn each of the following sentences into impersonal <u>statements</u> (i.e. statements not using questions and not using "you" or "I"):

    a) I think there is obviously too much junk food being sold in cities.

    b) Don't you think that there is a ridiculous amount of paranoia concerning the diet of teenagers today?

    c) I've noticed that people get more and more bad-tempered the closer they live to heavily polluted areas, and I think that something needs to be done about it.

15) Explain why you should cover the pros and cons of an argument in your essay.

16) What should you include in the conclusion of an 'analyse, review and comment' essay?

Worked Exam Answer

I've looked at this exam question and done a sample answer for you, with a few helpful notes scribbled on. It should really help you get an idea of what to do, so don't say I never do anything for you.

Worked Exam Question

1. Write a speech for your M.P. to use to persuade fellow M.P.s to vote for more money to be made available for foreign aid.

Essay plan:

1. *Begin by appealing to the M.P.s for their support in increasing aid.*

2. *Give examples of how people are suffering around the world.*

3. *Show how increasing foreign aid can make a difference.*

4. *Conclude with an emotional appeal about how they should vote.*

Essay:

Use formal address.

My right honourable friends, I come before you to appeal for your help, in providing aid to the poorest countries in the world. I come before you certain that you will want to help those in this world of ours, who are suffering.

This kind of detail really helps to bring the images home.

In Somalia, children are starving. They exist on meagre amounts of rice. No doubt, you have seen the pictures of them on television, with swollen round bellies and legs like sticks. In South Africa, many people are dying from AIDS. Mothers and fathers look on helplessly, whilst their children waste away with the disease. In Romania, for many years, the old, the disabled and the orphans have been locked away. We have all seen pictures of young children in orphanages who have no toys to play with and instead, rock backwards and

Emotive language helps to persuade.

Worked Exam Answer

forwards, their shaved heads making them look as if they are from a concentration camp. In other parts of the world that are torn apart by war, there are children who have lost limbs due to mines exploding on land where they have been playing.

Can _we_ look away? Can we allow such suffering to continue? Can we go on with our lives, whilst in another part of our world children are crying to be fed?

Using "we" makes it sound as if the listeners will agree already.

These rhetorical questions emphasise the points.

I went into politics, hoping to make a difference. I am sure each one of you did too. Now is the time to make your vote matter. _We_ have the resources to be able to help the poorest people of the world. Increasing our foreign aid by a mere 2% will ensure that those starving in Africa will receive, at least, one meal a day. Increasing our foreign aid by such a small amount will ensure that every child in the Third World will be inoculated against diseases that kill so many of them each year. Increasing the aid we send will, furthermore, help to provide an education for all.

Addresses the listeners' concerns.

You may ask, why should we give to those in other parts of the world? By helping set up projects in the Third World, we can give men and women the tools to help themselves – to build a future without poverty, illness and lack of education. That is what they ask of us – not handouts, but the chance to make a difference to their own families, communities, countries and, ultimately, to this world that we share. We cannot deny them this chance. Our constituents, I am sure, would feel that by using resources carefully we can help situations both here and abroad.

The list of three words adds power to the argument.

Vote to increase foreign aid.

Vote to end sickness, hunger and poverty.

Repetition helps to persuade.

Vote for a brighter future for every citizen of the world.

Exam Questions

Q1 Argue for or against the proposition that children are spending too much time at home using computers, instead of taking part in sporting and social activities.
Remember to:
- Choose the right language to present an argument.
- Sequence your ideas appropriately.

Q2 Write a speech for your M.P. to use to persuade fellow M.P.s to vote for a ban on violence in children's television programmes.
Remember to:
- Choose the right language for a speech.
- Use persuasive language.

Q3 Write an advice sheet for parents, about their children using computers at home.
Remember to:
- Set out your writing as an advice sheet.
- Concentrate on advising parents about the benefits of children using computers at home.
- Provide suggestions for other activities their children might take part in.

Q4 Write an article for a tabloid newspaper where you aim to:
- Argue the case for less violence in children's television programmes.
- Persuade the reader that watching violence on television can make children more aggressive.
- Choose language that will argue, persuade and advise.

Revision Summary

Arguing skills and analysing skills are really important — you'll end up using the same techniques for lots of different essays in the exam and in your coursework. In a way they're quite an easy sort of essay to get to grips with — factual, clinical and (mostly) detached. A bit like Science really. Anyway, make sure you can do all these questions. If not, you need to go back over the section again.

<u>Arguing and Analysing</u>

1) What is an 'arguing and analysing' essay trying to achieve?

2) Why is it important to be logical in your thinking?

3) Write a brief essay plan in response to the following question — "Should you try to get good grades in your GCSEs?" (use p.54 as a guide if you don't remember properly).

4) Explain why structuring your essay is important.

5) What's an analogy and why are analogies effective?

6) Why is it important to support your argument with facts?

7) Explain why it's better to use simple facts rather than complicated statistics.

8) Which of these quotes would be appropriate in an essay on getting good grades, and why?

    a) "All teachers are fascists" (source: unknown)

    b) "Most University Admissions staff look at how well students did in their GCSEs" (Prof. J. Morgan: University of Leeds, 2002)

9) Why are real-life examples more effective than fictional ones?

10) Explain why you need to keep your writing style polite and non-aggressive.

11) Why do you want your reader to feel as if you're on the same side as them?

12) What is a rhetorical question and why are rhetorical questions effective?

13) Do you need to try to put yourself in the reader's shoes when writing your essay? Why?

14) Why should you address any concerns you think your reader might have about your argument?

<u>Analyse, Review, Comment</u>

15) Why should an 'analyse, review and comment' essay be more clinical than an arguing essay?

16) Should your writing be a) clear, b) logical, c) precise or d) all of these?

17) Why should you try to cover all the different sides of an argument in your essay?

18) Explain why using the first person ("I") is not appropriate for this type of essay.

19) Read this question, then answer parts a) and b) — "Analyse the state of the current top 40".
    a) Write an essay plan where you discuss the good and bad points separately (as on p.60).
    b) Write an essay plan where you discuss the good and bad points simultaneously (also on p.60).

20) Is either one of the two suggested essay plans from Q.19, better than the other?

21) Explain why your essay needs a conclusion.

22) Which things should you check for at the end of the exam?
        a) clarity of argument
        b) proper use of English
        c) use of details and facts

Getting Your Answer Right

In the exam, you'll have to do a question where you need to either <u>inform</u>, <u>explain</u> or <u>describe</u>. Each type needs to be tackled in a different way — and you'll lose marks if you don't do it right.

Pick out the **Key Words** in the Question

To answer any question well, you need a clear idea of:

1) Your <u>purpose</u> — What are you writing about? And do you need to inform, explain or describe?
2) Your <u>audience</u> — The tone, structure and words you choose will depend on who your reader is.

<u>Key words</u> in the question will tell you what sort of answer the examiner is after. Scribble a circle around them and keep them in mind as you write:

> *Q1. There are many pressures on young people today. Explain what you think are the main pressures and how they affect your life and the lives of people you know.*

> *Q2. Write an article describing an ideal holiday place. It could be somewhere you have been to, or an imaginary destination.*

> *Q3. Write an informative article for teachers about "Clothes and Today's Teenager".*

Informing is about Giving Information to Your Reader

For this type of question, imagine you're teaching your reader something that they don't know much about. You want to give them a good outline of the topic so they can understand it better.

Whether you're writing to inform or explain, it's important to go into detail and back up your statements with <u>evidence</u>. An essay that is just personal opinion will get you zero marks.

Give <u>examples</u> every time you make a <u>statement</u>, to explain what you are saying.

There are two ways to do this:
- Give an <u>example/fact</u>.
- Give an <u>expert's opinion</u>.

STATEMENT

Smoking is really bad for your health.

EXAMPLE/FACT

• For example, smoking is one cause of cancer and heart disease.

• A link was found between lung cancer and smoking in 1950.

EXPERT OPINION

• The scientist Geraldine Hunt writes that smoking is "a vicious killer."

Always, always, always think "What is this question asking me?"
This can never be said enough. You MUST spend a little time pondering over what the question is actually ASKING you. Don't just start scribbling without a thought. THINK and you'll be just fine.

Getting Your Answer Right

Explaining *Means Giving a* **Detailed Discussion**

You might be asked to explain what you think about something.
You need to explain what your beliefs are, in a logical way:

- Decide what your main arguments are, then write a paragraph explaining each one.

- Make sure that each point is backed up with evidence —
reasons why you think what you say.

Make Descriptions **In-depth**

When you answer a describing question, it's all about giving a variety of interesting details.
Entertain your reader by using loads of unusual and exciting words and different kinds of sentences.
Describe sensations and feelings to give them a picture of what you're describing, in their mind's eye.

> The beach is yellow and the sun is
> really hot. You can order drinks
> whenever you want.

ADD DEPTH

+ INTEREST

> The sun's bright rays sparkle down on the golden sand
> dunes, where you can sprawl out while a handsome waiter
> fetches you ice-cold cocktails.

Make Descriptions **Interesting**

Don't be obvious. Add in any little details that will make it more interesting.

BORING

> Choose what food you want to eat.

BRILLIANT

> Decide what food you want to eat. Pasta is quick
> to cook and provides lots of carbohydrates.
> Roasted meat is really tasty but it takes longer.

Giving good descriptions — the proof is in the paragraph
Paragraphs. I'll say that again: PARAGRAPHS. It's an easy way to organise your essay but it'll get
you good marks. Each paragraph should be a statement, followed by evidence to back it up.

Starting Your Essay

As I said, in your exam you'll have to write an essay that explains, informs or describes. No one's trying to trick you — it really should be pretty simple, as long as you know what you're doing.

4 Ways Not to Mess it Up

1) Write About What You Know

If you have a choice of topics you should always choose one you know a lot about.
For example, a question might ask you to describe how to look after a pet.
You should choose a pet your family or friend owns, because you'll know more to write about.

2) Scribble Down a Plan

Note down the things you need to cover. It'll make sure you cover all the points and do it in a logical order. That'll make it much easier for the reader to understand what you are writing about. You should spend 5 minutes on the plan.

Question:
Write an essay to explain how to do an everyday task

Task selected:
To explain how to make dinner.

Plan:
Introduction
What to eat (how to decide)
How to cook it (reading labels, etc.)
How to serve the food / eat it...
Conclusion

The stages are listed in a clear order...

3) Write an Introduction

Start the essay with an introduction to say what the essay is going to be about. This should give the reader an idea of how you are going to tackle the topic.

Introduction:
Cooking dinner is one of the most useful things you can learn — it's cheaper and usually healthier than eating out. You might find it a bit difficult at first but there are a few simple steps to make sure you can cook successfully. This essay is going to explain each stage of preparing dinner: choosing what to eat, cooking it and serving it up.

4) Stick to Your Plan

- Once you start writing, don't get carried away, don't go off at a tangent and don't forget about your plan.

- Have some discipline in the way you write — keep your points in a logical order and don't wander off the topic.

- Write in paragraphs.

- Try and write at least two sides.

Stay logical and the conclusion will be good marks

Examiners aren't nasty people — they're just following their mark schemes. This kind of essay should be coherent, logical and persuasive. Do it like that and they will love you for it.

Make Sure Everyone Can Understand

It's no good if you're the only one that understands what you're writing about — you've got to make sure that everyone will be able to get their head round it.

Think About Your Readers

You're supposed to be explaining something.

1) Explain things which might be obvious to you, but not necessarily obvious to other people.

This is no good —

> Get a plant and grow it.

You need to explain what you mean —

> Buy some seeds from a garden centre. Dig a small hole and put the seeds in the hole. Water the area regularly.

2) Try to anticipate any bias your reader may have. Then try to respond to what they might be thinking. A balanced argument is more likely to persuade people than a ranting one.

Your reader might not agree with your argument...

> Everybody should be a vegetarian because eating meat is terrible.

> There are many different arguments for and against eating meat. To a lot of people, the idea of giving up meat is a difficult one. However, more and more people are becoming concerned about the rights of the animals and the treatment they receive.

The writer recognises what the reader may be thinking...

...but still puts across their point.

3) Try to anticipate where the reader might get confused and make those bits especially clear.

4) Always read over what you've written. Think, "If I were reading this for the first time, would it make sense?" If not, you need to change it so that it does.

Explain Unusual and Technical Language

1) If you're writing about something you know well, it's easy to forget that your reader won't understand all the technical words you're using.

2) Your aim should be to make your writing clear enough for anyone to understand what you're saying.

3) Take care even when you're explaining something as ordinary as cooking dinner. You might think it's obvious what "boil the potatoes" means. But a reader who doesn't know about cooking needs you to explain that "boil" means, "put in boiling water."

The underlined words here are technical terms. They'll be understood by tennis experts...

> The serve-volley game of Williams dominated Davenport's ground strokes. She repeatedly got to the net allowing her to take the first set, despite facing three break points in the second game.

...but others won't understand and will get confused.

DON'T confuse your readers

Technical jargon is really good for impressing examiners. BUT you MUST explain the tricky stuff properly, to show you're trying to help your reader, and you'll get more lovely, lovely marks.

Finishing Off Your Essay

At the end of your essay you need to tie up what you've been saying...

Finish Your Essay with a *Conclusion*

Before you start your conclusion look back at the <u>introduction</u>. Make sure that your conclusion agrees with the introduction. This will make the examiner feel as if the essay's a <u>complete package</u>, not just some random thoughts strung together.

Your conclusion should:

1 *Remind the reader about the <u>most important facts and ideas</u> in your essay.*

2 *<u>Give your opinion</u> on the topic you've been writing about.*

1 This bit reminds the reader about the main facts covered in the essay — how to get water, food, fire and shelter.

I hope you are never stranded on a desert island, but if it *does* happen remember that following these steps will massively increase your chances of survival: find water, find food, and then make a fire and shelter. Following these steps ensures you have the basic essentials for life. It will also make you feel more confident, and confidence is as much a key to survival as water, food, fire or shelter.

2 The final sentence has got an opinion about the facts in the essay.

You *Must Check* What You've Written

Once you've got a conclusion, go back over the whole essay and <u>check</u> these points:

Have you written a clear introduction which explains what the essay is about? ☐

Have you added some interesting and colourful details? ☐

Have you thought about your reader — where they might be confused or might disagree with what you've said? ☐

Have you explained all the technical terms you've used? ☐

As far as you can tell, is all the spelling and punctuation OK? ☐

1) If your answer to any of these questions is 'no', then do something about it.

2) There isn't much you can do if there are just 15 seconds to go — but five minutes is enough to <u>make a difference</u>. That's why it's so important to leave time for checking.

3) If you want to <u>add</u> anything, put a star (*) where you want the extra words to go and write them as clearly as you can in the margin.

4) If you want to <u>get rid</u> of anything, just cross it out <u>neatly</u>. Don't scribble all over it.

Conclusions are your chance to wrap up your argument
The conclusion is your chance to hammer home what you've been talking about, and finish things off nicely. It (and the introduction) are really vital for grabbing the reader's attention and making your point.

Warm-up Questions

You must be getting used to the routine by now — the warm-up questions run over the basic information, the worked example shows you how to tackle an essay question, and then after that it's all up to you.

Warm-up Questions

1) Explain what is meant by each of these essay instructions:
   a) explain
   b) inform
   c) describe

2) How would the vocabulary you use differ in a letter to a child and a letter to a parent?

3) List two ways you can support statements you make in an informative essay.

4) When should you not use technical or unusual language?

5) Which of these is the less interesting and less vivid description? Why?
   a) He wore a long, black overcoat that was ragged at the edges and fading in colour. His tattered hat was tilted to cover his eyes. As he loomed over me, I felt my heart in my mouth. I couldn't breathe.
   b) He wore an old coat and when he came near me, I was scared.

6) Which is the better explanation and why?
   a) Put some beef in a pan and cook it.
   b) Over a low heat, warm three tablespoons of olive oil in a large, deep frying-pan. Add 200 grams of stewing beef that has been sliced thinly. Cook until the meat is a light brown colour on both sides.

7) Why is it important to think about how your reader might react towards your piece?

8) Which is more likely to persuade your reader — a balanced argument or a ranting one?

9) What should you include in a good conclusion?

10) List five things you should check for at the end of the exam.

11) There are 4 photos below showing different landscapes. Write a paragraph describing each one. Explain how each one is different from the others.

A

B

C

D

Worked Exam Answer

Exam questions are the best way to practise what you've learnt. After all, they're exactly what you'll have to do on the big day — so go through this worked essay very carefully.

Worked Exam Question

1.   Places can seem different at different times of year. Choose one of the following places:
                a school playground
                a High Street
                a pond
                a country lane.
        Describe it in winter and summer.

Essay plan:

1.   *Begin by describing the country lane in winter — concentrate on the sensations of cold.*

2.   *Describe the harshness of the landscape and the wildlife struggling against the elements.*

3.   *Describe the country lane in summer — contrasting the beauty of the landscape with that of winter.*

4.   *Describe the wildlife and all of nature coming to life again.*

Essay:

Country Lane in Winter

Freezing rain, like shards of glass, pelted the long country lane. The leaves, that had once been fiery crimson and gold, had become a <u>dull brown mush. They squelched underfoot</u> and clung to boots and shoes. The once-proud poplar trees appeared ravaged by the winter's cold, each branch was now empty and barren. The undergrowth, around the trees, appeared dark and gloomy, as if it held dark secrets. The whole scene was grey, as if life had been sucked from it.

Detailed, interesting descriptions.

Describes sensations

Paints a vivid picture

Worked Exam Answer

The clouds moved in formations across the sky. They looked like monstrous faces, as if Nature itself were angry. The debris from a fallen tree, from the night before, was strewn across the lane – a danger to cars that might pass that way. The driving rain continued to come down, forming muddy pools and filling potholes. A lone bird struggled to fly, whilst the wind and rain battered its wings. It kept on fighting, in search of safety and shelter. Most of the wildlife had long since looked for refuge and some protection from the cold.

Contains depth and interest

Country Lane in Summer

The country lane wound its way through a row of poplar trees, that swayed gently in the summer breeze. It was as if their branches were waving, welcoming all who would pass by. A young girl, in a dark blue shirt meandered along; her jumper was casually tied around her waist.

Conveys a positive atmosphere

The sun's rays were warm and gentle, as they flickered through the trees. The hue of the sky was of the deepest azure blue. As a plane soared overhead, a white trail could be seen in the sky as if it were leaving its mark. In the haze of heat, little flies buzzed around. A butterfly, with the purest white wings, alighted upon a foxglove that stood proud and tall. In the hedgerows, delicate red poppies contrasted with the lush green grass and ferns. A chaffinch trilled out its welcome call to its mate, in the branches of a tree overhead. All around was flourishing with new life.

Depth and interest added

Variety of unusual and interesting words

Contains contrasting details to the lane in winter

Exam Questions

Q1   Choose a place that has been significant in your life.
      Write about it in a way which will inform other people.

Q2   Think about a time when you fulfilled an ambition.
      Explain what the ambition was and why it was so important to you to achieve it.

Q3   Choose one of the following places:
          a café
          a market place
          a fairground
          a seaside resort
      Describe it during the day and at night.

Q4   What job would you most like to do one day?
      Describe what it would involve and explain why you would most like to do it.

Revision Summary

It's definitely quite tricky to figure out the subtle differences between 'informing', 'explaining', and 'describing', but it <u>is</u> important for you to know what those differences are.
The main thing is that you're trying to give information to the reader. Otherwise, the basic rules for writing this essay are the same as for any other one. You've got to think about who you're writing for, and how to keep your writing lively, engaging and believable. So run through these questions and make sure that you've got all this knowledge locked up safe in your head.
You'll be thankful for it, come exam time.

1) Explain what is meant by each of these essay instructions in turn —
   a)   inform
   b)   explain
   c)   describe

2) Pick out the key words in the questions below and say what you think the question is asking —
   a)   Explain some reasons for the use of speed cameras by police.
   b)   Write an article describing an ideal profession. The job could be real or imaginary.
   c)   Write an informative article for parents about music and the teenagers of today.

3) When choosing a topic to write about, why is it important to choose one that you know a lot about?

4) Explain what a good essay plan should achieve.

5) Why should you use lots of interesting details in your essay?

6) Which of these is the better explanation? Explain why.
   a)   Feed your dog some food.
   b)   You must feed your dog the right amount for its size. You can find out what this is from your vet or from books on your dog's breed.

7) Why do you think a balanced argument is more likely to persuade people than a ranting one?

8) Which of these descriptions is more suited to an essay? Why?
   a)   Pilots should be able to deploy the chute, now fitted to all Cirrus SR20 light aircraft for test purposes, and float the entire bird to safety from 1000m high over Lexington, KY.
   b)   A new type of emergency parachute for aircraft is being tested in Kentucky.

9) Why do you need to think at all about how the reader will react?

10) What's the point of writing a conclusion?

11) Explain what makes a really good conclusion.

12) Write down all the things you need to check for at the end of the exam.

13) Explain why it's important to leave yourself time at the end to go over your essay.

Starting Your Writing

This section is full of useful hints and ideas for writing your own stories — something most people find really scary.

Use What You **Know** to Get **Ideas**

You'll need a plot — a basic outline of what happens in your story.
You'll also need some main characters.
Start off by scribbling down some ideas. You could:

1) Write about something you're interested in. If you already know stuff about it, your story will be more realistic and it'll be easier to give lots of detail.

   If you know loads about science fiction, base your story in outer space. If you're into ballet then write about a dance class.

2) Write about something that's happened to you. It'll be easier for you, and your story will seem more lifelike and genuine to the reader.

   If you saw a solar eclipse or won a donkey race, write about that.

Get Your Story Straight **Before** You Start Writing

Once you've got a rough idea of what's going to happen you need to plan your structure. Write a brief synopsis of your story — a breakdown of the plot.

Beginning   1) Start by introducing your key characters. What do they want to achieve, and what obstacles stand in their way?

A lot of stories are about conflict or struggle to achieve something. That's because characters have different motives — they have to compete or clash to get what they want.

Buildup   2) What's going to happen — how will you build up to the climax of your story?

Give your characters a challenge. There has to be uncertainty or an element of risk to make it exciting.

Climax   3) Bring the action to a head. The main event or turning point should happen now.

You need to build up the suspense and keep your reader guessing, up until this point. Otherwise the story will be boring.

Ending   4) Be sure that your conclusion makes some kind of point. Don't just tail off — you must tie up all loose ends.

You could give it a moral, so that the characters learn something. Or you could give the story an unexpected twist.

Don't be afraid of original writing — learn to trust your ideas

Don't panic about starting your writing. This section will show you how to turn a simple idea into a great story. Just try to relax — it's really not as terrifying as you might think.

Say What Happened

Give it lots of **Style** and **Substance**

To impress the people giving out those C - A* marks, you need to show you can write with <u>imagination</u> and <u>flair</u>. Check that your story has these things:

1) An entertaining plot that says something — there must be some <u>point</u> to it.

2) A clear <u>structure</u> — a beginning, middle and end that flow fluently together.

3) A variety of <u>styles</u> — different sentence lengths and structures, and interesting vocabulary.

4) <u>Grammatically correct</u> sentence- and paragraph-structure, punctuation and spelling.

5) It does what it's supposed to do. It must be written in a <u>style</u> that suits the audience it's aimed at.

Tell Your Reader **What Happened** and do it **Clearly**

1) Your story needs to have a good <u>structure</u>. An epic adventure with hundreds of characters and loads of action is no good if your reader can't follow what's going on.

2) Everything you write should be <u>relevant</u> to the plot— in other words, leave out anything that's boring or doesn't need to be there.

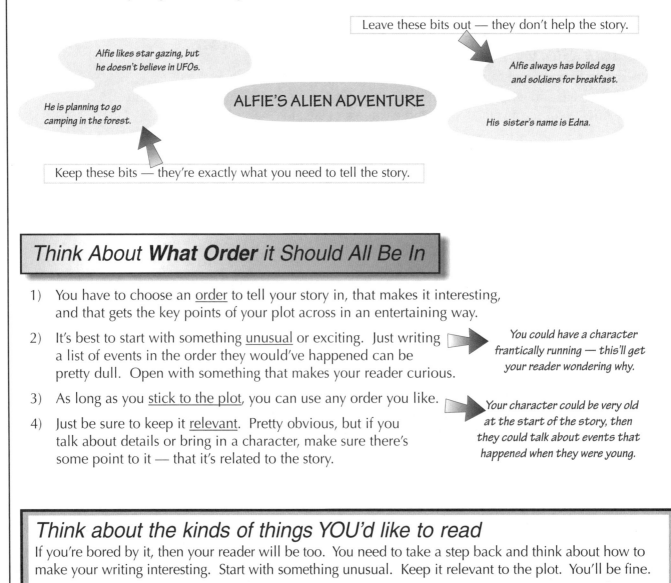

Leave these bits out — they don't help the story.

Alfie always has boiled egg and soldiers for breakfast.

His sister's name is Edna.

Alfie likes star gazing, but he doesn't believe in UFOs.

He is planning to go camping in the forest.

ALFIE'S ALIEN ADVENTURE

Keep these bits — they're exactly what you need to tell the story.

Think About **What Order** it Should All Be In

1) You have to choose an <u>order</u> to tell your story in, that makes it interesting, and that gets the key points of your plot across in an entertaining way.

2) It's best to start with something <u>unusual</u> or exciting. Just writing a list of events in the order they would've happened can be pretty dull. Open with something that makes your reader curious.

You could have a character frantically running — this'll get your reader wondering why.

3) As long as you <u>stick to the plot</u>, you can use any order you like.

Your character could be very old at the start of the story, then they could talk about events that happened when they were young.

4) Just be sure to keep it <u>relevant</u>. Pretty obvious, but if you talk about details or bring in a character, make sure there's some point to it — that it's related to the story.

Think about the kinds of things YOU'd like to read

If you're bored by it, then your reader will be too. You need to take a step back and think about how to make your writing interesting. Start with something unusual. Keep it relevant to the plot. You'll be fine.

Go Into Detail

Make the *Important* Parts Really *Stand Out*

You have to make sure your reader really <u>understands</u> which bits are important.
It's not enough to write long lists of facts and events — that's boring. You need to add
<u>details</u> and <u>vary your style</u>. Instead of just saying that a character is grumpy, explain
why they're like that and what reaction other people have to them, like this:

> As he brushed the crumbs off his lap, Roger looked up and noticed that his sister had begun
> to sulk. He was used to this, because she had been grumpy ever since she was a baby.
> Even then she would spit her dummy across the room and scream at the top of her lungs.

<u>Explain why what you're describing matters:</u>

1) Who cares about it?
2) What effect does it have on your characters?
3) How does it influence what happens?

> If your character is going to
> run a race, make it clear
> just how much they want
> to win and how nervous
> they are.

Always Say *Where* it Happened

English examiners <u>love</u> detail — it brings characters to <u>life</u> and makes things more <u>interesting</u>.

1) You have to make sure you're really <u>specific</u> — so the reader always knows exactly where
   the action is taking place. Then they can create a picture of what's happening, in their heads.

2) Make sure you keep it up <u>the whole way through</u>. This means more than just
   saying what town the story happened in. What was the house and the room like?
   Be as clear as possible — down to the last detail.

> Sam lived with her mum
> in Chorlton, Manchester.

> Sam lived in Chorlton, Manchester with her mum and brother.
> She spent most of her time playing the guitar in her bedroom,
> which was a tiny attic right at the top of the house. It was a
> damp, musty place, and she could often hear rats scuttling
> under the floorboards.

Give your readers structure — or they might lose the plot

The examiner will notice if your story doesn't make sense or has irrelevant bits, and you'll lose marks.
Emphasise important events by going into detail and using different styles.

Go Into Detail

Think About Each of the *Senses* When You Write

Clearly you can't use every single one all the time — that would get boring and be far too silly. But think about each of the senses as you write and use them to make your story <u>sensational</u>:

Sound — How things sounded...

Sam heard a faint, dripping sound echoing from somewhere deep inside the cave.

Taste — How things tasted...

The broth tasted salty and strange. It was probably the worst thing she had ever eaten.

Sight — How things looked...

The wall crumbled away to reveal a small tunnel with moss-covered walls winding into the distance.

Smell — How things smelled...

As she approached the door, a pungent smell like rotting vegetables suddenly filled her nostrils.

Touch — How things felt...

There was a sharp crunch under her foot. It felt like the shell of a snail or some other small creature cracking.

Think About the Characters' *Thoughts* and *Feelings*

The examiner will be impressed if you <u>get inside the characters' heads</u>.

    — What are they thinking about?

    — What motivates them?

    — How do they feel about the things that happen to them?

A good way of showing this is to write a section that is an <u>interior monologue</u> — this means writing down the thoughts the characters are having, just as if they were speaking them out loud.

> Emily stood by her window, getting ready to lower a basket of treats from her bedroom to children in the street below.
>
> "I must remember not to lean out too far," she thought to herself, "as I am so nervous of being seen by strangers. I hope the children enjoy the treats, and let me draw the basket up again without any trouble."

◄ This paragraph just shows Emily's <u>thoughts</u>.

This is a simple but effective trick. It puts the reader into the character's shoes — so they feel closer to them, as though they can <u>understand</u> their feelings.

Bring your feelings into it — you know it makes sense

Using some of the different senses is a BRILLIANT way of making your story come alive. It's quick and easy to do, and will make your writing more evocative so you can pick up extra marks.

Pace and Style

Stories written at the same pace the whole way through can be dull — you must vary the pace and style.

Vary The Pace to Make it More Interesting

You can <u>change the pace</u> — by switching between long, descriptive sentences and shorter, explanatory ones. The trick is to adjust the pace according to the mood of what is happening at that point in your story.

These sentences are short.
They sound slower.

This sentence is longer. It speeds up, and ends up sounding more energetic.

It was Ahab's turn to keep watch. All his shipmates were gently nodding off to sleep. Even the waves seemed to nod slowly as if in a trance. Out of nowhere a gigantic sperm whale surfaced right by the boat, blowing out a thousand bubbles, and everyone woke up and shouted, clutching at the rails for safety.

Of course, short sentences don't always have to slow the pace down. Sometimes they can be <u>short</u> and <u>punchy</u> to describe action scenes. You just have to make them as effective as you can.

He saw me and yelled. I turned and ran. I was scared. I didn't see the step. I hit the deck. That's all I know.

*Write Good **Descriptions** Using **Images***

Give <u>specific details</u> that set the scene for the reader, and help emphasise the important points.

Use <u>inventive images</u> to get the reader to conjure up a mental picture of what's happening — it makes them feel more involved.

This... *Billie Holiday was a good singer.*

...is not as effective as this.

When Billie Holiday sang, it was like listening to her heart pouring out of her mouth. She sang with her entire body and soul, and put enough emotional force into her singing to make you want to cry.

*Think About **Shifting Perspectives***

<u>Perspective</u> is the way you look at a situation — it's your point of view. Switching between perspectives is another effect that'll make your story more interesting to read — and it'll get you those top marks.

This could mean writing from <u>one character's perspective</u>, then switching to that of another.

Billy's eyes widened as James took him by the arm and led him aside. He couldn't believe that his old friend looked so different.
"It's been a long time, but you haven't changed a bit," said James, "Come with me and I'll explain everything."

Or it could mean writing about a character's perspective <u>a long time ago</u>, then commenting on their feelings today.

It was thirty years since they had last seen each other. In those days James had followed Billy's lead as he caused chaos in school and wreaked havoc all over the town. Now, as they made their way to the lake, Billy began to suspect that his friend would be taking charge from now on.

Pace yourself Ahab — we've a little whale to go yet...

It's vital to vary the pace in your story to keep the reader interested. You really have to think hard and not let the story get dull, or else the reader will just switch off and you won't get many marks.

Finishing Your Essay

Examiners really love a good ending. Your conclusion should make a point, have a twist or have some kind of moral. And then of course it's time to check it over.

Finish With a *Conclusion*

1) You need a paragraph at the end of your story that rounds up the plot nicely — it needs to <u>tie up all the loose ends</u>. There's nothing more frustrating than a story that leaves the reader hanging.

So <u>don't</u> end it with:
"Then I woke up — it had all been a dream."

2) The very <u>last line</u> is important — it needs to be written clearly and cleverly, so that it <u>sums up</u> the story for the reader and leaves them happy.

"Though life would never be the same again, he was glad to be home."

3) For the best marks, aim for the unexpected — finishing your story with a <u>twist</u> will really impress.

Drop a hint earlier on in the plot, then you can refer back to it later.

4) Another good device is to give your plot a <u>moral</u> — so that the story proves a point.

Think of the morals in different fairy tales — you could borrow one of these for your plot.

Keep Re-drafting — Until it's *Just Right*

1) <u>Edit</u> what you've written when you've finished your first draft.

2) Take time to tweak your story to get it as near-to-perfect as possible.

3) <u>Read</u> each paragraph through carefully and <u>underline</u> the bits you could improve on:

- Could you go into more detail or change the wording to make yourself clearer?
- Is there a better word you could find to describe something?
- Have you repeated or over-used words or expressions?

Check Your *Grammar* and *Presentation* Carefully

Think you've finished editing it? Then you need to read through the whole thing at least <u>two more times</u>.

1) Check that your <u>sentence formation</u> is accurate and correct.

2) Check that you've <u>spelt</u> all those interesting and unusual words right.

When you're doing coursework, you can't always rely on a PC spellchecker to spot everything.

3) Check that your <u>punctuation</u> is sound.

4) Check that you've got your <u>paragraphs</u> sorted and they flow nicely.

Finally, have a think about the <u>title</u> of the story. Is it snappy, is it clever? It should tell the reader something about your tale — but at the same time keep them guessing as to exactly what's coming.

I conclude with the observation that this section is almost over

Don't panic. People often find this the scariest bit of all, but it really isn't. Just learn everything in this section really well, and you'll be fine. You might even surprise yourself.

Warm-up Questions

These warm-up questions should ease you gently in and make sure you've got the basics straight. If there's anything you've forgotten, check up on the details before you do the exam questions.

Warm-up Questions

1) Your title should be relevant to the plot. Say which of the following points are appropriate to the title "The Haunting at Oakfield Park."

   a) David often went to the park to play football.
   b) David had blue eyes and fair hair; his best friend was called Ian.
   c) As darkness fell, strange shadows seemed to be moving near the bushes.
   d) As David stooped to pick up the football, a tall shadow fell across the grass at his feet.

2) An interesting or unusual beginning will grab your reader's interest. Which two of the following openings make you want to read on, and which ones are boring? Explain why.

   a) Ali had lived in Slough all his life. He lived with his parents and four sisters in a terraced house. They lived near the railway station.
   b) The neighbours had always thought that there was something strange about Ali. Even as a small boy he had caused heads to turn.
   c) Ali had black hair and brown eyes. He wore earphones. He listened to music as he walked along the road. He liked lots of music. There was lots of music he didn't like too.
   d) Ali had seen something terrible, and his life would be changed forever.

3) Add your own details to explain what is said about each of the following characters (one or two sentences for each answer will be enough):

   a) Rachel burst into tears at least five times during the school day — everyday.
   b) Dominic hated children. He was always chasing them away from his large garden, or raising his walking stick menacingly in their direction as he walked along the road.
   c) Paul was a bundle of energy; he never walked when he could run; and he spoke so fast that he made you gasp for breath.
   d) Charley turned out to be the best cat that we had ever had, in spite of everything.

4) List the five human senses that can be used to make your story more realistic. Write a brief example for each of the five senses as they might be used in a story.

5) a) Write one paragraph of your own, varying the pace by using a combination of long and short sentences.

   b) Write one paragraph using short, punchy lines to describe an action scene (a sports scene, or an action scene from a story).

6) Descriptive writing needs good images to bring it alive. Add details and inventive images to make the following sentences come alive:

   a) Claire was superb dancer.

   b) The black stallion reared up, his muscles rippling under his sleek coat.

   c) Alice played basketball well.

7) What should every piece of original writing end with?

8) Why is the very last line of your conclusion vital?

Worked Exam Answer

Sometimes it's hard to see how to answer exam questions. This worked essay will really set you on the right track — then you'll be ready to tackle some exam questions yourself.

Worked Exam Question

1. Write about a journey that you have made, and that you enjoyed very much.

Essay plan:

1   important info about the journey — where, with whom, preparation, plans

2   start of journey, feelings, changing terrain, observations of other people

3   progression to guesthouse, observations of other people

4   arrival at guesthouse, waiting to begin pre-dawn ascent, feelings

5   conclusion — feelings at end of journey

Mount Kinabalu

Good introduction giving important information about the journey.

Last year my family and I 'climbed' Mount Kinabalu, the highest mountain in S.E. Asia. The journey took a day and a half, ascending to a guesthouse by the first afternoon, and making the final ascent before dawn. It was a challenging adventure but I enjoyed the sense of achievement. Our journey began in the Kinabalu National Park, where we met our guide, Mario. I felt apprehensive, and uncomfortable about having a stranger with us.

Good range of feelings mentioned — "challenging", "enjoyed", "apprehensive", "uncomfortable" etc...

Repetition of wording from the question is good.

Change in feelings.

I was subdued as we set off through the rainforest but, when Mario showed us insect-eating plants, I began to feel excited. Soon, the terrain changed from lush forest to steps hewn from the mountainside. Then the terrain changed dramatically. Short tea trees grew out of a yellow,

Excellent choice of vocabulary. "Lush" and "hewn" give sense of richness and strength.

Worked Exam Answer

Senses mentioned successfully in this paragraph — sights, colours, feeling.

rocky landscape. I <u>felt tired</u>, because of the oxygen depletion as we ascended. We began to <u>see</u> the first groups of people descending the mountain.

Carefully chosen vocab to show short refreshment breaks (e.g. sip, nibble)

We stopped frequently to <u>sip</u> water, <u>nibble</u> energy bars and to take photographs. By midday everyone was breathing heavily; the air had turned cold, and a silver mist was swirling around us. We were now walking on grey rock. We were amazed to see <u>three local women carrying large gas cylinders in wicker baskets on their backs</u> - supplies for the guesthouse!

Observations of both terrain and people add interest.

We reached the guesthouse by late afternoon. After a simple meal we tried to sleep, before the pre-dawn ascent - but we were too excited. Everyone was awake when Mario called us. <u>We set off in the pitch-dark, our torches illuminating the thick white rope marking the route to the summit.</u> No one spoke; we were all suffering in the thin air.

Clever image — combining light / dark and also excitement / suffering.

Journey's end comes abruptly, emphasising the strangeness of the experience.

Suddenly, I saw other torchlights. We had arrived! We had walked to the top of the highest mountain in S.E. Asia! I was very excited! The wind was icy so we pulled on hats and gloves. The sunrise was magnificent, <u>staining the peaks caramel</u>.

Punctuation adds to excitement.

Very evocative use of the word "staining".

<u>Exhilarated</u>, we began our descent, which took about four hours. I hardly remember the return journey. I had ascended the highest peak in S.E. Asia, and I was <u>elated</u>!

Good words to show excitement.

Exam Questions

Q1 Describe two or three significant events in your life, and say what effects the incidents had on you.

Q2 Write about your first day at your present school.
What were your feelings at various times during the day?

Q3 'Do you remember the time when...?"

Complete this question to make the title of a story.
Then write the story that will fit the title.

Q4 Describe a time when you were very frightened. You may write about this in any way you like — a real or an imaginary situation.

Revision Summary

Lots of people get really worried over this original writing bit — they think creative writing is something you can either just 'do' or you can't. That's nonsense, and that is what this section is all about. You just need to learn the tricks of the trade that make stories seem really interesting and clever. And this is something that you can do without too much hassle for GCSE.
So make sure you go through every single one of these questions and examples, and you'll see just how easy it can be to do "original writing".

1) Why should you write about things you're interested in and already know about?

2) Explain what each of the following parts of a story should do:
   a) Beginning
   b) Buildup
   c) Climax
   d) Ending

3) Write out five things your story needs to have, to make the reader super-impressed.

4) Which of the following pieces of information could be used to put together a story?
   Say why you selected those particular bits and left the others out.
   a) Jess lives in Bristol.
   b) Jess loves wearing spangly bracelets and dancing.
   c) Jess's birthday is in November.
   d) Jess once got abducted by alien lizard creatures in her lounge.
   e) Jess likes cheese.

5) Explain why it's important to tell your story in an unusual or interesting order.

6) How can you make the really important bits of your story stand out to the reader?

7) a) Write a <u>good</u> and a <u>bad</u> description of someone's face (a few sentences is fine).
   b) Explain why one is better than the other.

8) Give an example of how each of the five senses might be used in a short story.

9) What is an 'interior monologue' and why should you use one?

10) Explain what is meant by the term 'perspective' and why you need to think about it when writing.

11) Let's say you've been abducted by aliens.
   a) Write a really dull paragraph about your abduction.
   b) Write a more interesting paragraph about your abduction (tips on p.81).
   c) Explain how you tried to make your second paragraph more interesting than the first one.

12) Why is a conclusion important in an original writing essay?

13) What should you check for, once you've finished?

Reading The Question

Writing about non-fiction and media is pretty much <u>the same</u> as writing about <u>fiction</u>, except you have to be able to spot <u>bias</u> and distinguish between <u>fact and opinion</u>.

4 Things To Get You Marks in Media Questions

These are all things that the examiner wants to give you marks for:

 Showing that you've <u>understood</u> and thought about what's in the text.

 Making <u>clear</u>, <u>logical points</u> that are backed up with <u>references</u> to the text.

 Telling the difference between <u>fact and opinion</u> (and spotting bias).

Using <u>technical words</u> confidently and successfully in your writing.

<u>Don't panic</u> — this section'll show you how to do all these things, and the examiner will have to give you more marks for doing them...

The main thing is to stay calm, and to try and focus. Above everything else you must write <u>clearly</u>.

Be Sure To Read the Question Before the Text

Look at the question <u>before</u> you start on the text — it'll tell you exactly what to look out for. Having an idea of what you're looking for will help to <u>focus</u> your reading. Pick out the <u>key words</u> in each question. Underline them, so you can see at a glance what the main point of each one is.

> 2. (c)   Explain, using your own words, the writer's <u>opinion</u> about the <u>decline of line dancing</u> in the last 8 months.

> 1. (a)   Write down <u>two facts</u> about the <u>need for security</u> at the Reading Festival.

Think About How Much the Question is Worth

1) The questions are worth different amounts of marks.

2) Spend a <u>shorter</u> time on the questions that are worth <u>less</u>.

3) Think about what the question is asking you to do.
   If it wants 5 examples of something, then try and find them <u>quickly</u>.
   If it only wants 2 examples, you'll have to go into more <u>detail</u>.

Don't waste too much time on questions worth one or two marks

All the examiners want is for you to show you've <u>understood the text</u>. It's hard to do that just through the short-answer questions. You need to get going on the ones that are worth more marks.

Writing Your Answer

Find the Bits that **Answer** the **Question**

1   You've got 15 minutes at the start of the exam just for reading. Go through the text at least _twice_, slowly. You'll have read the question, so you should be able to pick out everything _relevant_.

2   Keep track of the argument. It helps to mark the _key points_, as shown below.

3   Think about the _language_ and _tone_ of the piece as well, and write down anything that occurs to you.

---

1. (a)   In your own words, explain the attitude of the article towards Ben Kilham's approach, as well as towards those who criticise him.

GENTLE BEN

Most bear rehabilitators minimize human contact with their charges. Not Ben Kilham. When a forester brought him two bears, Anakin and sister Yoda, the frostbitten cubs moved into Kilham's guest room. "The bond isn't that hard to establish," he says, "They'd do anything to manipulate me into caring for them," — even raking him with sharp claws. Fattened on sheep's milk and applesauce, the cubs were soon moved to an enclosure outside of town where their education began. Some experts fear that such close contact may create a high proportion of nuisance bears. However, only two of Kilham's cubs are known to have become problems, preferring bird feeders to wilder fare.

Key point — Ben Kilham's approach is different from that of other bear specialists.

Key point — Ben says it's easy to bond with bearcubs.

The cubs were moved to an outdoor enclosure quite quickly.

This backs up the first point — namely that Ben's approach is not typical, and it worries people.

Language — scientific, authoritative, credible. The first sentence is a really good example.

Tone — humorous end. People are afraid for their own safety, worried that bears will eat them. The ending sides with Ben, saying that the only problems his bears have caused are feeding at bird feeders.

Think About the **Tone**

The _tone_ of the writing is tailored to specific audiences. Different types of writing will use different tones. Mention 'tone' and you'll impress the examiner. But just because it _sounds_ convincing, it doesn't mean it is.

A passionate, personal tone is often used by politicians in political speeches.
— it helps give the impression they believe sincerely in the argument they are making.

Articles in professional journals often use an impersonal, academic tone.
they want their arguments to appear to be well-grounded in fact and research.

Remember to read the question carefully BEFORE the text

The examiners want to know you've _understood_ the text. Even when you're still picking points out, always make notes in your own words. The examiner will spot any kind of copying.

Writing Your Answer

Start Your Answer Confidently

You've got to sound believable — ALWAYS use <u>impersonal language</u> (e.g. "It seems", not "I think").
Your <u>first line</u> should show the examiner that you know exactly what the question's asking.
Reword the question as a <u>statement</u>, and make certain you seem self-assured.

> 2. (b) How does the magazine 'Careless Talk Costs Lives' use images,
>   as well as text, to communicate meaning?

All this opening line does
is repeat the question.

*'Careless Talk Costs Lives' uses images and text to
communicate with its audience.*

This is much <u>better</u>.

*'Careless Talk Costs Lives' communicates with its readers using images
which explain and emphasise the points made in the text.*

Don't Just Copy From the Text

The examiner wants to know that you've <u>thought about</u> the text, and not just looked at it.
You'll get no marks for copying the text. Try and find interesting ways to <u>rephrase</u> the key points.

> *Rock'n'Roll eats its young — but sometimes
> they offer themselves up voluntarily. 'Manic
> Street Preachers' member Richey Edwards
> believed in the mythology of pop music; but
> rather than achieving some kind of
> transcendence, he met with a peculiar isolation.*

Awful — uses same
words and is <u>dull</u>.

*The text says Richey
Edwards believed in the
mythology of pop music
but was isolated.*

Better — sounds
<u>confident</u> and engaged
with the text.

*The text says Richey Edwards remained isolated, despite his belief that pop music could reach beyond everyday
life. It also suggests that he offered himself to this isolation, and brought it on himself.*

Be Selective in Your Use of Detail

<u>Detail</u> is good — you need to <u>explain</u> what you're saying fully. BUT — don't overdo it. Select specific
details that back up your point and help persuade the examiner — you'll get more marks.

*It says New Labour is
ineffective
because of the NHS.*

<u>Bad</u> — too brief
and badly phrased.

This one is so far removed
from the bad example, that
it'd probably get an <u>A</u>.

A bit better —
but still a <u>bit short</u>.

*It says New Labour is
ineffective because it hasn't
solved NHS problems.*

*It says New Labour has dealt inefficiently with
problems in the NHS, despite having made
election promises to solve them.*

Don't bury examiners with lots of detail

The big thing here is <u>no waffle</u>. Don't bury the examiner under loads of irrelevant details.
Be <u>precise</u>. Say what you think. Tell them why you think it, BASED on what the text has said.

Developing Your Answer

This is the bit where you need to be really critical about the piece of writing.

Don't Get Sucked in when there's No Evidence

1) Back your statements up with evidence to make them convincing
— the more evidence used (from different sources), the more convincing it is.

2) Where there is no evidence, the writer will try to persuade you, using language.

3) Words to watch out for are POSSIBLY, ALLEGEDLY, APPARENTLY, SUPPOSEDLY, BELIEVE...

4) Don't get sucked in. Instead, write about the language in your answer.

5) Say that the language attempts to persuade you even though there are no concrete facts,
and be sure to give a few examples. This will show the examiner that you can think for yourself.

Decide Whether Ideas Work or Not

Evaluating an idea means deciding whether it's any good or not. BUT — the examiners don't want
your personal rant — they want to know why you think that. Back all your ideas up with evidence.

What's the point being made?	Does the idea make sense?	Is there any evidence?
Sacco and Vanzetti were two poor Italians convicted of murder in the 1920s — the text says the judge and jury were biased against them.	Yes. People in U.S. at that time were scared of radical violence and the jury might have assumed they were guilty only because they were anarchists.	WEAK SPOTS 1) It's all "alleged" — not hard fact 2) We don't know what the actual trial evidence against them was.

Think Beyond The Text

1) What questions do you have about the idea that are left unanswered by the source?

2) Ask questions — it'll show the examiner that you've really thought about it.

How could you extend the idea?

• Did the evidence at the trial support a verdict of guilty or not guilty?

• Why were people scared of left-wing radicals?

• What was the reaction of the general American public to the verdict?

Compare and Contrast the Texts

1) Be sure to compare the bits of text you're given in the exam
(as long as they've actually asked you to do that).

2) Examiners think it's a really good thing if you can pick out differences and similarities in texts.

3) Try to figure out which text you think works best and say why.

Don't believe everything you read

So — the crucial three questions are: 1) What's the point? 2) Does the point make sense?
3) Is there any evidence? Answer all of those in your essay, and you're well on the way.

Writing About The Format of a Media Text

The media isn't just about making life hell for the rich and famous — nor is it just about text.
Newspapers, adverts, films, etc. use a lot of tricks to make a point — e.g. layout, pictures, music.

Show You Can Understand **Media Concepts**

1) The examiner wants you to judge it as a media text, not just as any random exam text.
   You need to comment on the format — what it's trying to do and how well it works.

2) The text in the exam might be a magazine, radio or T.V. adverts, film scripts,
   scenes from films or other printed material like articles, press releases or fliers.

3) So, you have to think about other things besides the words — things like presentation,
   layout, graphics, structure, and actually comment on the choice of the medium itself.

Think About What the **Graphics** are Trying to **Do**

If you get asked to comment on graphics, the examiner expects you to be clear and logical. This just means that if you use common sense you'll get more marks. Literally just say what you see.

Do they look good?
Do they complement the text?
What do you think they're trying to achieve?

Mention the **Layout**

Different layouts are aimed at different audiences. You should be able to work out who the target audience is, for each text.

This layout is dull. There's hardly any colour, the text is all of a similar size, and is justified, the header looks boring and the picture is formal. It's aimed at professionals.

This layout is more fun. There's lots of colour, more space, the text size is varied, the picture and headers are more eye-catching and interesting. It's aimed at young people.

It Looks Great if You Can Use **Technical Terms** Appropriately

CAPTION: a short line to explain a picture.
COLUMN: newspapers and magazines are normally laid out in columns.
LEAD: the main story on the front page.
HEADLINE: the phrase at the top of an article which tells you roughly what the story's about.

FEATURE: longish story with more detail.
EDITORIAL: opinion column stating newspaper's opinion.
HUMAN INTEREST STORY: focuses on a personal story — often sentimental.

Learn all the technical terms and sound like a pro
Well, after that page you should be able to sit down and read your favourite magazine,
and scientifically spot all the "media tricks" they use to manipulate you.

Warm-up Questions

People often find non-fiction and media texts tricky to write about until they have seen how to go about the task and are equipped with some nifty technical terms. Remember though – almost all non-fiction and media questions will want you to talk about the language and format used in the article. If you learn all of the terms used in the section off by heart, then you should have lots of impressive things to talk about in the exam. Go through these quick questions, and look up any answers you're not sure of. Keep on going over it until you don't have to look any of the answers up – then you'll know you've got enough information to sound knowledgeable in the exam.

Warm-up Questions

1) Media and non-fiction questions are great because you don't need to quote from the text to back up your answers.
   True or false?

2) Is it best to read the question before or after you read the text? Why?

3) Why is it a good idea to underline key words in the question?

4) Why should you use impersonal language in your answer?

5) How can you make it really obvious that you're answering the question in your first sentence?

6) Which of these questions would help you think about the <u>argument</u> in a media text?
   a) Roughly how long is the piece?
   b) What's the point being made?
   c) Is the piece written by a man or a woman?
   d) Is the piece from a newspaper or a magazine?
   e) Does the idea make sense?
   f) Is there any evidence in the piece backing up the ideas?

7) Apart from the actual text, what else do you have to think about and write about with media texts?

8) Write a definition for each of these words:
   a) headline
   b) caption
   c) lead story
   d) feature
   e) editorial
   f) human interest story

9) Would you say that the layout of the random article shown on the right is intended for a teenage audience or for an older audience? Explain why.

The Daily Sun

Worked Exam Answer

I know that you'll be champing at the bit to get on to the practice exam question, but it'll help you out a lot to carefully read this article, question and answer first. So make sure you do.

Worked Exam Question

My child, the fire risk

Regulations that were introduced to care and protect are being used to discriminate against the disabled.

Dea Birkett   **Friday April 4, 2003**   <u>**The Guardian**</u>

My daughter is a fire hazard. When I called the National Film Theatre to book tickets for both of us, I was told there was no seat for her because of the fire risk she posed. It wasn't because she's only 10 — it was a children's film, after all. It was simply because she uses a wheelchair.

As the Disability Discrimination Act has been extended, making it more and more difficult not to include people with disabilities, health and safety has become the last resort of the exclusion scoundrel. My daughter isn't the only person with a disability who faces a continual battle to prove that her very existence isn't a danger to us all. A man was refused gym membership because his diabetes posed "a risk to safety"; another person with a visual impairment was denied admission on the same grounds. When a local leisure centre was taken over by a new management team, she was told she could no longer take part in school swimming classes, even though she had been doing so for the previous two years. The grounds given were that she was "a danger to other children" in the pool.

Earlier this year, it took a high court ruling, backed by the Disability Rights Commission, to overturn local authorities imposing blanket bans on home care workers manually lifting any disabled person and deeming all lifting as too "hazardous". The government has even considered making third-party insurance compulsory for powered-wheelchair users, regarding their mobility aids as a hazard to others. (Disability rights groups point out that shopping trolleys can do just as much damage — will we need insurance to go to the supermarket?)

Health and safety is an easy excuse for those who want to make no effort to include people with a wide range of disabilities. There couldn't be a more effective get-out clause; we'd love to have you here, but it's dangerous if we do. Not only, we're told, because disabled people put other people in jeopardy, but because they're perilous to themselves.

During the firefighters' strike, many disabled students at universities and colleges across the country found they were barred from attending lectures other than those held on ground floors for fear they would not be able to be evacuated in the event of an emergency, as if they were an incendiary device. This is despite the fact that several wheelchair users escaped safely from the World Trade Centre on September 11, including one woman who was carried down 68 floors. And is my own daughter, a slim 10-year-old, incapable of being safely carried out of a building like the National Film Theatre, if threatened by fire?

We all face risks, and judge how great a risk has to be before it becomes unacceptable. But implicit in the thinking of those who hide behind the excuse of health and safety to exclude is that those with disabilities are somehow more hazardous and more vulnerable than the able-bodied. Disabled people mustn't just meet the standard of acceptable risk, but be entirely risk free.

Since our visit, the National Film Theatre says it has revised its policy for allocating tickets to wheelchair users. Miraculously, after my vigorous complaint she is no longer a fire hazard! Similarly, the swimming pool has agreed to allow her to continue having lessons with her classmates. Still, being portrayed as a threat to health and safety is a battle every person with a disability has to contend with. But disability is not a danger. The real danger is sanctioning exclusion by the misguided application of health and safety regulations. That's a hazard we should all be warned against.

Worked Exam Answer

1. Read the article entitled 'My child, the fire risk.'
    a. Write down **two** facts and **one** opinion about the treatment of disabled people.

    (2 marks)

    b. Explain, using your own words, what problems face disabled people, according to the writer.

    (3 marks)

2. Choosing **three** examples from the article, explain the techniques the writer uses to support her argument.

(6 marks)

Part a is only worth 2 marks — it needs to be short and to the point.

1a — Two facts about the treatment of the writer's daughter are: When Dea Birkett tried to book tickets at the National Film Theatre she was 'told there was no seat for her'. Also, management at the swimming pool told Dea Birkett that her daughter was 'a danger to other children' in the pool.

An opinion is: 'health and safety has become the last resort of the exclusion scoundrel.'

Good opening statement that sets up the argument — 'should', not 'are' opens up a conflict to write about.

1b — Things should be changing for the better for disabled people: the Disability Discrimination Act has been 'extended' so it should now be easier for disabled people to gain access to facilities like sports centres and cinemas. In fact, the writer says that the people who run these places use Health and Safety regulations as an excuse, to avoid the effort and expense of making their facilities suitable for disabled people. The writer thinks that non-disabled people are allowed to decide for themselves what is an 'acceptable' risk, while disabled people have to prove they are 'risk free' before they can enjoy the same access.

This comparison makes the argument stronger.

This is a strong opening — shows you have some real points to make and you sound confident.

2 — Firstly, the writer uses a contrast in the headline – 'My child, the fire risk.' The contrast is between 'my child' which is a phrase that talks about something personal and 'the fire risk' which is an impersonal official-sounding phrase. She is saying that her child is being treated like a problem, not a person.

The writer goes on to use rhetorical questions. To prove the fact that her daughter is not a fire risk she asks 'And is my own daughter, a slim 10-year-old, incapable of being safely carried out of a building?' By doing this she forces the reader to engage with the question and persuades us to agree with the writer's answer, which is obviously 'no'.

It's good to quote from the text like here...

Thirdly, the writer uses humour. She exaggerates ideas to make them seem ridiculous. When considering the 'danger' posed by powered wheelchairs, she shows how ridiculous it is to ask users to pay insurance by asking whether everyone should be insured for using supermarket trolleys. She also refers to people being treated as if they were an 'incendiary device'.

...and here.

Exam Questions

How to avoid teen tantrums
Sarah Tucker has interviewed scores of teenagers for her new book.
Here, with the school holidays upon us, she explains what will make them happy.

Saturday July 20, 2002   The Guardian
Given the choice, teenagers prefer not to go on holiday with their parents. Given the choice, parents prefer not to holiday with their teenage children. Given no option, teenagers take a holiday with their parents because their parents pay.

According to more than 1,500 parents and teenagers I've interviewed over the past 12 months for my next book on the best holiday options on travelling with 13 to 18 year olds, the concept of the happy family holiday appears to go awry when the child hits puberty.

"Harry Enfield's Kevin is spot on," says Desmond Morris, author of Body Watching and Naked Ape. "Teenagers need to assert their independence at this age. They may begin to resent help from their parents, perceiving it as interference - at best misguided, at worst manipulative. And, above all, they like to be among their peers - especially on holiday."

He adds: "There are additional tensions on holiday when families are brought together for a prolonged period of time and, just like at Christmas, there is an expectation of everyone enjoying themselves without having to work at it. Only it doesn't always work that way."

So what does work with teenagers on holiday? Ski and safari holidays are successful, while city breaks are not. Self-catering villas are preferable to hotels. Specific countries as well as holiday options proved more popular than others. Italy is the most popular destination for teenagers, closely followed by Australia and Canada.

The popularity of these countries appears to be as much to do with the personality and culture of the people as the location and facilities on site. "The people are lively and funky and laid back," commented one 15 year old, who had just returned from a two-week break with his family camping along the Adriatic coast. "I met up with a group of Italian teenagers from Bologna, who would go down to the beach every evening and play guitars till dusk. The campsite was on the beach, so parents knew where we were."

Another teenager had just returned with his father, hiking the Chilkoot Trail, in the Yukon, in western Canada, and both found it a "bonding experience".

An option many of those families I interviewed had tried included going with another family who also had teenage children. One mother explained that this only works if the teenagers as well as the adults are compatible. Personality clashes may make tense situations worse.

For those who presently have pliable 12 year olds, all is not lost. A percentage (less than 10%) of those I met enjoyed being seen with their parents on holiday, and are appreciative that they are not paying for the break themselves. If they aren't the appreciative type, the best option is to choose a holiday which will suit their specific needs and energies.

© SARAH TUCKER

Questions
1. You are being asked to follow an argument, select material appropriate to purpose and tell the difference between fact and opinion.
   a)   Write down two types of holiday that teenagers prefer, according to the article.

   (2 marks)

   b)   Write down two opinions expressed by the author in the article.

   (2 marks)

   c)   Write down two opinions expressed by people other than the author in the article.

   (2 marks)

2. You are now being asked to read the text as a media text.
   What do you think the writer aimed to communicate in this article?
   How successful has she been in achieving her aim?
   In your answer, you should comment on the **content** and **language** of the article.

   (5 marks)

Revision Summary

Media texts can be a bit tricky to get your head around, but that's only because of one key element — you have to appreciate that they can rarely be trusted. Once you've realised that, and you approach every media text you read with a healthy dose of cynicism, you really will be well on the way to being able to answer these questions successfully. When you know that they're mostly just trying to influence you or sell you stuff, it gets easier to recognise the little tricks they have up their sleeves. You know the drill, anyway. If you can get through these questions okay, you'll be ready for the exam.

1) Name 4 things the examiners will definitely give you marks for.

2) Why should you read the question before the text?

3) Is there any point in thinking about how many marks a question is worth? Why?

4) Explain why it's important to read through the question slowly and make a few notes before you start thinking about where to start your essay.

5) Write one sentence on 'jam' as an example of each of the following tones —
   a) a passionate, personal tone
   b) an impersonal, academic tone
   c) an amused tone

6) What kind of initial impression do you want the introduction to your answer to make on the examiner?

7) Why do you think that simply copying from the text doesn't get you any marks?

8) "The Theory of Evolution is nonsense." — What is wrong with the way this is argued?

9) Why do you need to look for hard evidence that backs up the writer's opinions in media texts?

10) Explain why you think examiners give out good marks when students show they can criticise a media text, and can say whether the ideas in it make sense or not.

11) What's the point of trying to think of questions that are left unanswered by the text?

12) Why is it important to think about what <u>kind</u> of media text it is (e.g. article, review, flier etc...)?

13) Is the layout important to consider in a media text? Why?

14) Briefly describe an example of each of the following (a diagram might help) —
   a) good use of graphics on a newsletter aimed at teenagers.
   b) bad use of graphics on a newsletter aimed at teenagers.

15) Write a brief description of each of the following terms —
   a) caption
   b) column
   c) lead
   d) headline
   e) feature
   f) editorial
   g) human interest story

Make Your Writing Clear To Read

Writing **Properly** Gets You a Better Grade

To get an A or A* you have to:

- get all your <u>spellings</u> right
- get all your <u>punctuation</u> right
- write sentences which are grammatically correct <u>and</u> varied
- write in clear, linked <u>paragraphs</u>

Even if you're not aiming for an A you've <u>got</u> to get your spelling, punctuation, grammar and paragraphs sorted. The examiner will rob you of the marks you deserve if you make mistakes in basic language and grammar.

Writing **Properly** Makes Your Work Easier to Read

It's really important to get your language and grammar spot-on. This is <u>why</u>:

Spelling

- If you don't spell words correctly then people won't even begin to know what you're trying to write.
- Bad spelling can really distract readers.

Punctuation

- Using correct punctuation makes your writing punchier.
- Punctuation breaks sentences up into little bits so it's easier to make sense of them.

Grammar

- Structuring sentences well means that no-one can get the wrong end of the stick.
- It makes your writing varied and easier to read.

Paragraphs

- Paragraphs make writing easier to read by dividing it into chunks.
- Paragraphs show where you're starting on a new idea.

Always Check For **Stupid Mistakes**

1) Getting this stuff right comes easily to some people.

2) For the rest of us it's tricky. The first thing to do is learn the rules in this section and use them when you're <u>actually writing</u>.

3) The second thing to do is to get into the habit of <u>checking</u> your work. If you check your work you can find the glaringly obvious mistakes and <u>correct</u> them.

Don't make any stupid mistaches

It will just make you look foolish in front of the examiner. There's a really important rule here, and I think you know what it is — CHECK YOUR WORK before you finish.

Standard English

Use **Standard English**

1) Everyone in Britain uses <u>different versions</u> of English — with different local words that can be difficult to understand.

2) <u>Standard English</u> is formal English. The point is that it avoids any local dialect words and helps people all over the country to understand each other.

3) And more importantly, it's what the examiners want you to use.

Use **Vocab** and **Grammar** With **Care**

Using Standard English means following some <u>simple rules</u>.

1) Avoid writing as you'd speak, e.g. putting, 'like' or 'ok' after sentences.

2) Don't use slang or local dialect words that some people might not <u>understand</u>.

3) Don't use <u>clichés</u> (corny phrases that people use all the time), e.g. 'at the end of the day'. They're very boring and won't get you any marks.

4) Standard English means using the <u>correct</u> forms of words with correct spelling and grammar — so make sure you learn this whole section really well.

Avoid these **Common Mistakes**

Follow these <u>rules</u> in the exam — otherwise it could push you down a whole grade.

1) **RULE:** don't put the word '<u>them</u>' in front of names of objects — always use '<u>those</u>'.

Let me see <u>them</u> books. ✗   Let me see <u>those</u> books. ✓

2) **RULE:** '<u>who</u>' is used to talk about people and '<u>which</u>' is used for everything else.

King Lear had two daughters <u>who</u> lied to him.   Androcles met a lion <u>which</u> did not kill him.

3) **RULE:** Don't write '<u>like</u>' when you mean '<u>as</u>'. And don't put '<u>like</u>' at the end of sentences.

✓
Othello did <u>as</u> Iago told him.
She looks <u>like</u> him.
He sings <u>like</u> an angel.

✗
Othello did <u>like</u> Iago told him.
He seemed a bit confused, <u>like</u>.

You'll <u>lose</u> loads of marks if you do this.

You must write with GOOD Standard English
The examiners will just sigh with exasperation if you write your essays the same way that you might talk to your friends. You MUST be formal, and precise with your use of language, if you want good marks.

Punctuation

Punctuation means all the dots, commas and other symbols that you need to put in your writing. And it's not just to make your essays look pretty — it's there for a reason.

Use **Capital Letters** and **Full Stops Properly**

Pretty basic stuff — you NEED to use them correctly to get anything beyond a grade F.

1) Always start sentences with a <u>capital letter</u>...

2) ...and always end sentences with a <u>full stop</u>.

3) Full stops mark a definite <u>pause</u> before the next sentence starts.

Use **Commas** to Put **Pauses** in Sentences

You need to use commas to get decent marks. Learn the <u>3 rules</u> below to improve your grade, instantly.

1) Commas are used to <u>separate</u> words or groups of words so that the meaning is made clear.

In the valley below, the villages all seemed very small. ← Without the comma, the sentence could be read as 'in the valley below the villages'.

2) Commas are also used to break things up in a <u>list</u>: *I bought onions, mushrooms, peppers and pasta.*

3) You need to use commas to add <u>something extra</u> to sentences:

The twins, who had their blue shirts on, were eating grass. ← The sentence would still work without the bit in the middle.

Semicolons Link Sentences

1) Semicolons <u>link</u> sentences to make one big sentence.

2) The two parts on either side of the semicolon must be <u>equally important</u>.

It's getting late; we won't get there on time.

Both parts are equally important.

Semicolons and colons are tricky, so don't use them unless you're 100% sure how they work. BUT do use them (when appropriate) if you want to get a grade A or B.

Colons Divide Sentences

1) Colons are used to <u>divide</u> sentences if the second half explains the first half:

The ballroom had become very empty: most of the guests had left.

2) You should <u>only</u> use a colon if the first part leads on to the second part.

3) Colons can also be used to introduce <u>lists</u>.

You will need: an apple, wool, and glue.

Ellipses and **Dashes** Mark a **Long Pause**

1) Ellipses are just '<u>dot dot dot</u>' to you and me.

2) Ellipses mark a <u>really long pause</u>... even longer than a full stop.

3) Dashes do basically the same thing — and they <u>separate</u> parts of a sentence nicely.

4) Dashes and ellipses are quite <u>informal</u> so only use them in original writing.

You NEED to learn this stuff on punctuation

just think how hard it would be to read something without punctuation i'm sure it would drive you up the wall it's the same for the examiners they can't stand it at all so use it I tell you use it use it use it

Apostrophes

Lots of people get apostrophes wrong. You need to get them figured out to get more than a C.

You've Got to Add 's to Show Who **Owns** Something

The dog belongs to Montel so you add an apostrophe + 's' to the name of the owner.

Montel's dog is less scary now.

There's always a catch, though:

Have you fed the dog its dinner?

This is just like saying '...his dinner'. You don't use an apostrophe with 'his' so don't use one with 'its'.

> Its = something belongs to it.
> Its doesn't follow the apostrophe rule.

It Gets a Bit **Tricky** with **Groups of People** or **Things**

They found the killer eels' lair during the underwater men's race.

1) If it already ends in s, stick an apostrophe on the end.

2) Words like men, women and mice follow the normal rule.

Apostrophes Can Show Where There's a **Missing Letter**

1) You can shorten some pairs of words by cutting out letters.

2) You put an apostrophe to show where you've removed the letters from.

I am ➡ I'm

The letter 'a' has been removed, so an apostrophe goes in its place.

Watch out — this isn't the same as 'its' in the dog example above.

we are ➡ we're		they are ➡ they're	
I will not ➡ I won't		who is ➡ who's	
I would ➡ I'd		do not ➡ don't	
I had ➡ I'd		does not ➡ doesn't	
It is ➡ it's		can not ➡ can't	

WARNING — Don't Use **Apostrophes** for Anything Else

NO!   Fresh brown banana's, 5 for £1.   ✗

This is wrong — it'll lose you points. Never use an apostrophe for plurals.

Make sure you know how to use apostrophes properly

You must use apostrophes, and you need to use them correctly. Just think how some songs would sound without them — "Cannot get you out of my head", "Do not stop moving, everybody is grooving", etc...

Speech Marks

Speech marks (quotation marks) are yet another thing the examiner will be looking out for.

Speech Marks Show Someone's *Actually Speaking*

Start of
speech

End of
speech

"You're going to lose that pretty hat," said Bob.

These are the words Bob said
— they go in the <u>speech marks</u>.

Always *Start Speech* with a *Capital Letter*

"Let's have a game of golf," said Claude.

Here's the <u>capital letter</u>.

Doug asked, "Where's the nineteenth hole?"

The speech bit <u>always</u> has a capital letter —
even if it isn't at the start of the sentence.

End Speech with a *Question Mark*, *Full Stop* or *Comma*

"Who will fight me in a duel?" asked Louise.

Remember — spoken <u>questions</u> have
to have a QUESTION MARK.

*Remember that you can
use exclamation marks to
end speech too...*

Tracey shouted, "I'm not afraid to fight."

This speech isn't a
question. It's got
to end with a <u>full
stop</u> instead.

"You're no match for me," replied Louise bravely.

This isn't a question either. The speech has
finished but the sentence hasn't — you
need a <u>comma</u> here.

> The punctuation rules are <u>exactly the same</u> whether you're writing dialogue in a
> story, or quoting from a poem in a literature essay. For more on quoting, see P. 8.

You have to get your punctuation RIGHT

Actually remembering to use speech marks is easy enough — it's working out where all the
punctuation goes that's the problem. But it's not impossible, so stop worrying and learn the rules.

Negatives

'No' Isn't the Only Negative Word

1) Negative sentences are the opposite of positive sentences.

2) The easiest way to make a phrase negative is to add 'no' or 'not'.

3) Words ending in -n't are also negative.

Positive sentence:
My aubergines are rotten.

Negative sentence:
My aubergines are not rotten.

Don't Use Double Negatives

I don't want no aubergine. **REALLY MEANS** I do want some aubergine.

Two negative words in the same
phrase will make it positive.
You should use only one negative at a time.

1) The main thing to remember is that words ending in '-n't' are negative...

2) ...so you don't need to add 'no' or 'not'.

The Word "None" has Three Meanings

1) 'None' is a word that can cause problems. As a pronoun it means 'not one' or 'not any':

"Did you see any film stars?"
"We saw none."

"Have you got any aubergines?"
"I'm afraid there are none left."

2) As an adverb, 'none' means 'not at all':

Surprisingly, the fish were none the worse for living in a different kettle.

3) 'None' should not be used with other negative words (see double negative rule):

He's not got none. ✗   He has none. ✓

Stop being so negative — it's not that bad
"I can't get no satisfaction," sang The Rolling Stones. But I bet they wouldn't be feeling so smug with their fancy lifestyles if they knew they'd broken one of the basic rules of English grammar.

Warm-up Questions

You could read through this page in a few minutes but there's no point unless you check over any bits you don't know and make sure you understand everything. It's not quick, but it's the only way.

Warm-up Questions

1) Which of these should you check for when you finish a piece of writing?
   a) correct punctuation
   b) cauliflowers
   c) paragraphs properly divided up
   d) clever bits so you can pat yourself on the back
   e) spelling all right
   f) each sentence grammatical
   g) bookworms

2) What's 'standard English'?

3) Do you need to use standard English in your GCSE exam?

4) Can you think of any parts of your English GCSE when it would be alright <u>not</u> to use standard English?

5) Rewrite the clichés in the sentences below in your own words:
   a) Juliet should have realised that you win some and you lose some.
   b) Sophocles' plays are all Greek to me.
   c) I am writing to inform you that I am slinging my hook.
   d) "Come on, comrade. It's eight o'clock.
      Let's go out and paint the town red."

6) Choose the grammatically correct sentence in each of the following pairs:
   a) *Give me them pens.*
      or *Give me those pens.*
   b) *Macbeth is a general who kills a king.*
      or *Macbeth is a general which kills a king.*
   c) *The boy did as the teacher said.*
      or *The boy did like the teacher said.*

7) What do you <u>always</u> have to have at the beginning and end of a sentence?

8) Write down three places in a sentence where you would need to put a comma.

9) Would you use a colon or a semi-colon to replace the * in the sentence below?

   "I saw these items in your bag * a shirt, some shoes and a pair of trousers."

10) Which creates a longer pause, a dash or a full stop?

11) Write out these sentences with the correct punctuation:
   a) the man who still hadnt recovered from his cold was writing his shopping list bananas milk tea and bread
   b) why wont Roberts dog the childrens dog and the ladies dog play with cats
   c) Sarah asked has anyone seen Liz today
   d) does anyone want another cup of tea Andy asked because Im having one

12) What will the examiners think you mean if you write 'I don't want to do no English exam'?

Spelling

Some Words **Sound** the **Same** but have **Several Spellings**

1) affect/effect

1) <u>Affect</u> is a <u>verb</u> meaning to act on or influence something.
2) <u>Effect</u> is a <u>noun</u> — it is the result of an action.
3) <u>Effect</u> can also be used as a <u>verb</u> meaning to achieve.

> Global warming is <u>affecting</u> Earth's climate.
> The <u>effect</u> of global warming is climate change.
> He <u>effected</u> his escape through a secret tunnel.

2) practise/practice

1) <u>Practise</u> is a <u>verb</u>.
2) <u>Practice</u> is a <u>noun</u>.

> I <u>practise</u> the piano daily. She <u>practises</u> medicine.
> I enjoy football <u>practice</u>.   The <u>practice</u> of polygamy is rare nowadays.   A dental <u>practice</u>.

3) where/were/wear

1) <u>Where</u> is used to talk about <u>place</u> and position.
2) <u>Were</u> is a past tense form of the verb '<u>to be</u>'.
3) <u>Wear</u> is a <u>verb</u> used with clothes, hair, jewellery etc.

> <u>Where</u> is the Frenchman?
> They <u>were</u> hidden behind a statue.
> He <u>wears</u> armour of burnished gold.

4) there/their/they're

1) <u>There</u> is used for <u>place</u> and position.
2) <u>Their</u> shows <u>possession</u>.
3) <u>They're</u> is the short form for '<u>they are</u>'.

> Where's the ball? Over <u>there</u>.
> <u>Their</u> dog bit me!
> <u>They're</u> my favourite shoes.

Watch out for these **3 Silly Spelling Mistakes**

1) Words with a silent 'h' — you don't say it, but you must write it: e.g. <u>ch</u>emistry.
2) Words written with 'ph' and pronounced with an 'f' sound: e.g. gra<u>ph</u> or philoso<u>ph</u>y.
3) Never end any word with '-ley' except some names: e.g. Heading<u>ley</u>, Bottom<u>ley</u>.

Get **Writers' Names** and **Literature Words** Right Too

1) There's <u>no excuse</u> for spelling a writer's name wrongly — or the name of a book, come to that.
It's the kind of mistake that makes you look as though you've got <u>no idea</u> what you're talking about.

2) Literature words like the ones on P. 23 and P. 39 have to be spelled right too.
If you spell them wrong the examiner will start wondering if you <u>really</u> know what they mean.

Get your spelling write

Spelling words right is <u>really</u> important. That's what I say. That's what the examiners say. That's what your teachers say. That's what everyone says. So don't be an idiot — make sure you learn it all.

Sentences

Every Sentence Needs a *Verb*

1) Verbs are 'doing' words or 'being' words...

2) ...and every sentence needs to have one.

They walk through the shopping centre.

Here's the action in this sentence — it's the 'doing' word.

Past tense

I was the first person there.

These are both 'being' words — but they're in different tenses.

I will be the first person there.

Future tense

Make Sure that *Numbers Agree* Too

The verb ending has to match whether the number of the subject is singular or plural.
When you're writing a verb in a sentence, say it out loud. Decide whether it sounds right or not.

This sounds wrong.

Jill like cheese sandwiches. **✗**

Much better — that sounds right and it makes sense too.

Jill likes cheese sandwiches. **✓**

NO!

The mice hates crusty bread. **✗**

That's better.

The mice hate crusty bread. **✓**

Don't Change *Verb Tenses* in Your Writing By *Mistake*

This is past tense.

As they tried to get the sail up, they could hear distant splashes — then they see a canoe.

Another past verb.

This one's wrong — it's present when it should be past.

You MUST follow these rules

If you don't follow these three rules, then you're asking for trouble.
People forget how important this stuff is, if you want to sound good.

Remember to put a verb in every sentence you write.

Sentences

Vary the Style of your Sentences

Sentences have to make sense to get any grade above an F. To get grade C to A* you need to make your sentences <u>interesting</u> to read, as well as clear. There are easy ways of doing this:

1) Use <u>parallel structure</u> — it basically means repeating words within a sentence.

The Spanish, French and Italians all have a snooze every afternoon. → The Spanish, the French and the Italians all have a snooze every afternoon. ← *Repeating '<u>the</u>' makes it sound loads better.*

You can also use parallel structure to <u>remind</u> the reader what you're <u>talking about</u>:

I used to write essays with ink, while now mustard is used. → I used to write essays in ink; now I write them in mustard. ← *The repetition of '<u>I write</u>' keeps the reader focused on the point of the sentence.*

2) <u>Start</u> your sentences in different ways:

There was a chill in the air as Jo walked towards the house. There was nobody around. There was a big oak door and Jo knocked on it. There was a scream from inside the house.
Boring — the word 'there' is repeated all the time.

This says the same things, but in a more interesting way. →

There was a chill in the air as Jo walked towards the house. Nobody was around. Jo knocked on the big oak door. A scream came from inside the house.

3) Vary the <u>length</u> of sentences. Mix together long and short sentences to make your essay more interesting to read — you'll get better marks for it.

Cornwall is in trouble. The tourists flock to this lovely area every year, clogging up the roads with slow-moving caravans and leaving behind piles of litter to endanger the local wildlife and pollute the sea. Something has to be done.

The contrast of long and short sentences works well.

Chronological Order Makes Things Easy to Follow

Your sentences need to be in the right <u>order</u> — if the examiner can't follow them easily you'll lose marks. <u>Chronological order</u> (the order in which things happened) is the most logical order.

Harry went flying and landed in a silage pit. Unfortunately it was faster than him and, just before he reached the gate, it headbutted him with all its force. Harry turned to run as the angry bull careered towards him.

What's happening <u>isn't clear</u>, because the sentences aren't in chronological order.

The chronological order <u>should</u> be:

1. Harry turned to run as the angry bull careered towards him. → 2. Unfortunately it was faster than him and, just before he reached the gate, it headbutted him with all its force. → 3. Harry went flying and landed in a silage pit.

Make your writing easy to follow

Thinking about the style and order of your sentences is a good way of making your writing more sophisticated. Examiners like sophistication, so they'll give you more marks.

Writing Varied Sentences

Use *Different Words* for the *Same Thing*

Don't fall into the trap of using the same word all the time — especially adjectives like "<u>nice</u>" or "<u>weird</u>". Examiners don't like it and you'll lose loads of marks.

DULL

> I went to a <u>nice</u> Indian restaurant last night. The waiters were <u>nice</u> to us and the walls were painted in a <u>nice</u> shade of red. I had an onion bhaji to start with and it was really <u>nice</u>. Then I had a <u>nice</u> curry. After the meal the waiters brought us mints, which was <u>nice</u> of them.

It may be 'correctly' written, but it's not going to score you any points because it's so <u>boring</u>.

This is lots better. Using lots of different adjectives paints a more <u>interesting picture</u> — and you'll get loads more marks for it.

GREAT

> I went to a <u>fantastic</u> Indian restaurant last night. The waiters were <u>friendly</u> to us and the walls were painted in a <u>lovely</u> shade of red. I had an onion bhaji to start with and it was really <u>tasty</u>. Then I had a <u>delicious</u> curry. After the meal the waiters brought us mints, which was <u>kind</u> of them.

It's the same with <u>verbs</u>...

> I <u>ran</u> to the post box with a letter, then I <u>ran</u> to the shop for some chocolate. After that I <u>ran</u> home so I wasn't late for tea.

> I <u>ran</u> to the post box with a letter, then I <u>hurried</u> to the shop for some chocolate. Finally I <u>raced</u> home so I wasn't late for tea.

Fancy Words Impress the Examiner

Using <u>different</u> words is a good start. If you can use different <u>and</u> clever words, then you're laughing — they can really improve your grade.

> United played badly on Saturday.

> United played lamentably on Saturday.

> The flooded pitch didn't help the standard of play.

> The saturated pitch was detrimental to the standard of play.

> The referee made some very stupid decisions.

> The referee made some exceedingly moronic decisions.

You can't use long, fancy words <u>all</u> the time — that'd sound rather odd. But you'll get extra marks if you use them <u>now and then</u>. So remember this rule:

sporadically   endeavour   substitute   concise
Every now and then, try to replace a short and simple word with a <u>long</u> and <u>clever</u> one.
elementary   complex   intellectual

Using long words is an exceedingly good idea

Get a dictionary and learn some new words. That might sound thoroughly ridiculous, but using the odd long and impressive word really will make a good impression on whoever is marking your work.

Writing Varied Sentences

This page will show you a couple more tricks to help win the examiner over.

Describe Things by Comparing them to Other Things

For more on similes and metaphors see page 23.

Comparisons create interesting visual images for readers. It's good to use them instead of adjectives sometimes. There are two different ways of comparing:

1) Less than, more than, the least, the most...

Lisa's face went blotchy. ➡ Lisa's face went more blotchy than a dalmatian's.

It was very cold. ➡ It was colder than an Arctic winter.

She was beautiful. ➡ She was the most beautiful woman this side of Stockport.

When you're making a comparison, you must EITHER say "more ... than" or "the most...", OR use the form of the word that ends in "er" or "est". DON'T do BOTH.

WATCH OUT: You are the most sporty person I know. Jenny is prettier than her sister.
NOT the "most sportiest". **NOT "more prettier".**

2) Use similes (say that one thing is like another). There are two ways of using similes:

1 The first is to take an adjective, think of a comparison, and then instead of using "more" and "than", you use "as" and "as".

Beth felt as happy as a hippo in a mud pool.

2 The other way of saying one thing is like another is nice and simple — you use the word "like".

I'd forgotten my gloves and soon my fingers were like blocks of ice.

It's OK to exaggerate when you make comparisons. If you were 100% accurate you'd have to write things like " Jack was as tall as a six foot two inch tree" — that'd just bore the reader.

Use Metaphors

You use metaphors when you talk about one thing as if it were something else, rather than as if it were *like* something else. It's quite a sophisticated way of livening up your writing. Use them for a C or above.

Leela cried so hard that a river flowed down her cheeks.

Wai Yin needed a glass of water — there was a desert in her mouth.

There wasn't literally a river flowing down Leela's cheeks, or a desert in Wai Yin's mouth, but the language creates a strong visual image and gets the point across well.

I've told you a million times — stop exaggerating
Using similes and metaphors will make the examiners see your work as an oasis of loveliness in the lonely desert of tedious, unimaginative essays that they all too often have to mark. So USE THEM.

Nouns, Verbs, Adjectives and Adverbs

A *Noun* is a *Person*, *Place* or *Thing*

There are four kinds of noun:

Proper Names

Gloria, Tuesday, Texas

Proper names always have capital letters.

Groups of people or things

class, pack, squad

Names of things or places

hedge, hair, woman

These are just everyday words.

Words for ideas

truth, beauty, fear

You can't see, hear, or touch them — but they're still nouns.

Verbs are 'Doing' or 'Being' Words

'Doing' words

riding   thinks

ate   belches

'Doing' words tell you what's happening in a sentence. Don't always use the same ones — or the examiner will be bored and will give you bad marks.

'Being' words

Today was a good day.
I am happy.

'Being' words tell you how something is or was or will be.

Adjectives Describe Things and People

Global warming is bad.

Too boring...

Global warming is a serious and very worrying issue.

Much better — the adjectives will help to impress the examiner.

Adverbs Describe How an Action is Done

The army retaliated, attacking the fortress.

Not much fun, this.

The army promptly retaliated, viciously attacking the fortress.

The adverbs make the sentence more exciting — which means more marks coming your way.

Make sure you know what an adverb is

Use different verbs, adjectives and adverbs to spice up your writing. It'll get you more marks, and that's really the point of all this revision. Now get on to the warm-up questions and you'll be ready.

Warm-up Questions

Here are a few more warm-up questions. Make sure you go through ALL of them properly.

Warm-up Questions

1) Choose the correct spelling:
   a) How you spell will <u>affect</u> / <u>effect</u> your grade.
   b) The <u>affects</u> / <u>effects</u> of spelling writers' names wrongly can be dire.
   c) Tony <u>effected</u> / <u>affected</u> a high grade by checking his spellings.

2) Write a sentence using the word "practise".

3) Write a sentence using the word "practice".

4) Write out each of these sentences, correcting all the words starting with W.
   a) I don't know wear I'm going; don't know were I've been.
   b) If I where the only boy in the world and you wear the only girl.
   c) This wearwolf is whereing me out.

5) Choose the correct sentence from each of the following pairs:
   a) I left my bicycle over their. / I left my bicycle over there.
   b) The twins invited they're friends to tea. / The twins invited their friends to tea.
   c) They're the wrong chickens! / There the wrong chickens!

6) Write down three words with a silent 'h'.

7) Write down three words with a 'ph' that's pronounced 'f'.

8) Complete the following sentences by putting the verb into the correct tense:
   a) When I got home, I (turn) _____ the television on.
   b) Sit down, turn over the question paper and (write) _____ your name at the top.

9) Rewrite 8a) and 8b) so they're talking about the future.

10) Put the sentences below into chronological order.
   I left reeling with satisfaction. The crème brulée was an exquisite end to an exquisite meal, with a silky texture and a diamond-hard crust. We began with a terrine of lobster and crayfish which played against the flavours of the champagne like a kitten patting at a butterfly. The beef was perfectly roasted and so tender that one hardly needed to chew.

11) Which sounds more formal?
   a) I go rollerblading now and then. / I go rollerblading occasionally.
   b) Evacuate the building immediately! / Leave the building now!
   c) Fruit and vegetables are extremely nutritious. / Fruit and vegetables are very healthy.

12) Which is correct?
   a) Katy's essay is much more better than Clare's. / Katy's essay is much better than Clare's.
   b) Today was the most hottest day of the year. / Today was the hottest day of the year.
   c) Murgatroyd is the tallest twin. / Murgatroyd is the taller twin.

13) What's the difference between a simile and a metaphor? Write an example of each.

14) Pick out the noun, the verb, the adjective and the adverb in each of the following sentences (sometimes there is more than one noun, verb, adjective or adverb):
   a) The enormous horses easily pulled the heavy carriages.
   b) Sonia desperately wanted to know the whole truth.
   c) The naughty little boys waited nervously outside the headteacher's office.

Revision Summary

There's quite a lot to take on board here. Have a browse back over this section, and when you feel confident, try these questions. Nip back and check the ones you get wrong, then have another bash. It'll probably take a little while — but you need to be able to sail through the questions like a knife through butter.

1) What four things do you need to do in your writing to get an A or an A* grade?

2) When you have finished, why is it important to check through your writing?

3) Write a paragraph to show that you know what standard English is.
Jot down one example of standard English and one of non-standard English.

4) True or false: You should try to use dialect words, slang and clichés when writing in standard English.

5) Name three things you need to remember so that you don't make mistakes when writing standard English.

6) What are the three places where you can use commas?

7) What are semicolons used for?

8) What are colons used for?

9) What do ellipses and dashes do? When should they be used?

10) Correct the mistakes in these sentences:
   a) The hamster has looked very happy since I brushed it's coat.
   b) Its nice to see a smile on its little face.

11) Cut out letters and replace them with apostrophes. The first one is done for you.
   a) I will not = I won't   b) can not   c) I had   d) It is   e) they are

12) True or false: You should use apostrophes for plurals.

13) What should speech always start with when you're writing? And what should it end with?

14) What is a double negative and why are they bad?

15) Which of these statements is correct?
   a) We where going to a fancy party.
   b) I decided to wear my birthday suit.
   c) I don't know were that idea came from.

16) What kind of word does every sentence need to have in it?

17) What is it important to remember about verb tenses when you are writing?

18) When you are writing, why would you use:
   a) parallel structure?   b) sentences of different lengths?

19) What is chronological order? Why is it a good thing to stick to it?

20) True or false: Using different and fancy words will impress the examiner.

21) When you're writing, why is it good to make comparisons between things?

22) What are two ways of using similes?

23) Name the four kinds of noun and give two examples of each.

24) What are verbs?

25) What do adjectives describe?

26) What do adverbs describe?

SECTION TEN — LANGUAGE AND GRAMMAR

Speaking and Listening

For some lucky people, the speaking bit's great — but for everyone else it can be a nightmare. It's much less scary if you've worked out what to say first — so make sure you learn everything in this section.

There are **Three Main Categories** of Practical Test

Any particular test you have to do will be assessed according to which <u>category</u> it is in.

Categories are:

1) explain – describe – narrate

2) explore – analyse – imagine

3) discuss – argue – persuade

A <u>debate</u> would be category 3. Giving a <u>talk</u> or having a <u>discussion</u> could fit any category, depending on the subjects asked for.

Examiners are on the lookout for certain things in the speaking tests. You've got to do these things if you want to get the marks:

What you need to do for an A*:
Use standard English vocabulary and grammar.
Listen carefully to other people who are talking.
Express tricky ideas clearly.
Adapt your talk to the task and audience, and make it original and interesting.

Remember the **CAP Rule** When You Speak

Think about these things <u>before</u> you start any speaking practical — <u>learn</u> and remember them.

1) <u>COURTESY</u> — Be <u>polite</u> at all times, especially when other people ask questions, or when they're doing their tests. If you're polite, they'll be on <u>your side</u> when you do your tests.

2) <u>AUDIENCE</u> — Adapt your speech to the audience. You'll be speaking to a big group, so you'll have to keep people's attention. Tell a <u>joke</u>, or use a <u>visual aid</u> to make your talk more interesting.

3) <u>PURPOSE</u> — Get your information across in an <u>interesting</u> way, as <u>clearly</u> as possible. Just keep it short, clear and to the point.

<u>REMEMBER</u>: CAP (Courtesy, Audience, Purpose)

Don't panic about the speaking exam

It's only your best mark in each category that counts — you get more than one go. That's got to be reassuring. Just remember to breathe, and to speak slowly. It's too easy to rush when you're flustered.

Speaking and Listening

Use Standard English

For more on
Standard English,
take a look
at P. 99.

Standard English isn't only useful when you're writing.
The examiner wants you to speak in standard English, so do it.
It doesn't mean you have to hide your accent — just speak clearly.

Don't use slang if you're giving a speech or a talk. You'll lose marks.
In a discussion it's OK to speak a bit more normally.

Make Your Talk Clear

1) Don't mumble into your collar. Speak up and look
   around the room while you're talking. That way you
   can at least be sure everyone can hear you.

2) Give your talk a clear structure. Don't just ramble on
   through a fog of disconnected points.

> Work out the most important piece of
> information you have to communicate.
> Use that at the beginning of your talk
> — it'll get people interested.

> Don't repeat yourself.
> Once you've finished making a point
> then move on to the next point.

> Talk clearly and plainly. Long fancy
> words are useless if no-one
> understands what you're saying.

> Draw attention to the
> most important facts.
> Then the audience will
> remember them.

Writing notes will stop you from getting off the point of your talk.
Don't write out every single word you want to say — you'll end up reading out your notes.

Clearly spoken standard English is what you need

Learn everything in this section to be really sorted for your exam. It may not seem like a big section,
but there are definite tricks you can learn in order to get good marks in your speaking exam.

Speaking and Listening

You might have to do a debate. Don't worry. If you stick to the debating rules, you'll get the marks.

Debates Argue *For* and *Against* a Motion

The subject to be debated is called the <u>motion</u>. Debates are always structured the same way:

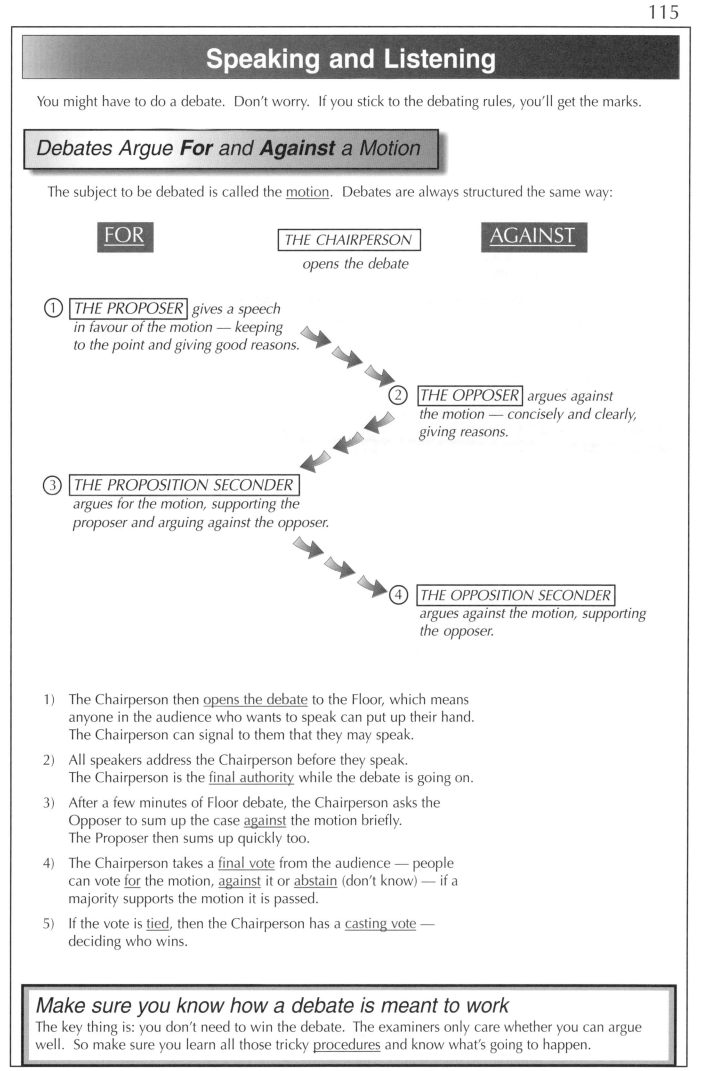

FOR   THE CHAIRPERSON   AGAINST
opens the debate

① THE PROPOSER *gives a speech in favour of the motion — keeping to the point and giving good reasons.*

② THE OPPOSER *argues against the motion — concisely and clearly, giving reasons.*

③ THE PROPOSITION SECONDER *argues for the motion, supporting the proposer and arguing against the opposer.*

④ THE OPPOSITION SECONDER *argues against the motion, supporting the opposer.*

1) The Chairperson then <u>opens the debate</u> to the Floor, which means anyone in the audience who wants to speak can put up their hand. The Chairperson can signal to them that they may speak.

2) All speakers address the Chairperson before they speak. The Chairperson is the <u>final authority</u> while the debate is going on.

3) After a few minutes of Floor debate, the Chairperson asks the Opposer to sum up the case <u>against</u> the motion briefly. The Proposer then sums up quickly too.

4) The Chairperson takes a <u>final vote</u> from the audience — people can vote <u>for</u> the motion, <u>against</u> it or <u>abstain</u> (don't know) — if a majority supports the motion it is passed.

5) If the vote is <u>tied</u>, then the Chairperson has a <u>casting vote</u> — deciding who wins.

Make sure you know how a debate is meant to work
The key thing is: you don't need to win the debate. The examiners only care whether you can argue well. So make sure you learn all those tricky <u>procedures</u> and know what's going to happen.

Having a Debate

Prepare to Defend Your Corner

During a debate, the examiner will be watching to see how well you've <u>prepared</u> your case.

1) <u>Research</u> your case carefully — then you'll know the facts inside out.

2) Work with the other person in your team. The seconder should <u>back up</u> the other person, and make their argument seem even more convincing.

3) Keep to the point. You need people to remember exactly what your opinion is.

4) Use two or three strong arguments with your best point for a <u>conclusion</u>.

5) You're allowed to be one-sided here — but use <u>facts</u> to support your ideas.

6) Don't attack people personally. You won't get any marks for being a bully — you'll only get marks if you argue calmly and <u>methodically</u>.

Listen Carefully and Be Polite

Even when you're not talking, you're being assessed.
You've got to show you're following what other people say too.

1) <u>Concentrate</u> on what the other person is saying.
   That means you won't miss anything.

2) If you're unsure of a point they've made,
   politely ask for it to be <u>repeated</u> more clearly.

3) <u>Don't interrupt</u> speakers in mid-flow.
   Let them finish before you have your say.

4) Always respond constructively — talk about
   any <u>good</u> things that the other person said.

5) If you want to <u>criticise</u>, then be critical about their <u>opinion</u>,
   explaining why you think their argument is wrong. Never attack
   people personally — you'll lose marks in a practical test.

6) You've got to be sure that your own views make <u>sense</u>.
   Never criticise people if they are talking about subjects
   you don't understand. Ask them to explain.

Try to stay calm and you'll be fine

Well there you go. End of the book. All you've got left are practice papers and a few spellings you should learn. Blast through the papers and remember — you're ready for the real thing. Well done.

[The end.]

Warm-up Questions

There's no point in skimming through the section and glancing over the questions. Do the warm-up questions and go back over any bits you don't know. It's hard to study for a speaking exam, but it's well worth you going through all these questions and learning what to do.

Warm-up Questions

1) Write down the three main categories of the Speaking and Listening practical test.

2) What are the four things you need to do for an A*?

3) What does CAP stand for?

4) How could you make your talk more interesting for the audience?

5) What sort of English would you normally use in the Speaking and Listening practical test?

6) What sort of English shouldn't you use if you're giving a speech or a talk?

7) Write down four ways to make your talk clear.

8) Right or wrong?

   a)   Don't bother to listen when other people are talking.

   b)   It's OK to ask for something to be repeated.

   c)   Let other speakers finish before you say something.

   d)   If you disagree with another person's opinion, it's wrong to criticise it.

   e)   It's acceptable to explain why you think another speaker's argument is wrong.

   f)   Make sure your own views make sense.

9) What is the subject to be debated called?

10) Who opens a debate?

11) What do the 'Proposer' and the 'Opposer' do?

12) Who argues for the motion and supports the Proposer?

13) Who argues against the motion and supports the Opposer?

14) Which is correct?

   a)   The Proposer opens the debate to the Floor.

   or:

   b)   The Chairperson opens the debate to the Floor.

15) Which is correct?

   a)   The Chairperson takes a final vote from the audience.

   or:

   b)   The Chairperson takes a final vote from the Opposition Seconder.

16) Why is it important to research your case carefully?

17) What should you use for a conclusion?

18) What should you use to support your ideas?

Commonly Misspelled Words

Here is a list of the most common words that people spell wrongly. Cross off the ones you can already spell and then learn the rest. If you don't you'll just be throwing marks away.

absence	ceiling	exaggerate
accelerate	changeable	exceed
acceptable	chaos	except
accommodate	cheque	excitement
accurate	chief	exercise
achieve	chimney	existence
acknowledge	choose	extremely
acquaintance	chose	fascinate
acquire	college	feasible
across	colourful	February
address	column	financial
aerial	commit	foreign
aeroplane	conceit	forty
agreeable	condemn	fulfil
aisle	conscience	fulfilment
amount	conscious	fulfilled
anxious	criticism	gauge
appalling	deceive	gorgeous
appoint	decision	government
argue	definitely	grammar
ask	describe	grief
assistant	desire	grievance
association	despair	handkerchief
athlete	desperate	height
authorise	develop	holiday
autumn	disappear	humorous
awkward	disappoint	humour
beautiful	disciple	illegible
beige	dissatisfy	imaginary
belief	double	immediately
benefit	dread	immensely
benefited	eccentric	incidentally
bicycle	ecstatic	independent
biscuit	eerie	indispensable
build	efficient	innocence
business	embarrass	insistent
cease	endeavour	install

Commonly Misspelled Words

installation
interruption
irrelevant
irritable
jewellery
judge
knack
knock
knowledge
labour
laughter
leisure
library
likeable
loveable
manoeuvre
maintain
marriage
miscellaneous
mischievous
mortgage
murmur
necessary
neighbour
niece
ninety
noticeable
occasionally
occur
occurred
occurrence
omission
panic
panicked
parallel
pastime
permissible
personal
personnel
philosophy

physician
possess
prejudice
preliminary
prescribe
privilege
proceed
profession
psychiatrist
psychology
pursue
quay
questionnaire
queue
realm
reassure
receive
receipt
recommend
relief
repetition
resource
restaurant
rhyme
rhythm
ridiculous
secretary
scene
scenery
schedule
seize
separate
similar
sincere
skilful
solemn
soliloquy
sophisticated
souvenir
stationary

stationery
style
succeed
successful
sufficient
supersede
surprise
suppress
symbol
syntax
temporary
theatre
thief
thieves
thorough
tongue
transfer
typical
tyre
umbrella
unmistakable
unnecessary
unnoticed
until
vague
vegetable
vicious
view
Wednesday
weight
weird
whole
wilful
woollen
wreath
wreck
yacht
yeast
yield
zodiac

Practice Exam

Once you've been through all the questions in this book, you should feel pretty confident about the exam. As final preparation, here is a **practice exam** to really get you set for the real thing. It's split into **three papers** — two for English Language and one for English Literature. These papers are designed to give you the best possible preparation for the differing question styles of the actual exams, whichever syllabus you're following.
If you're doing Foundation then you won't have learnt every bit — but it's still good practice.

General Certificate of Secondary Education

GCSE
English (Language)

Centre name				
Centre number				
Candidate number				

Paper 1

Surname
Other names
Candidate signature

Time allowed: 2 hours 10 minutes

The first 10 minutes are for **reading the passages on pages 4 and 5**.
You **must not write anything** during the first 10 minutes.
You will then have **2 hours to work on the tasks**.

Instructions to candidates

- Write your name and other details in the spaces provided above.
- Answer **both** questions in **Section A** and **one** question from **Section B**.
- Spend about 1 hour and 15 minutes on Section A and the rest of your time on Section B.
- Cross through any rough work that you do not want marked.
- You must not use a dictionary in this examination.

Information for candidates

- You are reminded of the need for good English and clear presentation in your answers. All questions should be answered in continuous prose.

SECTION A: READING

Answer **both** questions in this Section.
Spend about **1 hour and 15 minutes** on this Section.
Plan your answers and write them carefully.

This question paper is based on 'Deadly monsters of the air spawned by nature',
and John Ezard's piece from Oklahoma. The passages are printed on pages 4 and 5.

Question 1

Look again at the article 'Deadly monsters of the air spawned by nature' **and the diagram which accompanies it.**

Summarise the information given about how tornadoes are formed, their general characteristics and their effects.

Write **about 250 words** in total.

Use your own words as far as possible.   [20]

Question 2

Read again **both** passages.

Explain how each writer, through his content and use of language, engages the interest of the reader.

[20]

OCR, 2001

SECTION B: WRITING TO ARGUE, PERSUADE OR ADVISE

Answer **one** question in this Section

Spend about **45 minutes** on this Section.

> **Remember:**
> - spend 5 minutes planning and sequencing your material
> - you should not write more than about two sides of your answer book
> - spend 5 minutes checking your:
>   - paragraphing
>   - punctuation
>   - spelling.

Ignore these marks — different boards use different systems. Pretend they're all worth the same mark.

EITHER

1 Write a speech for a Governor's meeting where you, as a student, aim to try to **persuade** Governors to change the rules about some controversial issue in your school or college.

(27 marks)
AQA, 2004

OR

2 You are a journalist. Write an **advice** column aimed at teachers about the best ways to keep fit for the job.

(27 marks)
AQA, 2004

OR

3 Your class has the opportunity to take part in an adventure weekend. This will involve such activities as rock-climbing, abseiling, canoeing and go-karting.

Write **two** letters, one to members of your class persuading them to go on the weekend and the other to their parents or guardians advising them of the precautions which are being taken to ensure children's safety.

Start your letters: *Dear ....*

[20]
OCR, 2002

OR

4 'We all need some excitement and risk in our lives.'

How far do you agree with this statement?

[20]
OCR, 2002

Deadly monsters of the air spawned by nature

Tornadoes: creatures of a clash between warm, moist air and cool breezes

Tim Radford

Science Editor

The fusillade of tornadoes that tore across Kansas and Oklahoma wrecking towns and taking at least 36 lives was the worst in more than a decade – but still only a taste of nature's worst.

Most tornadoes hit the ground, tear up anything in their path and then lift again swiftly.

But the worst tornado ever recorded was a monster which in March 1925 travelled 219 miles across Missouri, Illinois and Indiana, killing 742 people and injuring 2,771. Others have been seen hurling railway wagons into the air, and even tearing up stretches of roads.

Tornadoes are nature's special effects: creatures of a clash between warm moist air and cool dry breeze. Tornado Alley, a stretch of the United States which runs from South Dakota to northern Texas, via Oklahoma, Kansas and Nebraska, is a kind of natural pressure cooker.

A stream of cool, dry air flows south and east from the Rockies to meet a warm moist flow from the Gulf of Mexico, and fuels an updraft, which tends to spiral. Just as a skater accelerates her spin by tucking in her arms, so the updraft accelerates and narrows as it makes its way up to the stratosphere, to create a storm cloud.

A downdraft spills from the top of the storm to the ground. This creates a vortex: the cool and warm streams roll against each other like barrels. By this time, the conditions are right for a tornado.

A tornado is a kind of thunderstorm condensed to a small point: it can move across the plains at 30 mph or more, but

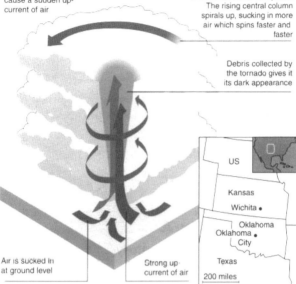

Birth of a tornado

Surface heating of air pockets or convergence of different air masses can cause a sudden up-current of air

Natural (anticlockwise) spin of air in northern hemisphere. The rising central column spirals up, sucking in more air which spins faster and faster

Debris collected by the tornado gives it its dark appearance

Air is sucked in at ground level

Strong up-current of air

US
Kansas
Wichita •
Oklahoma
Oklahoma •
City
Texas
200 miles

the winds inside it will be swirling at between 200 and 300 mph, its low pressure core sucking up moist air, dust and debris.

This debris has been known to include railroad freight cars, telephone poles and even a huge strip of the tarmac off Texas Route 86.

One tornado tore off an aircraft wing and "flew" it for 10 miles; lighter objects have been carried 200 miles. The trail of damage can be more than a mile wide and 50 miles long.

Anyone in the way is at risk. Cats and dogs have had fur ripped from their bodies, horses have had their harnesses torn away, chickens have literally been plucked alive by tornadoes.

Human victims overtaken together have been carried for miles in separate directions. Tornadoes are capricious – a three-year-old girl was picked up in Fort Smith, Arkansas and set down unharmed three miles away.

Others have demolished houses but left the furniture untouched.

A farmer watched from the doorway of his barn while the tornado carried the rest of it

away. Another man walked to the door of his house – and fell 30 feet to the ground as his house sailed away in the air.

But other tornadoes have driven roof shingles into trees, and straws right into car tyres. The classic wooden houses of the American plains collapse, or seem to explode, or occasionally get lifted away. The only safe place is in the storm cellar – for those who can get there in time.

"We can only prevent damage by giving people good design advice," said Scott Steedman, of Sir Alexander Gibb and Partners, one of a team of British scientists and engineers involved in the UN international decade for natural disaster reduction (ID-NDR).

"It's usually the thrown objects, the debris thrown at lightweight buildings that does the damage and causes the fatalities. So much debris is

> 'It's usually the debris thrown around that does the damage and causes the fatalities'

being thrown around.

"You know what it is like yourself, just out in the street in a windy day in London, with dust being thrown in your eyes. "Just imagine you are doing that with two-by-fours eight feet long, and trees and things thrashing around at sixty miles an hour, ground level. They would just go straight through normal walls.

"And bear in mind that much American construction is lightweight. Brick construction would be much more resistant. It's that terrible story of the three pigs, isn't it?"

The US records 800 tornadoes in an average year: and each year, up to 80 people die and 1,500 get hurt.

Tornadoes occasionally form over the Gulf coast as water spouts and move inland; some last only minutes and evaporate before they do any damage, some can last longer than an hour.

They can occur singly, or in scattergun blasts: in one April night in 1991 a total of 54 tornadoes killed 21 people and injured 308, besides doing $277 million damage.

Scientists from the US National Severe Storms Laboratory in Norman, Oklahoma go on the tornado hunt every spring and summer, when conditions are at their ripest, and researchers have been trying to predict their formation.

They have warned citizens for more than 50 years, after a "twister" raked the entire length of the Tinker US Air Force Base outside Oklahoma City.

It was a tornado that carried off Dorothy in the classic story The Wizard of Oz – but tornadoes can happen anywhere. Aristotle records them.

A tornado damaged the astronomer Patrick Moore's garden telescope and lifted off roofs in Selsey, West Sussex. And they happen in the Middle East: the Bible records that God spoke to Job from the centre of a whirlwind.

OCR, 2001

Travel writer John Ezard was in Oklahoma during the recent tornado. Here is his reaction.

Oklahoma is a highly distinctive American state; and that shows in the reaction of its people to their spasmodic catastrophes. Three years ago when 168 men and women were killed in the state capital's worst single disaster, the bombing of the Alfred Murragh federal headquarters, staff in the city's largest tower block arranged their office lighting so that it projected the sign of the cross. Yesterday morning, as they commuted to work past the confetti-like debris of more than 7,000 homes in the suburbs of Mid West City and Moore City, they did something rare on a freeway and almost unprecedented here. They slowed their cars down to 15 miles per hour.

Mostly it wasn't to gawp because you couldn't see much detail past the police barriers and the tall walls of the highways. It was a mark of respect, almost of reverence, for the ending of 38 lives and, temporarily at least, of the proud, earnest material dreams of thousands more families. The passers-by turned their vehicles into an impromptu, collective, funeral cortege. It might so easily have happened to them, the series of vortexes that sucked humans and the fabric of their lives towards the sky and spat them back to earth in these aspiring middle-class satellite townships within a few seconds. At dawn yesterday, which broke with a clear sunny sky after the torrential thunder storms and continuing statewide tornado alerts of Tuesday, you could for the first time realise what had struck these new model Main Streets.

Sound brick houses, built around traditional timber frames, have been at best left looking like shanty town remnants and at worst like Dresden after the fire storm. You can still see what neat places Moore and Mid West used to be. Now they are flimsy death traps which need bulldozing. Yesterday afternoon thousands of survivors were allowed back for a strictly limited two hours to fumble through the ruins of Mid West City and salvage possessions by the car load. They are desperate to retrieve not only their family photos and videos and their children's clothes but their TVs and microwaves. These possessions had to be saved for, or paid off by credit card, and if you can recover them then rebuilding your life is a mite easier. 'First nature shatters my life. Now the government is going to bury my possessions,' said one frantic woman, her face still blood-flecked with cuts from the flying debris.

In time the dead will get their public memorials, like the one which is due to be opened next year to the Murragh bomb victims. Here, the bomb is seen as an incomprehensible atrocity from another planet, an event to be buried deep in memory. But the twisters come every year, their spouts grubbing up and spewing out soil, property and sometimes people, like giant malignant earthworms reaching down from the sky. Moore City had its last tornado as recently as October.

Moving at 35 miles an hour, engorged with sucked-up debris, this evil killer grew to a base more that a quarter of a mile broad which started to twinkle with grey flashes as it brought down power lines. "My God. This thing is a monster," said a TV weather man. Then another twister developed nearby and they marched together like twin Hiroshima mushroom clouds. "God, it just hit. It was so loud, much louder than last time." Ronna Johnson said. "Our house was covered with mud. And then I started crying. I said 'This is not right...' "

Within minutes the response was as practised and organised as in a disturbed ant hill. Neighbours trained in mouth-to-mouth resuscitation were sought to treat the heart victims that twisters always cause. Six designated emergency hostels were re-opened, and within an hour Wayland Bonds, Moore's school superintendent, who lost two schools and a technology centre, was planning how to complete the school year without them. Less than two days afterwards, the event is beginning to lose its grip on public interest. Last night, even on local radio bulletins, the topic of tornado damage had dropped to third place. And during the commercial breaks – "in this difficult time" – the Prudential Insurance Company was urging prudent people to take out policies to protect those material dreams during the next big blow.

OCR, 2001

[BLANK PAGE]

General Certificate of Secondary Education

GCSE
English (Language)

Centre name					
Centre number					
Candidate number					

Paper 2

Surname	
Other names	
Candidate signature	

Time allowed: 1 hour 15 minutes

Instructions to candidates
- Write your name and other details in the spaces provided above.
- Answer **one** question in **Section A** and **one** question from **Section B**.
- Spend about **30 minutes** on Section A and about **45 minutes** on Section B.
- Cross through any rough work that you do not want marked.
- You must not use a dictionary in this examination.

Information for candidates
- For Section A, candidates must have a copy of the current *Anthology*. This may be annotated, but candidates must not use any additional notes or materials.
- You are reminded of the need for good English and clear presentation in your answers. All questions should be answered in continuous prose.

SECTION A: POETS FROM OTHER CULTURES AND TRADITIONS

Answer **either** Question 1 **or** Question 2, using your *Anthology*.
Spend **30 minutes** on your chosen question.

EITHER

1   How do **two** of the poets show you something important about
     the culture or cultures they are writing about?   *(27 marks)*

OR

2   Write about the use of description and its effects in **any two** poems.   *(27 marks)*

*If you're doing the OCR syllabus, your
"Different Cultures" works will be short
stories, not poems. You can still do one
of the questions above — just write
about authors and short stories
instead of poets and poems.*

AQA, 2001

SECTION B: WRITING TO INFORM, EXPLAIN OR DESCRIBE

Answer **one** question in this Section
Spend about **45 minutes** on this Section.

> **Remember:**
>
> - spend 5 minutes planning and sequencing your material
> - you should not write more than about two sides of your answer book
> - spend 5 minutes checking your:
>   - paragraphing
>   - punctuation
>   - spelling.

EITHER

*Ignore these marks —
different boards use
different systems.
Pretend they're all worth
the same mark.*

1   People often enjoy reading about the interests and hobbies of others.
    Choose something you are interested in and know a lot about.

    Write about this in a way which will **inform** other people.   *(27 marks)*

AQA, 2004 Specimen

OR

2   Decisions can be difficult to make.
    Think about a difficult decision you have had to make.

    Explain what the decision was and what happened as a result of it.   *(27 marks)*

AQA, 2004 Specimen

OR

3   Do you look for friendship in people who are like, or unlike, yourself?
    Explain how similarities and differences may affect a friendship.

[20]

OR   **OCR, 2001**

4   'The Odd Couple.'
    Write a story with this title.   [20]

OCR, 2001

[BLANK PAGE]

NB: All of these questions look like they're worth different amounts, and some don't have any marks next to them at all. Don't worry about this — they're all different because I've taken them from different exam boards. **DON'T WORRY ABOUT THE NUMBER OF MARKS FOR EACH ESSAY — THEY'RE ALL WORTH THE SAME AMOUNT.**
All of these questions cover the syllabus. It's okay to answer questions from **any board**, even if it's not the board you're studying.

General Certificate of Secondary Education

GCSE
English (Literature)

Centre name				
Centre number				
Candidate number				

Paper 3

Surname	
Other names	
Candidate signature	

Time allowed: 1 hour 45 minutes

Instructions to candidates
- Write your name and other details in the spaces provided above.
- Answer **one** question from **Section A** and **one** question from **Section B**.
- You should spend about **45 minutes** on Section A and about **1 hour** on Section B.
- Cross through any rough work that you do not want marked.
- You must not use a dictionary in this examination.

Information for candidates
- The marks available are given in brackets at the end of each question.
- This is an open text examination. Candidates must bring copies of texts into the examination room. These may be annotated, but candidates must not use any additional notes or materials.
- You are reminded of the need for good English and clear presentation in your answers. Quality of written communication will be assessed in all answers.

SECTION A

PROSE AND DRAMA

SECTION B

POETRY (FROM YOUR ANTHOLOGY)

SECTION A — PROSE AND DRAMA

- Answer **one** question from this Section
- You should spend about **45 minutes** on this Section.

Shakespeare: Romeo and Juliet

JULIET   O God, she comes!
Enter NURSE *and* PETER
O honey nurse, what news?
Hast thou met with him? Send thy man away.

NURSE   Peter, stay at the gate.
Exit PETER

JULIET   Now, good sweet Nurse — O Lord, why look'st thou sad?
Though news be sad, yet tell them merrily,
If good, thou shamest the music of sweet news
By playing it to me with so sour a face.

NURSE   I am a-weary, give me leave awhile.
Fie, how my bones ache! What a jaunce have I!

JULIET   I would thou hadst my bones, and I thy news:
Nay, come, I pray thee, speak, good, good Nurse, speak.

NURSE   Jesu, what haste? Can you not stay awhile?
Do you not see that I am out of breath?

JULIET   How art thou out of breath, when thou hast breath
To say to me that thou art out of breath?
The excuse that thou dost make in this delay
Is longer than the tale thou dost excuse.
Is thy news good, or bad? Answer to that.
Say either, and I'll stay the circumstance.
Let me be satisfied, is't good or bad?

NURSE   Well, you have made a simple choice. You know not
how to choose a man. Romeo? No, not he; though his face
be better than any man's, yet his leg excels all men's, and for
a hand, and a foot, and a body, though they be not to be
talked on, yet they are past compare. He is not the flower of
courtesy, but, I'll warrant him, as gentle as a lamb. Go thy
ways, wench, serve God. What, have you dined at home?

JULIET   No, no. But all this did I know before.
What says he of our marriage? What of that?

NURSE   Lord, how my head aches! What a head have I!
It beats as it would fall in twenty pieces.
My back o' t' other side — O, my back, my back!
Beshrew your heart for sending me about,
To catch my death with jauncing up and down!

JULIET   I'faith, I am sorry that thou art not well.
Sweet, sweet, sweet Nurse, tell me, what says my love?

NURSE   Your love says, like an honest gentleman, and a
courteous, and a kind, and a handsome, and, I warrant, a
virtuous — Where is your mother?

JULIET Where is my mother! Why, she is within;
      Where should she be? How oddly thou repliest!
      'Your love says, like an honest gentleman,
      Where is your mother?'
NURSE   O God's lady dear!
      Are you so hot? Marry, come up, I trow.
      Is this the poultice for my aching bones?
      Henceforward do your messages yourself.
JULIET Here's such a coil! Come, what says Romeo?
NURSE Have you got leave to go to shrift today?
JULIET I have.
NURSE Then hie you hence to Friar Lawrence' cell.
      There stays a husband to make you a wife.
      Now comes the wanton blood up in your cheeks,
      They'll be in scarlet straight at any news.
      Hie you to church; I must another way,
      To fetch a ladder, by the which your love
      Must climb a bird's nest soon when it is dark.
      I am the drudge and toil in your delight,
      But you shall bear the burden soon at night.
      Go — I'll to dinner, hie you to the cell.
JULIET Hie to high fortune! Honest Nurse, farewell.
         Exeunt

Question 1:

How does this extract add to your understanding of the Nurse's character,
and her feelings for Juliet?

In your answer you should make some reference also to other parts of the play.

OCR, 2003 Specimen

[TURN OVER FOR NEXT QUESTION]

John Steinbeck: Of Mice and Men

Question 2:

The following passage is taken from near the beginning of Chapter Four where Crooks is talking to Lennie.

How does Steinbeck present Crooks in this passage?
What is the importance of Crooks in the novel as a whole?

'But I know now.' He hesitated, and when he spoke again his voice was softer. 'There wasn't another coloured family for miles around. And now there ain't a coloured man on this ranch an' there's jus' one family in Soledad.' He laughed. 'If I say something, why it's just a nigger sayin' it.'

Lennie asked, 'How long you think it'll be before them pups will be old enough to pet?'

5 Crooks laughed again. 'A guy can talk to you an' be sure you won't go blabbin'. Couple of weeks an' them pups'll be all right. George knows what he's about. Jus' talks, an' you don't understand nothing.' He leaned forward excitedly. 'This is just a nigger talkin', an' a busted-back nigger. So it don't mean nothing, see? You couldn't remember it anyways. I seen it over an' over an' over – a guy talkin' to another guy and it don't make no difference if he don't hear or understand. The thing is, they're talkin', or
10 they're settin' still not talkin'. It don't make no difference, no difference.' His excitement had increased until he pounded his knee with his hand. 'George can tell you screwy things, and it don't matter. It's just the talking. It's just bein' with another guy. That's all.' He paused.

His voice grew softer and persuasive. 'S'pose George don't come back no more. S'pose he took a powder and just ain't coming back. What'll you do then?'

15 Lennie's attention came gradually to what had been said. 'What?' he demanded.

'I said s'pose George went into town to-night and you never heard of him no more.' Crooks pressed forward some kind of private victory. 'Just s'pose that,' he repeated.

'He won't do it,' Lennie cried. 'George wouldn't do nothing like that. I been with George a long time. He'll come back tonight—' But the doubt was too much for him. 'Don't you think he will?'

20 Crooks' face lighted with pleasure in his torture.

(27 marks)

AQA, 2004 Specimen

William Golding: Lord of the Flies

EITHER

Question 3:

The deaths of Simon and Piggy are both profoundly disturbing for different reasons.

Show how Golding makes us respond to the two deaths in different ways.

OR

Question 4:

You are Jack, immediately after the quarrel about letting the fire out.

Write your thoughts.

OCR, 2001

John Steinbeck: Of Mice and Men

EITHER

Question 5:

George says several times 'If I was alone, I could live so easy.'

Do you think he is right?

OR

Question 6:

You are Curley, after your first meeting with George and Lennie.

Write your thoughts.

OCR, 2001

Harper Lee: To Kill a Mockingbird

EITHER

Question 7:

'Our father didn't do anything. He worked in an office, not in a drug store. Atticus did not drive a dump-truck for the county, he was not the sheriff, he did not farm, work in a garage, or do anything that could possibly arouse the admiration of anyone.'

How does the writer present Atticus as a man that Scout learns to admire?

OR

Question 8:

Two of the novel's themes are prejudice and hatred. What other themes have you found? Write about any two of the themes that you have found and explain why you feel they are important in the novel.

Edexcel, 2001

George Orwell: Animal Farm

EITHER

Question 9:

Major tells the animals, 'Man is the only real enemy we have.'

To what extent does Orwell's novel persuade you that Major is right or wrong?

OR

Question 10:

You are Snowball on the day Mr Jones has been chased off Manor Farm.

Write your thoughts.

OCR, 2001

J.D. Salinger: The Catcher in the Rye

EITHER

Question 11:

Does Holden Caulfield change at all in the course of the novel? Write about **three** episodes, including one near the beginning of the novel and one near the end.

Write about:
• how he changes, or stays the same
• how the writer shows him changing or staying the same.   *(27 marks)*

OR

Question 12:

How does J.D. Salinger present the problems of teenagers in *The Catcher in the Rye?*
                                                                            (27 marks)

AQA, 2004 Specimen

Susan Hill: I'm the King of the Castle

EITHER

Question 13:

How does Susan Hill present Hooper and Kingshaw, and why do you think she presents them in the ways she does?

Write about:
• how the writer makes Hooper and Kingshaw speak and behave
• their relationship with each other and their relationships with other people
• the writer's purposes in presenting them like this.   *(27 marks)*

OR

Question 14:

Kingshaw dies at the end of the novel.

Who do you think Susan Hill wants the reader to blame for what happened to him, and why?   *(27 marks)*

AQA, 2001

Barry Hines: A Kestrel for a Knave

EITHER

Question 15:

Barry Hines says that *A Kestrel for a Knave* makes people realise that "it is possible to achieve something in life, however difficult the circumstances".

What do you think the novel has to say about the difficulties of someone like Billy "achieving something"?

Write about:
- how the writer shows the difficulties Billy faces
- the extent to which Billy overcomes these difficulties
- what ideas the writer conveys about the possibility of "achieving something in life"
- how the writer conveys these ideas.

(27 marks)

OR

Question 16:

When Kes dies, Mrs Casper says: "It's only a bird. You can get another, can't you?"

How does the writer show ways in which Kes is important to Billy?   *(27 marks)*

AQA, 2004 Specimen

Robert Cormier: Heroes

EITHER

Question 17:

What does *Heroes* have to say about the nature of heroes, and how does the writer present heroes in the novel?

(27 marks)

OR

Question 18:

How does the structure of *Heroes* help to shape the reader's response to the novel?

Write about:

- how the story is revealed
- the changes in time
- how the structure affects the reader.

(27 marks)

AQA, 2004 Specimen

Arthur Miller: The Crucible

EITHER

Question 19:

How does Miller use the character of Mary Warren to add to the dramatic impact of the play?

OR

Question 20:

You are John Proctor just after your conversation with Abigail Williams in Act One.

Write your thoughts.

OCR, 2002

George Orwell: Nineteen Eighty-Four

EITHER

Question 21:

To Winston, becoming an 'unperson' is worse than torture and death. Explain why.

OR

Question 22:

'The two main aims of the Party are to conquer the whole surface of the earth and to extinguish once and for all the possibility of independent thought.'

To what extent do you think the aims of the party are achieved in the novel?

Edexcel, 2001

Jane Austen: Pride and Prejudice

EITHER

Question 23:

'And so you like this man's sisters too do you? Their manners are not equal to his.'
(Elizabeth speaking to Jane)

In what ways does Jane Austen develop the differences between Mr Bingley and his sisters, Caroline Bingley and Mrs Hurst, in the novel?

OR

Question 24:

Mrs Bennet and Mrs Philips are conversing after learning that Charlotte Lucas is to marry Mr Collins and Mr Bingley has left Netherfield.

Write the conversation between them.

OCR, 2001

Thomas Hardy: The Mayor of Casterbridge

EITHER

Question 25:

Show how Hardy makes the opinions and traditions of the ordinary people of Casterbridge a significant part of the novel.

OR

Question 26:

You are Donald Farfrae just after the death of Lucetta, thinking over what she told you on the last night of her life.

Write your thoughts.

OCR, 2001

Arthur Miller: Death of a Salesman

EITHER

Question 27:

What does Miller's portrayal of Uncle Ben add to the dramatic impact of the play?

Remember to support your ideas with detail from the play.

OR

Question 28:

You are Bernard leaving your father's office after your conversation with Willy in Act Two.

Write your thoughts.

OCR, 2003 Specimen

Willy Russell: Educating Rita

EITHER

Question 29:

Explore the ways in which Willy Russell depicts aspects of the English class structure in *Educating Rita.*

OR

Question 30:

How far does Willy Russell succeed in bringing to life characters who do not actually appear on stage in this play?

OCR, 2001

J.B. Priestley: An Inspector Calls

EITHER

Question 31:

What do we learn about Mr Arthur Birling's character and attitude towards life as the play unfolds?

OR

Question 32:

In most plays all of the main characters appear on the stage. What is gained or lost by leaving Eva Smith/Daisy Renton unseen?

Edexcel, 2001

Arthur Miller: A View from the Bridge

EITHER

Question 33:

'I could see every step coming, step after step, like a dark figure walking down a hall towards a certain door. I knew where he was heading for, I knew where he was going to end.'

Consider how the writer's portrayal of Eddie makes his downfall inevitable.

OR

Question 34:

How does the writer use aspects of the Italian immigrant community to influence the course of events in his play?

Edexcel, 2001

[TURN OVER FOR SECTION B]

SECTION B — POETRY (FROM YOUR ANTHOLOGY)

- Answer **one** question from this Section
- You should spend about **60 minutes** on this Section.

EITHER

Ignore these little headings in brackets — they're referring to section titles in an old Anthology.

Question 35: *(Time and Place)*

Choose **at least three** poems from *Time and Place* in which time is important – either the time of day or historical time.

Explore the similarities and differences between the poems by comparing:

- the importance of time in the poems
- how the poets convey this sense of time.

OR

Question 36: *(Comparisons between Groups)*

Compare **two** poems from *Hearts and Partners* with **two** poems from *That Old Rope*, showing how different poets explore the conflicts between people in close relationships.

Explore the similarities and differences between the poems by comparing:

- conflicts and relationships
- feelings and attitudes about conflicts and relationships
- ways in which the poets use language, form and structure.

OR

Question 37: *(Comparisons between Groups)*

"Poetry is the best that has been thought and said, in the best words."
"Poetry is fancy stuff that's all right if you want to get away from the real world for a while."

From your reading of poems in the Literature *Anthology*, which of these statements would you agree with more, and why?

Refer to **any four** poems from anywhere in the Literature *Anthology* (pages 72-96), including **one** written before 1900.

AQA, 2001

OR

Question 38: *(Childhood)*

Choose **at least three** poems where children experience events which have a profound effect upon them.

Explore the similarities and differences in the poems by comparing:

• the events and the effects of the events
• how the poets use language and form to convey experiences and their effects.

OR

Question 39: *(War)*

Compare **two** poems which present the experiences of war positively with **two** poems which present it negatively.

Explore the similarities and differences between the poets' presentation of war by comparing:

• experiences and situations
• attitudes and feelings
• the poets' methods and purposes.

OR

Question 40: *(I Tell You I Don't Love You)*

Some of the poems in your *I Tell You I Don't Love You* are written in unusual or striking ways.

Compare the ways that **at least three** of them are written.

Your comparison should include comment on language, form and structure.

OR

Question 41: *(A Matter of Life and Death)*

Sometimes the way a poem is written can be as interesting as what it has to say.

Compare **at least three** poems from your *A Matter of Life and Death* where you think this is so.

AQA, 2001

Page 10 — Warm-up Questions and Short Tasks

1) Any reasonable answers — for example:
   a) School uniform has a negative effect on learning. Incorrect uniform causes conflict in the classroom.
   b) The school expects high standards at all times. Uniform rules will be adhered to, especially the banning of jeans and trainers.
   c) Expense is often used as an argument against school uniform, but keeping up with the latest clothing fashions can also be expensive.

2) a) Creative writing b) Persuasive writing c) Newspaper report d) Analytical writing e) Advice

3) a) time   b) character   c) setting   d) speaker

4) Any reasonable answer, as long as it uses all four paragraph changes — change of time, character, setting and speaker.

Page 11 — Warm-up Questions and Short Tasks

5) Any reasonable answer — for example:
   Firstly, listening to loud music can cause health problems for the future.
   Secondly, the nature of some lyrics encourages young people to commit violence.
   Thirdly, pop songs are mainly about image yet many of the idols are negative figures.
   Finally, pop music is limited in its scope and so gives young people very narrow horizons.

6) Any reasonable answer — for example:
   Although listening to loud music can cause health problems, this applies to all music and not just pop music.
   It has been argued that the nature of some lyrics encourages young people to commit violence, yet this is largely unproven and anecdotal.
   Many adults feel that pop singers are negative figures, yet having your own heroes and idols is an important part of identity.
   Although pop music can be limited in its scope, it is obvious that teenagers who develop a love for music will continue to listen and so will broaden their horizons as they get older.

7) Any reasonable answers — for example:
   a) '...it has the power to develop both mind and character.' / 'It is the gateway to other worlds.'
   b) 'On a practical level, it gives you the skills essential for everyday life...'
   c) The writer states that speaking and listening activities can increase confidence and improve thinking skills as students learn to argue their perspective and listen to others.

8) Any reasonable answer — for example:
   The writer thinks that English is essential on two levels. Firstly, it is vital for everyday communication as it equips us with 'life skills'. More than this though, it develops the whole person enabling us to broaden our minds and experiences. This way it really is '...the gateway to other worlds'.

9) In order of importance = persuasive writing; For and against alternated = discursive writing; Sequential = instructional writing;
   Flashback = creative writing; Chronological = account of an event.

10) "Kieron never realised how much his life would <u>change</u> after selling <u>his</u> comic book script. Now people <u>everywhere</u> would read his comics.
    He was starting to believe that he could <u>accomplish</u> anything<u>."</u>

Page 18 — Warm-up Questions

1) b) the writer's message
   d) the characters

2) a) bad advice
   b) bad advice
   c) good advice
   d) bad advice

3) bullet points

4) (a).

5) One.

6) In your conclusion, sum up all your points very briefly and say what your overall answer to the question is.

7)

| Step One: Work out what the questions are about. | → | Step Two: Choose the question that's best for you. | → | Step Three: Break the question into bullet points. | → | Step Four: Write a general answer then follow the plan. | → | Step Five: Write a conclusion. |

8) Almost every sentence in this passage helps you understand something about Jason, but these are some of the bits you could underline:
   Jason groaned and rolled over on the <u>grey and greasy sheets</u>. He reached out a <u>thick, hairy hand</u> and <u>grabbed</u> the alarm clock. He <u>battered</u> it against the floorboards <u>five times before he realised</u> that it wasn't the alarm clock ringing but the phone. He picked it up and <u>barked</u>, "<u>What the hell</u> do you want?" then <u>slammed</u> the receiver down and collapsed back onto his pillow. He sighed deeply. The phone began to ring again. Jason reached down for the cord and <u>wrenched</u> it out of the wall.

9) Any answer's OK, <u>so long as it's backed up with evidence from the story</u>. You could mention any of these points:
   Jason's a filthy slob — "grey and greasy sheets".
   He's quite rough-looking — "thick, hairy hand".
   He's violent — "battered...grabbed...slammed...wrenched". He tries to turn off the alarm clock by bashing it on the floor.
   He's a bit thick — it takes him five goes at turning off the alarm clock before he realises it's not ringing.
   He's rude — "What the hell do you want?"

10) e.g. pity, fear, love, money, anger, greed, power.

11) a) motivate – encourage to do something.
    b) manipulate – control other people so that they do what you want.
    c) revenge – getting your own back for something someone's done to you.

12) A 'third person narrator' is someone telling the story who isn't one of the main characters. They can tell you what all the characters think and feel.

13) A 'first person narrator' is one of the main characters. The first person narrator can only really tell you what he or she thinks and feels.

14) NO. You can't believe everything a first person narrator says – they're only telling the story from one point of view and they could be trying to twist the way you see things.

Page 25 — Warm-up Questions

1) The writer's message is what the writer thinks — the opinion or moral that's put across in the writing.

2) Events of the story, what happens to the characters, the tone of the writing, the title of the writing.

3) b) Show you understand the writer's point of view.

4) c) An excellent idea if you want to show that you know what you're talking about.

5) c) The sentences are very short — the longest is five words. There are no descriptive words at all.

6) a) nervous; tense.
   b) amused; entertained.

7) a) flashback: the story is in the present and then the scene shifts back to the past.
   b) foreshadowing: this point in the story provides hints about what will happen later.

8) True.

9) The metaphor is "Pigs". Tabitha says the boys are pigs, but she means they are behaving like pigs because they're eating in such a greedy way.

10) symbolism: making an object stand for an idea.
    allegory: where characters, settings and events can stand for something else.
    ambiguity: where words or events have more than one meaning.
    irony: where the writer says the opposite of what is really meant.

Page 31 — Warm-up Questions

1) a) get the facts straight about the story.
   d) quote relevant snippets to prove each point you make.

2) It would show you know the play in detail.

3) This depends on whatever plays you're doing — if you get stuck talk to your teacher or other people in your English class.

4) a)'s better because it refers to the audience.

5) a) Stagecraft — the writer's skill at writing for the stage and making the events come to life.
   b) Tragedy — a play concerning the downfall of the main character, usually as a result of a fatal character flaw.
   Tragedies often deal with serious topics like religion, love, death and war.
   c) Comedy — a funny play, often with events based on real life.
   d) Dialogue — conversation between two or more people in a play.
   e) Soliloquy — when a character talks to themselves but does it out loud so the audience can hear.
   f) Imagery — comparing one thing to another to give a more vivid picture of it.

6) The imagery used is personification. Time or life — "this petty pace" — is described like a person, creeping along.

7) It adds detail to the story and explains how they want the play to look on stage.

8) Poetic verse and blank verse both have 10 or 11 syllables per line, but only poetic verse rhymes.

9) Poetic — when a posh character's talking; at the beginning of a scene; at the end of a scene.
   Blank — most of the time.
   Prose — when it's a funny bit; when it's not a very important bit.

Page 34 — Exam Questions

1) Who do you consider to be most responsible for the death of Eva Smith?
   List of points for a good essay:

General	A good answer will show a strong argument supported by close references to the text. A top grade essay will carefully evaluate each character's responsibility.
Introduction	Briefly refer to the key words in the question: say each member of the Birling family has a responsibility for the death of Eva Smith.
Main Body	Show how the 'chain of events' began with Arthur Birling sacking Eva Smith for 'having too much to say'. When the Inspector questions Birling about sacking Eva he strongly defends his actions and shows no remorse. Sheila's responsiblility: Eva was given the sack from Milward's as a result of Sheila's jealousy and imperious behaviour. Unlike her father, Sheila accepts responsibility. She's the character most susceptible to the Inspector's lesson: the Inspector tells the others 'we have more effect on the young'. Gerald's role: When he meets Eva in the Palace Bar she's changed her name to Daisy Renton: perhaps to bring her luck. Gerald takes advantage of her and has an affair. This ends because Gerald doesn't want marriage: at the time the play is set relationships between two people from different classes/backgrounds were not socially acceptable. Gerald shows little acceptance of responsibility: he's more concerned about Sheila's reaction than Eva/Daisy's death. Eric's responsibility: They have an affair: Eva becomes pregnant. Eric gives Eva money but she knows he's stolen it. Eva ends the relationship. Eric shows remorse: he's changed and his relationship with his parents will never be the same. Mrs Birling: Her actions were the final straw, abusing her chairmanship of a charity to turn Eva away. Eva committed suicide shortly afterwards.
Conclusion	They all have responsibility but Mr and Mrs Birling seem to have the most.
Language and Structure	A top class essay has a proper introduction, middle and end — the conclusion should be concise and to the point, and ideally use a snappy quotation to emphasise your argument. Use interesting language and a varied vocabulary.

2) Explore the different forms of disguise and deception that feature in 'Twelfth Night'.
   List of points for a good essay:

General	A good answer will focus closely on the key words in the question with main points supported by close textual reference.
Introduction	This should outline how you will interpret the key words 'disguise' and 'deception': refer to Viola's disguise as Cesario, how the disguises and deceptions add to the comedy and how some characters are guilty of self-deception.
Main Body	Examine Viola's disguise as Cesario and show how: it helps her to work for Orsino, results in Olivia falling in love with her, stops Viola revealing her love for Orsino, adds to the dramatic irony and causes the complications of mistaken identity. Demonstrate how disguise or deception causes most of the comedy in the play by commenting on: the trick played on Malvolio, how Sir Andrew is led to think he has a chance with Olivia and how he is tricked into a duel with Cesario, how Feste adopts the disguise of 'Sir Topas' and how Sir Andrew thinks Sebastian is Cesario. Support your points with relevant brief quotations. Show how some characters are guilty of self-deception: Olivia pretends to be in mourning, Orsino convinces himself he is in love with Olivia but is only in love with the idea of being in love. Malvolio is fooled into thinking he could be a serious suitor for Olivia. Again, support your points with relevant quotations.
Conclusion	Refer back to the original question and sum up your main points. For a top grade essay add an extra idea in your conclusion, for example, word-play is also a kind of disguise and the use of so many puns in the play complements the theme; you could quote from the conversation between Viola and Feste in Act III Scene I.
Language and Structure	A top class essay has a proper introduction, middle and end — the conclusion should be concise and to the point, and ideally use a snappy quotation to emphasise your argument. Use interesting language and a varied vocabulary.

3) How far is Frair Lawrence responsible for the deaths of Romeo and Juliet?
   List of points for a good essay:

General	A strong answer will show focus on Friar Lawrence's character: to respond to the phrase 'how far?' you need to put his role into context.
Introduction	Briefly describe the Friar and his relationship with Romeo.
Main Body	Comment on the Friar's actions throughout the play: he marries Romeo and Juliet, advises and comforts them, sends Romeo to Mantua, he offers to help smooth things over whilst Romeo is in exile — Act III Scene 3: 'To blaze your marriage, reconcile your friends', gives Juliet the potion, tries to save her when things go wrong but then apparently runs away when he thinks he will be found in the tomb. Examine his motives; does he want to end the feud? Act II Scene 3: 'turn your households' rancour to pure love'. He shows superiority when advising the couple, he looks for appreciation and gratitude from others, he's aware of his weaknesses and wants to conceal them. Are his motives positive? He wants to end the feud but his plans show his naivety and he unwittingly contributes to the tragedy. Discuss how other characters are similarly responsible: the Nurse has also been taken into the lovers' confidence and has given advice, the fight between Tybalt and Mercutio is not caused by the Friar, the fued has been going on for a long time and would eventually result in tragic consequences.
Conclusion	Argue that the Friar set events in motion which ultimately led to the deaths of Romeo and Juliet but the tragedy would have happened anyway: the Friar is only partly responsible. A top class essay will admit in its conclusion that this is not a final answer to the question: there are other interpretations of the Friar's actions. The examiner will reward an essay that contains any well-supported argument.
Language and Structure	A top class essay has a proper introduction, middle and end — the conclusion should be concise and to the point, and ideally use a snappy quotation to emphasise your argument. Use interesting language and a varied vocabulary.

4) Discuss whether you think Macbeth is a tragic hero or a tyrant.
   List of points for a good essay:

General	A strong answer will provide an informed discussion of Macbeth's character supported by close textual reference.
Introduction	Define what constitutes a 'tyrant' and also a 'tragic hero'.
Main Body	Explore what Macbeth does and says which support these distinctions: a tyrant is all-powerful, in Act III Scene I Macbeth decides to have Banquo murdered to prevent him from voicing his obvious suspicions. Macduff justifiably refers to him as this 'tyrant' in Act IV Scene 3 after Macbeth has slaughtered his family: a very cowardly act. A hero is courageous and our first impression of Macbeth is that of a 'brave' soldier who has almost single-handedly saved Scotland from the rebellion and is valued highly by his king. To emphasise courage is a very important point when considering Macbeth's character: even before the audience first meets Macbeth he is defined by his courage and in the final scene of the play this courage returns: he does not die a coward's death. Lady Macbeth knows how important manhood and courage are to Macbeth and she plays on this when tempting and persuading him to murder Duncan. Because she fears he is 'too full o' the milk of human kindness'. Explain that whether Macbeth is a tyrant or tragic hero depends on the weight of the evidence. Some of his actions can be seen as tyrannical or heroic, or a combination of the two.
Conclusion	Remember that there is no right or wrong answer to this question: decide which view you support and sum up your argument. For a top grade essay you will produce a clear and persuasive argument in support of your view of Macbeth's character.
Language and Structure	A top class essay has a proper introduction, middle and end — the conclusion should be concise and to the point, and ideally use a snappy quotation to emphasise your argument. Use interesting language and a varied vocabulary.

5) Discuss whether you think the main character in a play you are studying is a hero or a villain.
   List of points for a good essay:

General	A strong answer will provide an informed discussion of the main character supported by close textual reference.
Introduction	Define what constitutes a 'hero' and also a 'villain'.
Main Body	Explore what the main character does and says which support these distinctions: How do other characters see the main character? Use quotes which refer to the main character's personality. How does the main character behave? Is there confusion or is it a clear-cut case? Use persuasive language to back up your argument.
Conclusion	Remember that there is not really a right or wrong answer to this question: decide which view you support and sum up your argument. For a top grade essay you will produce a clear and persuasive argument in support of your view of the main character.
Language and Structure	A top class essay has a proper introduction, middle and end — the conclusion should be concise and to the point, and ideally use a snappy quotation to emphasise your argument. Use interesting language and a varied vocabulary.

150

Page 40 — Warm-up Questions

1) It will make your writing sound more convincing.
2) A poem written for someone who has died.
3) Poetry written in lines of irregular length that do not have to rhyme.
4) A verse.
5) a) couplet   b) triplet   c) quatrain
6) e.g. A poem written in the first person that deals with a specific situation and involves some sort of revelation by the speaker.
7) Any reasonable answer – for example: all knowing, detached, authoritative
8) Any reasonable answer – for example: When there is a pause in mid-line. "The car was warm. The driver hoped to show me how to park."
9) Any reasonable answer – for example: When a sentence runs from one line of poetry into the next one.
   "The car was warm and the driver hoped
   To show me how to park."
10) It will help you to work out what to write about.
11) Topic, language and how the writer wants you to feel when you read the poem.
12) You should include quotes from the poem in your essay to strengthen your point.
13) This statement is very wishy-washy and does not sound convincing.
14) The examiner is expecting you to find the similarities and differences between poems.
15) False.
16) Empathy is when you can understand another person's feelings.
17) It's good because it means that there are no right or wrong answers, so any reasonable idea will get you some marks as long as you can back it up.
18) At least three times.
19) A sonnet is a poem with 14 lines that has a regular rhyme scheme. Shakespeare is very famous for writing sonnets.
20) A quatrain (4 lines).
21) Any of the following: implies conspiracy, often more engaging, access to secret thoughts, implies intimacy, about personal matters.
22) Alliteration is when consonants are repeated. Any reasonable example e.g. the green grass grew gradually.
23) Onomatopoeia is when a word sounds like what it means. Any reasonable example e.g. pop.
24) e.g. Tone means the feeling the words are spoken with e.g. angrily.
25) e.g. It is important to only use them if they are relevant and you can show that you know how to use them.

Page 43 — Exam Questions

1) 'Education for Leisure' and 'Havisham' by Carol Ann Duffy are regarded by many people as disturbing poems. Do you find the poems disturbing?
   Give reasons for your answer, referring to language, tone and structure.
   List of points for a good essay:

General	A strong answer will be equally balanced for each poem, showing good knowledge and understanding of both texts. Give an opinion, and support your answer by commenting on specific areas. Give specific reasons and quote from both poems.
Introduction	Refer back to the question in your introduction, and state clearly whether you agree with the statement for neither, one or both poems. Remember you are being asked if you find the poems 'disturbing' so you must use this word consistently within your answer.
Main Body	In order to achieve the highest grades possible you should compare both poems within your paragraphs rather than writing about each poem separately. Ensure that you give good reasons as to whether you find the poems disturbing by quoting from the texts and referring to language, tone, structure AND imagery of BOTH poems. Find the most disturbing lines or images and use them as a starting point.
Conclusion	Refer back to the question in your conclusion and restate your personal opinion as to what extent you find the poems disturbing.
Language and Structure	Make sure that you use the correct technical vocabulary in your answer, but only comment on techniques such as alliteration if you are making a valid point that is relevant to the question. You should also remember to paragraph, using formal language and ensure that you quote accurately, remembering speech marks for quotes and inverted commas for titles of poems.

For a top grade essay you must compare the two poems consistently throughout your answer, using comparative language. You must also quote directly from the text and thoroughly analyse quotes, in detail. Vary your vocabulary, including as much technical language as you can. Above all, make sure every point you make is DETAILED and RELEVANT to the question.

2)   In 'My Last Duchess' by Robert Browning, what techniques does the poet use in order to convey a negative impression of the Duke to the reader?
     List of points for a good essay:

General	A good answer for this type of question will examine very specifically the poetic techniques you have learned about so far. These include language, imagery, tone and structure, which are the elements you must cover in any poetry question. Make sure that in your answer you do not just focus on one technique but discuss several, since the question asks for techniques.
Introduction	Always refer back to the question in your introduction and use the same language. With this type of question you should agree with the statement so do not attempt to write about the positive impression given. In this instance you are not being asked for your own opinion on the matter although you may include this at the end in your conclusion if you want to.
Main Body	Remember you are only writing about one poem, so you need to give a detailed answer. Keep referring back to the question and explain how the techniques convey a negative impression and quote from the text to give an example of each technique. It is not good enough just to name some techniques; you must link them to the question. Comment on each technique in turn, but remember to link your paragraphs using appropriate connectives and by constantly referring back to the question.
Conclusion	In your conclusion you should attempt to summarise the key points you have made in the body of your essay without going into too much detail and repeating yourself. You could also give an opinion in your conclusion as to how negative your own opinion of the Duke is.
Language and Structure	For a top grade essay, make sure that you analyse in detail the language and techniques used by the poet and remember to focus your answer on the question. Your writing must form a coherent argument, so your paragraphs must be linked by connectives and you must make your points confidently and authoritatively.

3)   "Simon Armitage's poem 'Those bastards in their mansions...' is a poem about the antagonism between the upper and lower classes." What evidence is there in the poem to support this statement, and to what extent do you agree with this suggestion?
     List of points for a good essay:

General	In order to write a strong answer, you will first have to find evidence to support the statement before you explain how far you agree with it. Don't try to do this the other way round because if you do, you may find that you are not actually answering the question.
Introduction	It would be a good idea to begin your answer by repeating the statement made in the question. You can then explain that there is a lot of evidence in the poem to support it, and then you can go on to find and analyse the evidence in the main body of the essay.
Main Body	In this essay you are being asked to find evidence, therefore you MUST quote from the text, but you must then analyse how these particular lines, words or images support the statement. Be careful that you do not just analyse language, but also the tone suggested by the poet, the different images used and, very importantly in this poem, the structure. You do not need to use comparative language within the main body of this essay, but you will need to make very clear when you are analysing the lower class attitudes and when you are analysing the upper class attitudes.
Conclusion	You should address the second half of the question in your conclusion. Here you get to give your personal opinion on how far you agree with the statement. Be very clear about this and state that you agree entirely, partially or not at all. However, you must remember that you have provided lots of evidence so if you say you don't agree at all you must give an alternative theme that is more obvious or important. It is usually best to agree with the question to avoid confusion.
Language and Structure	As always, for a top grade essay, analysis is the key word. It is not sufficient to just quote from the text; you MUST analyse the quotes and explain how they are relevant to the question.

4)   'Ozymandias' by Percy Bysshe Shelley is a poem with a very clear moral. What do you think this moral is, and how is it conveyed by the poet through language, imagery and tone?
     List of points for a good essay:

General	In order to write a strong answer to this question, you must decide what you think the moral is before you begin to write. If you do not decide this first, you will have difficulty structuring your answer and keeping it focused on the question.
Introduction	Use the language of the question and state immediately what you consider the moral of the poem to be. This then signals to the examiner the direction in which your answer should be going.
Main Body	The three aspects of the poem referred to in the question are a guide to how to structure your essay, so you should aim to write a paragraph on each of them. If you miss out one of these aspects you will not be fulfilling all the criteria for a top grade answer. You should also make sure that your answer is equally weighted between the three. Quotes are essential and should be analysed in detail in order to show how they are examples of particular language, tone or imagery and how they convey the moral. Remember that you decided the moral, so if you are struggling to find evidence, re-word your moral slightly to make it fit your answer.
Conclusion	Refer back to the question, re-state your moral and briefly summarise how language, imagery and tone all contribute to conveying this message.
Language and Structure	Make sure that you structure your answer so that one paragraph covers each aspect mentioned in the question. No comparative language is needed here, but make sure you are using the technical language relevant to poetry.

For a top grade essay, your answer should be clearly structured and your argument should be clear from the beginning and sign-posted using appropriate connectives. Your language should be varied and your analysis should be sensitive and critical. Remember that you must convince the examiner that your opinion is correct and that you know exactly what you are talking about.

Page 49 — Warm-up Questions

1) It shows the examiner that you know how the book fits in with what was going on at the time, e.g. whether it describes those times, or criticises them.

2) It means the writer can criticise events that are going on at the time, or make people think about them from a different perspective, without having to actually criticise them openly.

3) I can't help you with this one. It depends what books you're studying. If you get stuck, talk to your teacher or other people from your English class.

4) b) Stick it in the essay — the examiner will be pleased to see that you can think for yourself.

5) Quoting to <u>back up</u> your points is <u>vital</u> in any English Literature essay.

6) c) Write about how this extract fits in with the rest of the book, and why it's important.

7) b) "The writer heads the chapters with prime numbers instead of numbering them normally." This sentence mentions 'the writer' — it shows you realise the book is a result of conscious decisions by the author, not just a big accident.

8) a) no.
   b) no.
   In any fiction the narrator is made up by the author, just like all the other characters.

9) Any 5 from: Why are they important? Do they change? What have they learnt? How does the writer reveal their personality? How are they similar or different to others? Do you sympathise with them? What does the writer want us to think about them?

10) Any reasonable answer, e.g. There seems to be a difference between what her mum says and how she behaves. Her mum says Rhi's really excited, but all Rhi does is stare out of the window blankly. Her mum says she talks about it all the time, but here she says nothing. You could deduce that Rhi is perhaps not as excited as her mum says she is, and we have to wonder why there is this discrepancy between Rhi's behaviour and what her mother says about her.

Page 52 — Exam Questions

1) Compare and contrast the characters of Atticus Finch and Robert Ewell.
   List of points for a good essay:

General	A strong answer will show a close understanding of each character which explores the similarities and differences supported by close textual evidence.
Introduction	Refer briefly to the question: although they have many differences, they have some things in common.
Main Body	Explore their different attitudes to their families and children: both are widowers but Atticus is caring and responsible towards his family: quote from Chapter 1 where Scout says he '...treated us with courteous detachment'. He sets a good example whereas Robert is the total opposite; he allows his children to truant and neglects them physically and emotionally. Examine how both men are victims of prejudice: Atticus because he supports and legally represents Tom who is black and therefore an outcast in racist Maycombe, and Ewell because he represents the 'white trash' of the community. Contrast their attitude to the law: Atticus sends Scout to school and gets Jem to provide evidence in court after Ewell's death. Ewell allows his children to play truant, poaches on other people's land and is a bigoted liar. Discuss how when Atticus breaks the law at the end of the novel, he does so for a good reason.
Conclusion	Refer to the key words in the question: Atticus and Ewell 'differ' in many ways: what they have in 'common' is that they are both outsiders. Reinforce the point that they are total opposites.
Language and Structure	For a top grade essay you will need to show how these characters have been affected by the time and place in which the novel is set. You should also comment on the author's technique by stating that the language each character uses emphasises the difference between them: quote from the court-room episode in Chapter 17 to provide evidence.

2) Show how the sense of order on the island deteriorates over the course of the novel.
   List of points for a good essay:

General	A strong answer will explore why some characters feel the need for order on the island and discuss the reasons why others cause this to deteriorate.
Introduction	State the author's intention: to show how easily and quickly civilisation can deteriorate, particularly in the presence of a strong malevolant force. Golding uses the castaways to demonstrate this.
Main Body	Ralph = good: creates order, uses the conch as a symbol of order, gets the boys to build a fire for a signal. Ralph and Piggy make improvements — shelters are built. Order deteriorates: the fire gets out of control, the 'beast' is introduced providing fear by reminding the boys they're vulnerable. Jack = evil: encourages the others to hunt causing the fire to go out. Violence erupts: Ralph is angry about the neglect of the fire, Jack retaliates by breaking Piggy's glasses. The glasses are another symbol of order. Jack uses the 'threat' from the beast to undermine Ralph's leadership and organises a hunt. Order collapses: Jack challenges Ralph then sets up a rival camp with his 'tribe'. Most of the others join him. Jack's followers become savage and a symbol of chaos: they kill Simon who knows the truth about the beast. The violence escalates with the murder of Piggy. Finally: Ralph, isolated, is hunted like a pig. Ralph is saved from death by the arrival of 'civilisation' in the form of the naval officer.
Conclusion	Sum up your points to say that the author uses the boys to demonstrate how civilisation/order can easily be undermined by a strong malevolent force.
Language and Structure	A top grade essay will support the points made with evidence and comment on the author's technique of using symbols to represent order and chaos.

3) Consider the theme of loneliness in the novel 'Of Mice and Men.' How does it affect the friendships and relationships in the novel?
List of points for a good essay:

General	A strong answer will demonstrate a structured response to the question with an appreciation of the writer's ideas supported by close textual reference.
Introduction	Refer to the key words in the question: 'loneliness' and 'affect'. State that most of the characters are lonely because various things set them apart: age, race, sex.
Main Body	Discuss George and Lennie: their appearance, personalities, relationship: quote from Section 1. Comment on why they travel together. Introduce Candy: his age and disability make him lonely. Comment on the death of his dog in Section 3: why is he eager to join Lennie and George in their plans? Introduce Crooks: his colour excludes him: quote from Section 4 when he tells Lennie that without mixing with other people he feels 'he got nothing to measure by'. Introduce Curley's wife: being the only woman causes her loneliness. Comment on her behaviour, how she is treated, why she married Curley. Her true character is shown in Section 5 when she reveals her 'dream' to Lennie: her loneliness ultimately causes her death. Explore the incident in the barn in Section 5: explain what brings Lennie and Curley's wife together and what happens. Explain how the death of Curley's wife affects the relationships between George, Lennie and Candy.
Conclusion	Refer back to the key words in the question and sum up the points you have made, arguing that loneliness has a significant effect.
Language and Structure	For a top grade essay, explore how the author's technique creates an effect. For example, the difference between George and Lennie is immediately illustrated by the language he uses: words to describe George are 'quick' and 'restless', words to describe Lennie are 'slow' and 'bear-like'.

4) In Section 2 of the novel Billy tells his 'tall story': in what ways does this reinforce the themes of the novel and what does it reveal about Billy's life?
List of points for a good essay:

General	A strong answer will show insight into the themes of the novel and match this with an informed understanding of Billy's character.
Introduction	Stress the importance of the 'tall story': it illustrates the themes of the novel and reveals Billy's character.
Main Body	Explain that the story describes a day Billy dreams of having: for most boys this would be normal and not a dream. Note the poor technical skills reflect Billy's lack of education. Examine Billy's life in the 'tall story' and contrast this with reality. Billy dreams of living in 'Moor Edge', a wealthy area where he does his paper-round: the homes are extravagantly furnished, sharply contrasting with his council house. Billy's mother gives him breakfast in bed: in reality she neglects his meals. Jud has joined the army: in reality Billy hates Jud and wishes he would leave home. Billy's father returns: in reality he's left home permanently. Comment on how Billy is physically and emotionally neglected at home. Unlike the 'tall story', there are no treats. Show how he's also neglected in school: Mr Gryce canes him and Mr Sugden brutally humiliates him for not having his PE kit and making a fool of him. In the 'tall story', a teacher shows an interest in him: this doesn't happen in reality until Mr Farthing comes to see Billy training Kes.
Conclusion	Sum up your points to argue that there's a complete contrast between Billy's real life and the one described in the 'tall story': what is normal for others is an unattainable dream for him.
Language and Structure	For a top essay, focus on the key words in the question: 'reinforce' and 'reveal' and give close textual reference to support your points.

Page 62 — Warm-up Questions

1) yes
2) Any reasonable answer — e.g.: commonly held beliefs about things that are right and wrong. e.g. Violence is harmful.
3) e.g. a comparison to show a similarity. They help readers grasp the basic argument using simple ideas and they provide memorable images.
4) e.g. a rhetorical question is a question which is given which requires no answer. e.g. "Who knows?"
5) e.g. language which appeals to our emotions. e.g. If we do not act now, many more innocent, little children will die of hunger.
6) e.g. they are easy for the reader to understand.
7) e.g. they provide the argument with hard reality and are not based on groundless theory.
8) It makes it sound as if your readers agree with you already.
9) They give backing to your arguments.
10) e.g. by showing that you have thought about their concerns; by arguing against what might be a reader's counter-argument; by challenging biases and expectations.
11) It should be a) detached.
12) e.g. any two of the following — by writing simple and clear points; by using 'it' rather than 'I' or 'you'; by structuring the essay around the points that are in favour and those against; by not using emotive language or analogies.
13) 'It' makes your argument sound more detached, professional and authoritative than 'I', which sounds like only your personal, unimportant opinion.
14)a) There is obviously too much junk food being sold in cities.
   b) There is a ridiculous amount of paranoia concerning the diet of teenagers today.
   c) People get more and more bad-tempered the closer they live to heavily polluted areas — something needs to be done about it.
15) e.g. it makes the essay impartial, unbiased and authoritative.
16) The conclusion should sum up all the key points and, based on the whole report, it should say what should be done and why.

Page 65 — Exam Questions

1) Argue for or against the proposition that children are spending too much time at home using computers, instead of taking part in sporting and social activities.
List of points for a good essay:

General	A strong answer will consist of an argument which is easy to follow and persuasive. It will contain logical reasoning and points that are made will be supported with evidence. The question asks you to argue for or against the proposition, so you must be careful to convince the examiner of your point of view. Be confident and forceful. You need to persuade the examiner of the strength of your argument. For a top class essay you need to provide a rational, reasoned argument. Use a variety of vocabulary and a consistently formal tone. Your argument must be backed up with carefully chosen evidence and examples.
Introduction	Use the same language as the question — give one of the main benefits or disadvantages of computer use in the home.
Main Body	Develop your argument for or against the proposition with logical reasoning and definite language, in order to sound confident. Including analogies, emotive language and ethical beliefs will help to persuade your reader.
Conclusion	Summarise the main points in your argument with a vivid, punchy ending.
Language and Structure	You need to use formal language in order to sound authoritative. Your argument should be based on logic and emphasised with emotive language. Put forward your points with supporting evidence and challenge counter-arguments that the reader might think of.

2) Write a speech for your M.P. to use to persuade fellow M.P.s to vote for a ban on violence in children's television programmes.
List of points for a good essay:

General	A strong answer will be a very persuasive, formal speech. It will include a variety of tricks, such as rhetorical questions and lists of words to emphasise points. The question asks you to write a speech and it is important that you think about how it will sound to listeners. For a top class essay, your argument needs to be backed up with facts and real-life examples. You should use the persuasive tools of rhetorical questions, analogies and lists of three words, where appropriate, to emphasise your points.
Introduction	The introduction should be a strong appeal to the audience of the importance of your argument. It needs impact to capture their interest and for them to want to listen to the rest of what is being said.
Main Body	Extend your argument by providing examples of children's television programmes that have contained violence, and of the harmful effects this can have. Identify the M.P.'s concerns and address them.
Conclusion	Your conclusion should be a final, emotive appeal to your audience to support your point of view.
Language and Structure	You need to use a range of vocabulary and a variety of sentences. Rhetorical questions can be very effective. Your argument should be clearly and logically structured. Be assured and present your views persuasively and with authority.

3) Write an advice sheet for parents, about their children using computers at home.
List of points for a good essay:

General	A strong answer will be an advice sheet that uses vocabulary which is fitting for parents. The tone of the advice sheet should be quite formal but also understanding. It should inform in a clear and interesting way. Be clear and imaginative. You need to capture your reader's interest. Give an idea of the presentational features your advice sheet would include, such as bold print, highlighting, pictures and underlining, to make the information stand out and be memorable.
Introduction	The introduction should briefly make clear what the advice sheet is about. You should use language that grabs the attention of the reader.
Main Body	Provide information regarding the benefits of children using computers at home; address concerns parents might have. You should also make suggestions for other activities parents could encourage their children to take part in and why these would be helpful.
Conclusion	Your conclusion should give a brief summary of your advice. The sheet should end in a positive and reassuring way.
Language and Structure	It is important that your advice sheet is well organized and that your information is laid out in a clear way. Your language should be suitable for parents. For a top class essay, your language should be consistently varied and imaginative. You should show the examiner that you are aware of your readers' concerns and your information should be organized in a logical way.

4) Write an article for a tabloid newspaper where you aim to:
- Argue the case for less violence in children's television programmes.
- Persuade the reader that watching violence on television can make children more aggressive.

List of points for a good essay:

General	A strong answer will have an argument which is punchy and persuasive. It will be written in the style of a tabloid newspaper and will contain opinions, which should be supported with evidence.
Introduction	The opening should contain the main points of the article and should be written in a catchy and interesting way.
Main Body	Show an emotive view of the violence that is in some children's television programmes and persuade your reader of the harmful effects it can have. Give examples to illustrate your argument.
Conclusion	The final paragraph should be memorable and catchy. It should imaginatively summarise the most important point of your argument.
Language and Structure	You need to use emotive and persuasive language. The tone should be fairly informal and there should be a clear structure to your ideas, that readers will find easy to follow. Write forcefully and persuasively. You need to convince your reader that your viewpoint is right. For a top class essay, your grammar must be extremely accurate and the language you use should play effectively on the emotions of the reader. You should support your points with examples and, where appropriate, analogies and anecdotes. Using persuasive tools, such as rhetorical questions, will also make your argument more powerful.

Page 72 — Warm-up Questions

1) e.g. a) give a detailed discussion   b) give information   c) give in-depth, interesting descriptions
2) e.g. Language would be more formal for the parents.
3) e.g. Give a real example, state a fact, use a direct quotation, give an expert opinion.
4) If you are uncertain about their usage.
5) b) is less interesting, (e.g.) because there is no varied use of language or detail, and there is no attempt to build any suspense.
6) b) (e.g.) because it is more precise.
7) e.g. so you can anticipate their reactions and use that to make your writing more persuasive.
8) A balanced argument.
9) e.g. The most important points from your essay, as well as a final assertion of your own opinion.
10) i) is the intro clear? ii) are there interesting details? iii) have you thought about the reader? iv) have you explained all the technical terms? v) are spelling and punctuation okay?
11) Any reasonable answers accepted. This is an exercise in showing varied language and use of description. Answers should be imaginative. e.g.:

Picture A shows a desert. It is not an ordinary desert, with rolling sand dunes and soft pale sand — it is rocky, desolate and remote. Although the sky overhead is cloudy, the brightness of the blue sky peeks out from behind the clouds, and it must still be very warm there. In this place, one could walk for miles and miles, and never see another soul. The land is dry and arid, and who knows how many unfortunate creatures have died there in the heat.

Picture B also shows a desolate landscape, but where A is too hot, the temperatures in B must be below freezing. It, too, shows a rocky landscape, but one which is covered in deep, soft snow. Walking in this climate would only be possible with a multitude of layers of clothing, and a radio to call for help if it was required. In this place the snow looks peaceful, but it can hide many dangers, and lull climbers into thinking that they have nothing to fear.

Picture C contrasts both of the previous two photographs. It shows a field, possibly with some sheep grazing in the background. It is green, lush, and full of growing plants and tall grasses. A small hedge, fenced with posts, marks the boundary of the field, conjuring up images of the English countryside in springtime. You can almost hear the lazy flies buzzing around, and perhaps a friendly bee, scouring the land for flowers.

Picture D is the only one of these pictures to show any water. There is a dramatic coastline, the waves crashing on the shore before a blue sky. In the distance is the headland — a snake of rocks, dramatically eroded by countless years of being pounded by the ocean. At the end, the waters have worn a hole right through the stone, and it is no doubt a place which swimmers must avoid, so as not to be swept into the swirling depths and crushed against the walls of an ocean tomb.

All four pictures are very different, each showing a different area of the natural world — the dry and uninhabitable, the cold and imposing, the green and growing, and finally the coast at the mercy of the ocean's power. We are all at the mercy of the natural world, although we often try to persuade ourselves otherwise.

Page 75 — Exam Questions

1) Choose a place that has been significant in your life. Write about it in a way which will inform other people.

List of points for a good essay:

General	A strong answer will contain detailed information, which will allow the examiner to imagine the place clearly. It will also convey clearly why it is important to you.
Introduction	Use the same language as the question to answer it directly and extend it by pinpointing, and reflecting on, its imporance to you.
Main Body	Give the reader a detailed account of the place, so that they can understand what it is like much better. The tone you use, for example, humorous, affectionate, will be important in the impression you create for your reader.
Conclusion	End in an interesting way, stressing the main reason why the place is so significant for you.
Language and Structure	Your ideas need to be organized into well constructed paragraphs, with links between them. Your language should contain imagery to add interest and vitality; it will help in conveying your information to the examiner. Write in a lively way. Use details and examples so that your essay can be clearly understood. For a top class essay you need to use varied language, which fits the informative purpose. The essay must be well structured, with vivid images to add interest.

2)   Think about a time when you fulfilled an ambition. Explain what the ambition was and why it was so important to you to achieve it.
        List of points for a good essay:

General	The question asks you to explain what the ambition was and why it was important to you to achieve it. Therefore, a strong answer would contain clear, detailed reasons. Ideas would be organised in an effective order and the writing would be interesting.
Introduction	Briefly outline what the ambition was and explain in a lively way why it was so important to you.
Main Body	Give a detailed account of what achieving your ambition entailed, including when you first had the idea that you wanted to fulfil this goal, how you set about achieving it and what it felt like when you finally succeeded. Give examples of steps you took along the way.
Conclusion	Summarise, overall, why it was so important to you to fulfil this ambition and how it has affected you.
Language and Structure	Organise your ideas in a logical order. Your explanation will include factual details, but these need to be expressed using lively and interesting vocabulary. Be clear and confident. Convey your enthusiasm for what you achieved to the examiner. For a top class essay include details which engage the reader's interest. You must write logically and with consistent clarity. You need to use a variety of sentence types and vocabulary for effect.

3)   Choose one of the following places:
            a café
            a market place
            a fairground
            a seaside resort
        Describe it during the day and at night.
        List of points for a good essay:

General	To gain a high number of marks for this essay, you need to create contrasting moods and atmospheres for the place, by night and by day. You are asked to write a description — a picture of the place for your reader — so it is important that you do not end up telling a story instead.
Introduction	Begin by gaining your reader's interest, by using unusual words and images to create the atmosphere of the place by day.
Main Body	Extend your essay by describing in detail the sensations that are experienced in the place you are trying to give your reader a picture of. Use a point of focus to link ideas together. In describing the place at night, contrast the sensations, such as what is heard and smelt, with those during the day. Give a sense of the feelings the place evokes.
Conclusion	End your description in an imaginative way, so that the examiner has a clear impression of the atmosphere you are trying to convey.
Language and Structure	Make sure that you include lots of interesting detail, to paint pictures of the place at different times. Use different kinds of sentences for effect. Clearly get across to your reader how different the place is by night and by day. Use descriptive phrases that are imaginative and original. For a top class essay, you must create a convincing image of the place. Interesting language will subtley give a sense of the atmosphere and mood. Grammar and punctuation must be very accurate.

4)   What job would you most like to do one day? Describe what it would involve and explain why you would most like to do it.
        List of points for a good essay:

General	The question asks you to describe and explain, so it is important that, as well as giving a detailed account of the job, you also give fully developed reasons for your choice. You need to be able to reflect on what it is about the job that would excite and challenge you.
Introduction	Use the same language as the question to answer it, outlining the job you would undertake and your main reason for choosing this.
Main Body	Extend your essay by describing what the job entails. Include the most interesting details. Go on to give your reasons for choosing this job and what you would gain by doing it.
Conclusion	Provide a clear summary of the main points of your essay.
Language and Structure	Interesting phrases and images should be used. Your ideas need to be structured in a logical and coherent way. Be enthusiastic and lively in your writing, so that the examiner gains a clear impression of the choice you wish to make and your reasons why. For a top class essay, you need to explain your reasons in a logical way and they need to be supported with evidence. Ideas need to be well organised and good links need to be made between paragraphs. Your writing must be engaging and interesting.

Page 83 — Warm-up Questions

1)   Appropriate: (c), (d)
2)   These answers will be subjective. e.g. (a) and (c) are more boring because they just make bland statements, while (b) and (d) arouse curiosity by hinting at mysterious things and leaving them unsaid. They make the reader want to read on and find out.
3)   These answers will be subjective, as they involve creative writing. e.g.
   a) Rachel burst into tears at least five times during the school day – everyday. She wasn't sure she could face Sharon's harsh words any longer. If the teasing didn't stop soon, she might have to do something stupid.

b) Dominic hated children. He was always chasing them away from his large garden, or raising his walking stick menacingly in their direction as he walked along the road. People thought he was mean, but deep down he'd just never recovered from the death of his baby son, Simon.

c) Paul was a bundle of energy; he never walked when he could run; and he spoke so fast that he made you gasp for breath. Of course, some people suspected this was because he was embarrassed by his awful body odour, which didn't seem to go away no matter what he did.

d) Charley turned out to be the best cat that we had ever had, in spite of everything. Katherine refused to get rid of him even after the incident where he chased the next door neighbour's ferrets into our downstairs toilet. The ferrets wouldn't come out of the bowl for days — we ended up having to coax them out with bits of cheese tied to Auntie Julie's shoelaces. Mum never forgave him, but the rest of us still love Charley.

4)   Sight, sound, smell, taste, touch. Any reasonable examples are acceptable — answers will vary as it involves creative writing. e.g.:
Sight: The sky was ablaze with streaks of gold and pink, and we watched the sun set for a long time, grateful to be able to see it one last time.
Sound: The shade given by the forest's trees was cool, and we could hear a thousand tiny insects chirping in the scrub in a friendly hum.
Taste: As soon as I swallowed, I knew I'd made the worst mistake of my life. My throat was on fire, and all I could taste was the smouldering of my tonsils.
Touch: At first Jack was afraid, but once he put his hand onto the snake he realised that it wasn't cold and slimy at all. It was warm and soft, like a leather jacket on a radiator.

5) a) Any reasonable answer e.g. Peering through a thin slit between the window and the curtain, he glimpsed a ragged silhouette. He yanked the curtain open. Tom screamed. He staggered backwards, shielding his eyes with his hands.

    b) Any reasonable answer e.g. The bell went. It all kicked off. Guns were pulled out. Bystanders were pushed to the floor. The masks went on, and the robbery had begun.

6)   Any reasonable answers e.g.

    a) Claire was superb dancer. Her graceful swirls always mesmerised the crowds. Her arms arched above her head made her look like a flower waiting to bloom.

    b) The black stallion reared up, his muscles rippling under his sleek coat. Suddenly he was a giant — standing in front of me like a huge black tower of horse.

    c) Alice played basketball well. When she bounced that ball it was as though she was pounding out a jungle rhythm, keeping time to an unseen drummer.

7)   Some sort of conclusion.

8)   The last line rounds off the plot and ties the whole piece of writing together. It's the last thing that the reader will read, so it needs to have a strong impact.

Page 86 — Exam Questions

1)   Describe two or three significant events in your life, and say what effects the incidents had on you.
List of points for a good essay:

General	A good essay will be written in detail, and express your thoughts and feelings realistically. Planning is very important. Ensure there are enough details for a full-length essay. You need to grab the reader's attention immediately and introduce the two or three events. They need to be carefully linked to keep the essay flowing at both sentence and paragraph level.
Introduction	Grab the reader's attention immediately with a statement or an anecdote.
Main Body	Decide on the order of events - most recent or earliest? Give at least one paragraph to each event, and be sure to tell the reader its significance. Each event should have a clear beginning, climax and end. Avoid the temptation to repeat the same opening for each paragraph. Work on paragraphs individually then try to link them logically. Your writing should be logical, detailed, yet interesting.
Conclusion	Link the two or three events by making a point — restate the significance that each event has had on your life. Look for the opportunity to change tenses from past to present.
Language and Structure	Unusual vocabulary in interesting descriptions will maintain the reader's interest. Links between paragraphs are essential. Events must flow, and have a logical development.

For a top class essay, your writing will need to be well planned and well ordered at both sentence and paragraph level.
Your aim is to interest the reader with descriptions, thoughts and feelings at particular times. Tense changes in the final paragraph should be exploited.

2)   Write about your first day at your present school. What were your feelings at various times during the day?
List of points for a good essay:

General	A good essay will be written in detail, and express your feelings realistically. Planning is very important. Ensure there are enough details for a full-length essay. You need to grab the reader's attention immediately with an event that happened early in the day, followed by the other events you intend to describe. They need to be carefully linked to keep the essay flowing at both sentence and paragraph level. "At different times during the day" is a key phrase, so a variety of incidents is important.
Introduction	Write in the first person and in the past tense. Make it clear when your first day was, and if possible introduce the school.
Main Body	Be selective. Choose three or four events at different times during the day. Aim to cover a variety of feelings and situations to maintain interest. Include descriptions of people, places, sounds and activities as appropriate. Avoid listing everything that happened. Work on paragraphs individually then try to link them logically. Your writing should be logical and detailed, yet interesting.
Conclusion	Link the three or four events by making a point — restate what your feelings were. Look for the opportunity to change tenses from past to present or future, possibly in the final line.
Language and Structure	Unusual vocabulary in interesting descriptions will maintain the reader's interest. Links between paragraphs are essential. Events must flow and have a logical development. Stick to past tense for main body of essay.

For a top class essay, your writing will need to be well planned and well ordered at both sentence and paragraph level.
Your aim is to interest the reader with descriptions, thoughts and feelings at particular times.

3)   'Do you remember the time when…?" Complete this question to make the title of a story. Then write the story that will fit the title.
       List of points for a good essay:

General	A strong answer will be a well-structured story with clear plot, characterisation and atmosphere. Correct punctuation in dialogue is essential. You need a good title to grab the reader's attention. A top class essay will display imagination and flair, as well as excellent organisation and control of the plot.
Introduction	The first line and first paragraph need to be interesting and make the reader want to read on. You need to construct something that will draw the reader into the rest of the story.
Main Body	Decide on the order of events — this question could easily lend itself to using flashback sequences, so think about tense. If you successfully manage to vary the tenses and keep the story interesting, then you'll be able to pick up more marks.
Conclusion	Ideally, a good conclusion will give the reader a sense of satisfaction — i.e. that links back to the title and the opening in some way, and that possibly involves a twist or a dramatic ending, but at the very least it should try to tie up any loose ends. It should be inventive, instead of just tailing off.
Language and Structure	Structure is vital for creative essays. The flow must make sense to the reader. Images should be clear. Dialogue should be punctuated correctly. The story must flow.

4)   Describe a time when you were very frightened. You may write about this in any way you like — a real or an imaginary situation.
       List of points for a good essay:

General	A strong answer will be a well-structured story with clear plot, characterisation and atmosphere. The descriptions will be vivid and imaginative. The vocabulary should be carefully chosen to achieve the desired effect in describing fear. A top class essay will display imagination and flair, as well as excellent organisation and control of the plot, whether this account is factual or fictional.
Introduction	The question dictates the use of the past tense. Establish the narrator, create atmosphere and engage the reader.
Main Body	The writing should be clear, maintaining sense of atmosphere and successfully engaging the reader. Vary vocabulary and use clear paragraphs to keep the story flowing and interesting.
Conclusion	Ideally a good conclusion will give the reader a sense of satisfaction — it may involve a humorous twist, or else an appeal for empathy from the reader regarding the frightening event. In any case, it should be a strong ending, not a weak, indistinct one.
Language and Structure	Structure is vital for creative essays. The flow must make sense to the reader. Images should be clear. Dialogue should be punctuated correctly. The story must flow.

       A top class essay will aim for realism, and successfully evoke the frightening experience with carefully chosen vocabulary and story structure.

Page 93 — Warm-up Questions

1)   False.
2)   It's best to read the question before you read the text, so you know exactly what information you are looking for.
3)   It helps you concentrate on what the question's asking, so you can be sure your answer will stick to the point.
4)   It makes it sound like you're calmly explaining the facts, not just writing about your personal opinions.
5)   Rephrase the words of the question in your first sentence.
6) b) What's the point being made?   e) Does the idea make sense?   f) Is there any evidence in the piece backing up the ideas?
7)   Layout, graphics, structure, and the medium being used (e.g. if it's a wordy article about brushing your teeth for six-year-olds, maybe a comic strip would be more suitable).
8) a) Big text at the top of a page to tell you what an article's about.
   b) Short text explaining a picture.
   c) The main story on the front page.
   d) Longish story with more detail.
   e) Opinion column stating the newspaper's opinion.
   f) A personal story – often sentimental.
9)   Older audience, because (e.g.) there's no bright colours, the layout is very formal, the picture is black and white, there are lots of columns, the text is small, there are no flashy captions etc...

Page 96 — Exam Questions

1) a) Any two of the following: ski holidays; safari holidays; self-catering villa holidays; holidays in Italy; holidays in Australia; holidays in Canada.
   b) You could mention any two of the following: teenagers prefer not to go on holiday with their parents; parents prefer not to holiday with teenage children; the concept of the happy family holiday appears to go awry when the child hits puberty; the popularity of countries (like Italy, Australia and Canada) appears to be as much to do with the culture of the people as the location and facilities on site; if teenagers aren't the appreciative type, the best opinion is to choose a holiday which will suit their specific needs and energies.
   c) You could mention any two of the following: Harry Enfield's Kevin is spot on; teenagers need to assert their independence at this age; they may begin to resent help from their parents, perceiving it as interference; they like to be among their peers; there are additional tensions on holiday (all Desmond Morris); people in Italy are lively and funky and laid back (teenager).

2)   List of points for a good essay:

General	There are five marks on offer so it makes sense to go for one mark at the beginning by explaining what you think the aim of the article is, then to make a couple of points each on the content and language for the remaining four marks. Decide what all your points are before you start writing. Stick to one paragraph for each point. Keep the language impersonal so you sound objective.
Introduction	Start by clearly saying what you think the writer is trying to achieve with her article and why you think that. Mention briefly whether you think the writer succeeded, e.g. The article is called "How to avoid teen tantrums" and in the first paragraph the writer says that though neither teenagers or parents especially want to go on holiday together, they often do. This suggests that her aim is to help parents of teenagers make sure that the whole family enjoys their holiday. Although the article offers a few ideas about making holidays with teenagers work, these tend to be quite obvious or vague.
Main Body	Make a couple of points about the content, backing them up with plenty of references to the article, e.g. The article takes a long time to start supplying the information it promises at the beginning. The writer illustrates the difficulties of holidays with teenagers with quotes from the writer Desmond Morris. These quotes are interesting but lengthy and it takes readers some time to reach the information about what kind of holiday teenagers would enjoy. In the middle section the writer briefly mentions some holidays that are successful with teenagers, for example, ski and safari holidays, but does not go into detail. She does point out that it's not only the type of holiday that makes it a success. The country and the people make a big difference too. This is useful information, but could have been backed up with more examples. You also need to write about the language — you definitely need plenty of quotes here, e.g. the negative side of holidays with teenagers is described especially in the quote from Desmond Morris with words like 'resent', 'interference' and 'manipulative'. This makes the article more readable, and makes the reader eager to find out how to solve the problems of teenagers on holiday. The rhetorical question "So what does work with teenagers on holiday?" introduces the section outlining successful holiday options. The happier and more reassuring tone comes through in words and phrases such as 'popular', 'parents knew where we were' and 'a bonding experience'. The language used shifts the article from feeling quite negative at the beginning to feeling much more positive at the end. This makes it feel as though the article has been more helpful than it really is. The language is quite informal and conversational with phrases like 'given the choice' and the rhetorical question "So what does work with teenagers on holiday?". Short paragraphs add to the relaxed feel. This makes the writer sound friendly and sympathetic. This should help make the article appealing to parents.
Conclusion	You don't need a fancy conclusion. Just sum up what you've said above, e.g. At the beginning of the article the writer seems to be aiming to explain to parents how to organise a successful holiday. However, almost as much space is given to explaining what the problems are as to how to avoid them and there is little concrete advice. Although the language supports the writer's aims, the fact that the content is thin means the article does not fully achieve its aims.
Language and Structure	For a top essay you could mention alternative interpretations of the article e.g. the writer mentions her own book in the second paragraph, so maybe she deliberately held more practical information back hoping that readers would be more tempted to buy the book.

Page 104 — Warm-up Questions

1) a) correct punctuation.
   c) paragraphs properly divided up.
   e) spelling all right.
   f) each sentence grammatical.
2) Formal English.
3) You definitely need to use standard English in your GCSE.
4) If you were writing a story with direct speech it would be OK to put the speech in non-standard English — so long as that suited the character speaking.
5) Possible answers:
   a) Juliet should have realised that life does not run smoothly all the time.
   b) I find Sophocles' plays incredibly difficult to understand.
   c) I am writing to inform you that I am leaving.
   d) "Come on, comrade. It's eight o'clock. Let's go out and indulge ourselves in decadent pleasures and entertainments."
6) a) Give me those pens.
   b) Macbeth is a general who kills a king.
   c) The boy did as the teacher said.
7) Start with a capital letter and end with a question mark, exclamation mark or full stop.
8) Any three of these places: separating the parts of a list; after a phrase about time; around a phrase starting 'which' or 'who'; anywhere where the sentence wouldn't make sense without the comma.
9) a colon (:)
10) dash
11) a) The man, who still hadn't recovered from his cold, was writing his shopping list: bananas, milk, tea and bread.
    b) Why won't Robert's dog, the children's dog and the ladies' dog play with cats?
    c) Sarah asked, "Has anyone seen Liz today?"
    d) "Does anyone want another cup of tea?" Andy asked, "because I'm having one."
12) I want to do an English exam.

Page 111 — Warm-up Questions

1) a) affect.   b) effects.   c) effected.
2)   e.g. You'll never make it to Wimbledon, if you don't practise every day.
3)   e.g. My mother's a vet; her practice specialises in farm animals.
4) a) I don't know <u>where</u> I'm going; don't know <u>where</u> I've been.
   b) If I <u>were</u> the only boy in the world and you <u>were</u> the only girl.
   c) This <u>werewolf</u> is <u>wearing</u> me out.
5) a) I left my bicycle over there.
   b) The twins invited their friends to tea.
   c) They're the wrong chickens!
6)   Any three words will do. If they're not listed here, check the spelling in a dictionary. e.g. chemistry, orchestra, chorus.
7)   Any three words will do. If they're not listed here, check the spelling in a dictionary. e.g. geography, philosophy, physics.
8) a) When I got home, I <u>turned</u> the television on.
   b) Sit down, turn over the question paper and <u>write</u> your name at the top.
9) a) When I <u>get</u> home, I <u>will turn</u> the television on.
   b) <u>You will sit down, you will turn over</u> the question paper and <u>you will write</u> your name at the top.
10)   We began with a terrine of lobster and crayfish which played against the flavours of the champagne like a kitten patting at a butterfly. The beef was perfectly roasted and so tender that one hardly needed to chew.   The crème brulée was an exquisite end to an exquisite meal, with a silky texture and a diamond-hard crust. I left reeling with satisfaction.
11) a) I go rollerblading occasionally.
    b) Evacuate the building immediately!
    c) Fruit and vegetables are extremely nutritious.
12) a) Katy's essay is much better than Clare's.
    b) Today was the hottest day of the year.
    c) Murgatroyd is the taller twin.
13)   A simile says something is <u>like</u> something else. A metaphor says something <u>is</u> something else.
        Simile: e.g. Revising for GCSEs is like walking down an endless gravel road, barefoot, under a blazing sun.
        Metaphor: e.g. When you walk out of your last GCSE exam, you'll be in paradise.
14) a) noun   =   horses; carriages
       verb   =   pulled
       adjective   =   enormous; heavy
       adverb   =   easily
    b) noun   =   Sonia; truth
       verb   =   wanted; know
       adjective   =   whole
       adverb   =   desperately
    c) noun   =   boys; headteacher; office
       verb   =   waited
       adjective   =   naughty; little
       adverb   =   nervously

Page 117 — Warm-up Questions

1)   Explain — Describe — Narrate, Explore — Analyse — Imagine, Discuss — Argue — Persuade
2)   Any reasonable answer — for example: Use standard English vocabulary and grammar. / Listen carefully to other people who are talking. / Express tricky ideas clearly. / Adapt your talk to the task and audience. / Make your talk original and interesting.
3)   Courtesy — Audience — Purpose
4)   Tell a joke or use a visual aid.
5)   Standard English.
6)   Slang.
7)   Any reasonable answer - for example: Speak up. / Give your talk a clear structure. / Don't repeat yourself. / Talk clearly and plainly. / Draw attention to the most important facts.
8) a) Wrong.   b) Right.   c) Right.   d) Wrong.   e) Right.   f) Right.
9)   The motion.
10)   The Chairperson.
11)   The 'Proposer' gives a speech in favour of the motion.
        The 'Opposer' argues against the motion.
12)   The Proposition Seconder.
13)   The Opposition Seconder.
14)   b)
15)   a)
16)   Because then you'll know the facts inside out.
17)   Two or three strong arguments with your best point.
18)   Facts.

Please note: The answers to the past exam questions have not been provided by or approved by the examining bodies (AQA, OCR and London Qualifications Ltd - Edexcel). As such, AQA, OCR and London Qualifications Ltd do not accept any responsibility for the accuracy or method of the working in the answers given.
CGP has provided suggested solutions — other possible solutions may be equally correct.

Paper 1 — Section A
Question 1

BAND	DESCRIPTOR
A	An excellent range of points is chosen, very well organised with good synthesis. There is a complete grasp of all three elements of the question. A concise response uses excellent own words.
C	A good range of appropriate material has been covered in an organised fashion, although there is less evidence of synthesis. Consistent own words reveal good understanding. There is usually an attempt to be concise.
E	The treatment of general characteristics and effects is likely to be more successful than that of formation. There is likely to be some inefficient selection and also some lifting which may imply that points have not been clearly understood.

Question 2

BAND	DESCRIPTOR
A	This is a consistently analytical response, covering a excellent selection of critical points. Both passages elicit mature comments, which may contain original and impressive insights.
C	The candidate has a grasp of both writers' methods, and includes a range of points covering both passages in a balanced way. There will be some sound language judgements, well supported from the text.
E	The response is likely to concentrate on the content. Language points will be limited and obvious. There is likely to be some mention of the writers' choice of words, but any attempt to deal with language may well be descriptive rather than analytical. Points may have some limited textual support.

Paper 1 — Section B

<u>Question 1</u>

BAND	DESCRIPTOR
A	• persuades successfully and convincingly; well-informed, drawing on a range of sources • growing subtlety of purpose and ability to adapt tone to manipulate reader • controls a range of means to gain emphasis (e.g. one sentence paragraph) and demonstrates variety of possible consequences • fluent control of range of devices and discursive markers with an extensive vocabulary range • uses full range of appropriate sentence structures • achieves a high level of technical accuracy in spelling • achieves a high level of technical accuracy in punctuation
C	• persuasion is starting to become more detailed with a clear awareness of the alternative standpoint/interests of Governors. • some sense of varying emphasis for effect with conscious use of a chosen tone • paragraphs are competently linked by content and language • confident use of devices such as anecdote in context and rhetorical questions • discursive markers are becoming more integrated and are used to persuade • uses sentence forms for effect • generally secure in spelling • generally secure in punctuation which clarifies meaning and purpose
E	• linked material which may be developed in a generalised way. • addresses Governor audience directly and/or starts consciously to use a more formal register, though still evidence of colloquial language • begins to use rhetorical devices, for example, rhetorical questions with occasional evidence of language being used emotively • discursive markers e.g. the first point..., where used, are mechanical and obvious • more frequent use of linguistic/presentational devices e.g. repetition for effect • uses a range of securely demarcated sentence structures • some accurate spelling of more complex words • starts to use a range of punctuation

<u>Question 2</u>

BAND	DESCRIPTOR
A	• advises successfully and convincingly; well-informed, drawing on a range of sources • growing subtlety of purpose and ability to adapt tone to manipulate reader • controls a range of means to gain emphasis (e.g. one sentence paragraph) and demonstrate variety of possible consequences • fluent control of range of devices and discursive markers with an extensive vocabulary range • uses full range of appropriate sentence structures • achieves a high level of technical accuracy in spelling • achieves a high level of technical accuracy in punctuation
C	• advice is starting to become more detailed with a clear awareness of position, job, needs of teachers • some sense of varying emphasis for effect with conscious use of a chosen tone • paragraphs are competently linked by content and language • confident use of devices such as anecdote in context and rhetorical questions • discursive markers are becoming more integrated and are used to enhance the advice; may mark both cause and effect e.g. as a result of this... consequently ... • uses sentence forms for effect • generally secure in spelling • generally secure in punctuation which clarifies meaning and purpose
E	• linked arguments put forward which may be developed in a generalised way. • addresses teacher audience directly and/or starts consciously to use a more formal register, though still evidence of colloquial language • begins to use rhetorical devices, for example, rhetorical questions with occasional evidence of language being used emotively • discursive markers e.g. the first point..., where used, are mechanical and obvious • more frequent use of linguistic/presentational devices e.g. repetition for effect • uses a range of securely demarcated sentence structures • some accurate spelling of more complex words • starts to use a range of punctuation

Question 3

BAND	DESCRIPTOR
A	There is a consistent engagement with the task and a clearly structured argument. A good sense that the writer is in control of the material and opinions are supported by evidence and anecdote. Content is relevant and controlled. The essay develops towards a focused conclusion. *A fully rounded and incisive argument, clarifying and persuading to a point of view.* The candidate's writing is controlled and precise, in an appropriate register, showing a keen awareness of the purpose and audience. A wide and rich vocabulary is used and a precise, fluent style in which syntax, spelling and punctuation are almost faultless. Structures are varied skilfully to enhance meaning and arouse/sustain interest. Paragraphs have unity and are effectively linked with preceding and following paragraphs. *Writing is striking in its originality and complexity. It has flair.*
C	Some engagement with the task and a sense of structure are apparent. Some opinions are supported. Content may be underdeveloped or superficial. Ideas will be mainly relevant. Some evidence that the candidate is working towards an intended conclusion. *Clear sense of organising / presenting a case, or both sides, as appropriate; a grasp of persuasion.* The candidate's writing is controlled, coherent and in a suitable style. Purpose is clearly understood and the audience is addressed. There is a suitable vocabulary. Syntactical conventions are followed; most complex words are spelt correctly; punctuation is used effectively. Structures show appropriate variety of length and shape, although there may be a tendency to repeat types. The interest of the reader is maintained. Paragraphing is used to aid meaning. The writing is well presented. *Writing shows individuality and engages the reader's attention.*
E	Very little engagement with the task. Writing is poorly structured containing unsubstantiated assertions or opinions. Essays may be long, rambling and irrelevant or very short. There is little or no evidence of a planned conclusion. *Some argument with some sense of persuasion; not always controlled.* The candidate shows a measure of control and the use of form and style is generally appropriate to purpose. There is an awareness of audience being addressed. There is some range of vocabulary and grammar which is generally accurate, although there may be errors in more complex structures. The spelling of irregular words is generally accurate and punctuation helps to clarify meaning. Full stops are used to separate sentences, but their use is not secure. There is some range of sentence structure. Reader's interest is generally maintained. Paragraphing is fair. Quality of presentation will not impede communication. *Writing may be virtuously simple and correct, or over-reaching, making errors in attempting vivid writing.*

Question 4

BAND	DESCRIPTOR
A	There is a consistent engagement with the task and a clearly structured argument. A good sense that the writer is in control of the material and opinions are supported by evidence and anecdote. Content is relevant and controlled. The essay develops towards a focused conclusion. *A fully rounded and incisive argument, clarifying and persuading to a point of view.* The candidate's writing is controlled and precise, in an appropriate register, showing a keen awareness of the purpose and audience. A wide and rich vocabulary is used and a precise, fluent style in which syntax, spelling and punctuation are almost faultless. Structures are varied skilfully to enhance meaning and arouse/sustain interest. Paragraphs have unity and are effectively linked with preceding and following paragraphs. *Writing is striking in its originality and complexity. It has flair.*
C	Some engagement with the task and a sense of structure are apparent. Some opinions are supported. Content may be underdeveloped or superficial. Ideas will be mainly relevant. Some evidence that the candidate is working towards an intended conclusion. *Clear sense of organising / presenting a case, or both sides, as appropriate; a grasp of persuasion.* The candidate's writing is controlled, coherent and in a suitable style. Purpose is clearly understood and the audience is addressed. There is a suitable vocabulary. Syntactical conventions are followed; most complex words are spelt correctly; punctuation is used effectively. Structures show appropriate variety of length and shape, although there may be a tendency to repeat types. The interest of the reader is maintained. Paragraphing is used to aid meaning. The writing is well presented. *Writing shows individuality and engages the reader's attention.*
E	Very little engagement with the task. Writing is poorly structured containing unsubstantiated assertions or opinions. Essays may be long, rambling and irrelevant or very short. There is little or no evidence of a planned conclusion. *Some argument with some sense of persuasion; not always controlled.* The candidate shows a measure of control and the use of form and style is generally appropriate to purpose. There is an awareness of audience being addressed. There is some range of vocabulary and grammar which is generally accurate, although there may be errors in more complex structures. The spelling of irregular words is generally accurate and punctuation helps to clarify meaning. Full stops are used to separate sentences, but their use is not secure. There is some range of sentence structure. Reader's interest is generally maintained. Paragraphing is fair. Quality of presentation will not impede communication. *Writing may be virtuously simple and correct, or over-reaching, making errors in attempting vivid writing.*

Paper 2 — Section A

Question 1

BAND	DESCRIPTOR
A	•exploration of and empathy with writer's ideas and attitudes •references integrated with argument •analysis of variety of writer's techniques •concise, appropriate explanation of content of two poems •analysis of what is important about culture(s) •examination of specific examples of features of presentation demonstrating their effectiveness in revealing something important •integrated approach analysing and developing own response
C	•understanding of feeling(s), attitude(s) and idea(s) •effective use of textual detail and/or some cross reference •awareness of authorial techniques and purpose •some focus on culture in two poems and on presentation of them •extended comment on what poems are about •comment on how something important is shown by means of detail from the poems
E	•extended unsupported comment and generalisation on the text as a whole •appropriate reference and some use of quotation •simple comment on some aspects of presentation •some awareness of a writer at work •accurate description of content of one or more poems •identification of what is described •simple comment on how it is described •generalisation about effect(s)

Question 2

BAND	DESCRIPTOR
A	•exploration of and empathy with writer's ideas and attitudes •references integrated with argument •analysis of variety of writer's techniques •concise, appropriate explanation of content of two poems •analysis of what is described •examination of specific examples of use and effects of description •integrated approach analysing and developing own response
C	•understanding of feeling(s), attitude(s) and idea(s) •effective use of textual detail and/or some cross reference •awareness of authorial techniques and purpose •some focus on description in two poems and on presentation of them •extended comment on what poems are about •comment on how description is used •some explanation of effects
E	•extended unsupported comment and generalisation on the text as a whole •appropriate reference and some use of quotation •simple comment on some aspects of presentation •some awareness of a writer at work •accurate description of content of one or more poems •identification of what is described •simple comment on how it is described •generalisation about effect(s)

Paper 2 — Section B

Question 1

BAND	DESCRIPTOR
A	•cogent focus on subject with wide range of interesting information •growing subtlety of purpose and ability to manipulate reader's response •structured and developed using a range of means to effectively demonstrate points about chosen subject •fluent control of range of devices and discursive markers •extensive vocabulary range •uses full range of appropriate sentence structures •achieves a high level of technical accuracy in spelling •achieves a high level of technical accuracy in punctuation
C	•more evidence of selection of information for interest •information likely to cover a range of aspects e.g. personal/technical, and be drawn from different sources •may address reader directly, offering reasons why s/he would enjoy hobby •paragraphs are competently linked by content and language •control of question / answer approach, anecdote in context, emphasis etc. will be competent where used •discursive markers are becoming more integrated and are used to enhance the organisation of the information e.g. finally •uses sentence forms for effect •generally secure in spelling •generally secure in punctuation which clarifies meaning and purpose
F	•some focus on chosen subject with developed points •may be mainly anecdotal and/or narrative in approach though clearly intended to inform •may use simple rhetorical devices to interest reader e.g. have you ever...? •paragraphing may be tabloid and/or, at times, correctly placed •beginnings of variety in vocabulary •uses a range of securely demarcated sentence structures •some accurate spelling of more complex words •starts to use a range of punctuation

Question 2

BAND	DESCRIPTOR
A	•cogent focus on decision with wide range of interesting explanations •growing subtlety of purpose and ability to manipulate reader's response •structured and developed using a range of means to explain decision effectively •fluent control of range of devices and discursive markers •extensive vocabulary range •uses full range of appropriate sentence structures •achieves a high level of technical accuracy in spelling •achieves a high level of technical accuracy in punctuation
C	•more evidence of selection of material for explanation •explanations likely to cover a range of aspects •may write in first person consistently •paragraphs are competently linked by content and language •control of anecdote in context, emphasis etc. will be competent where used •discursive markers are becoming more integrated and are used to enhance the organisation •uses sentence forms for effect •generally secure in spelling •generally secure in punctuation which clarifies meaning and purpose
E	•some focus on chosen subject with developed points •may be mainly anecdotal and/or narrative in approach though clearly intended to inform •may use simple rhetorical devices to interest reader e.g. have you ever...? •paragraphing may be tabloid and/or, at times, correctly placed •beginnings of variety in vocabulary •uses a range of securely demarcated sentence structures •some accurate spelling of more complex words •starts to use a range of punctuation

166

Question 3

BAND	DESCRIPTOR
A	*Difficult tasks completed with absolute clarity and no ambiguity.* Candidate's writing is controlled and concise, in an appropriate style showing a keen awareness of purpose and audience. A wide and rich vocabulary is used and precise, fluent style in which syntax, spelling and punctuation are almost faultless. Structures are varied skilfully to enhance meaning and arouse/sustain interest. Paragraphs have unity and are effectively linked with preceding and following paragraphs. *Writing is striking in its originality and complexity. It has flair.*
C	*Secure response to challenging tasks; expression clear and sound.* Candidate's writing is controlled, coherent and in a suitable style. Purpose is clearly understood and the audience is addressed. There is a suitable vocabulary. Syntactical conventions are followed; most complex words are spelt correctly; punctuation is used effectively. Structures show appropriate variety of length and shape, although there may be a tendency to repeat sentence types. The interest of the reader is maintained. Paragraphing is used to aid meaning. The writing is well presented. *Writing shows individuality and engages the reader's attention.*
E	*Can sequence facts in appropriate language; secure language.* Candidate shows a reasonable control and the use of form and style are generally appropriate to purpose. There is an awareness of audience being addressed. There is some range of vocabulary and grammar which is generally accurate, although there may be errors in more complex structures. The spelling of irregular words is generally accurate and punctuation helps to clarify meaning. Full stops are used to separate sentences, but their use is not secure. There is some range of sentence structure. Reader's interest is generally maintained. Paragraphing is fair. Quality of presentation will not impede communication. *Writing may be virtuously simple and correct, or over-reaching, making errors in attempting vivid writing.*

Question 4

BAND	DESCRIPTOR
A	*Complete control of an imaginative idea; personal style.* Candidate's writing is controlled and concise, in an appropriate style showing a keen awareness of purpose and audience. A wide and rich vocabulary is used and precise, fluent style in which syntax, spelling and punctuation are almost faultless. Structures are varied skilfully to enhance meaning and arouse/sustain interest. Paragraphs have unity and are effectively linked with preceding and following paragraphs. *Writing is striking in its originality and complexity. It has flair.*
C	*Imaginative and personal; may use features such as an unexpected ending.* Candidate's writing is controlled, coherent and in a suitable style. Purpose is clearly understood and the audience is addressed. There is a suitable vocabulary. Syntactical conventions are followed; most complex words are spelt correctly; punctuation is used effectively. Structures show appropriate variety of length and shape, although there may be a tendency to repeat sentence types. The interest of the reader is maintained. Paragraphing is used to aid meaning. The writing is well presented. *Writing shows individuality and engages the reader's attention.*
E	*Interesting and quite adventurous ideas; story developed.* Candidate shows a reasonable control and the use of form and style are generally appropriate to purpose. There is an awareness of audience being addressed. There is some range of vocabulary and grammar which is generally accurate, although there may be errors in more complex structures. The spelling of irregular words is generally accurate and punctuation helps to clarify meaning. Full stops are used to separate sentences, but their use is not secure. There is some range of sentence structure. Reader's interest is generally maintained. Paragraphing is fair. Quality of presentation will not impede communication. *Writing may be virtuously simple and correct, or over-reaching, making errors in attempting vivid writing.*

Paper 3 — Section A

Question 1

BAND	DESCRIPTOR
A	Candidates will sustain a perceptive, convincing response, demonstrating clear, analytical understanding of the way in which Shakespeare draws the character of the Nurse throughout the extract. They will respond sensitively and in detail to the way language works to create this portrayal, making well-selected references to the text.
C	Candidates will begin to develop a personal and critical response to the way Shakespeare draws the character of the Nurse throughout the extract, supported from the text. They will make some response to the way language works to create this portrayal.
E	Candidates will make some relevant comment about the way in which Shakespeare draws the character of the Nurse throughout the extract, with a little support from the text/reference to language.

Question 2

BAND	DESCRIPTOR
A	•exploratory response to terms of the question •insight into writer's methods, purposes and characteristics •developed exploration of context/meaning/response •insight into structure and significance of patterns of detail •evaluative Answers are likely to include: •exploration of presentation of Crooks in passage and novel, eg his attitudes and position in society •measured/developed response to details of passage relevant to Crooks here and/or elsewhere, eg details relevant to loneliness/isolation of Crooks •measured/analytical comment on/response presentation of Crooks and/or his importance in novel, eg to the ways Crooks is described, or his language, and/or the significance of his colour •evaluative comment on writer's presentation of Crooks and/or his importance in novel, eg how the details of his language and situation reflects situations of other characters in the novel
C	•structured response to the question •sustained relevant knowledge •appropriate comment on meaning/style •understanding of how effects are achieved •effective use of details to support answer •sustained response to situations or ideas Answers are likely to include: •focus on presentation of Crooks in passage and novel, eg his appearance and attitude •explained/sustained response to details of passage relevant to Crooks here and/or elsewhere, eg details relevant to loneliness/isolation of Crooks •identification/explanation of writer's presentation of Crooks and/or his importance in novel, eg the ways Crooks is described, or his language, or how his situation reflects other characters' situations
E	•support points made •generalisation(s) about text/subject matter •some comment on specific details •some awareness of a writer at work •supported response to characters/situations/ideas Answers are likely to include: •selection of appropriate material about Crooks, eg details of passage •simple comment(s) on details of passage relevant of Crooks here and/or elsewhere, eg his disability and/or attitude to Lennie or other people •Some awareness of writer's presentation of Crooks and/or his importance in novel, eg the way Crooks is described, or his language, and/or the significance of his colour

Question 3

BAND	DESCRIPTOR
A	Candidates will show clear, sustained understanding of the way in which both deaths are presented with some flair, showing imagination and originality, sophistication and confidence. The text will be treated in considerable detail.
C	Candidates will show clear, sustained understanding of the way in which both deaths are presented. They will make careful and relevant reference to the text and respond with some thoroughness and detail to the way language works.
E	Candidates will begin to develop a response to both deaths supported by some detail from the text.

Question 4

BAND	DESCRIPTOR
A	Candidates will use a comprehensive understanding of the text to write with great assurance in Jack's voice, revealing, to a high level, their understanding of the character's thoughts, opinions and feelings.
C	Candidates will have a good knowledge and understanding of Jack and will be able to use this to produce writing expressed in a way that is fitting and authentic. Jack will be clearly recognisable through the voice assumed.
E	Candidates will show a basic understanding of what Jack has done and what he thinks after the argument. These ideas will show evidence of being expressed in an appropriate way.

Question 5

BAND	DESCRIPTOR
A	Candidates will show clear, sustained understanding of the various aspects of the relationship with some flair, showing imagination and originality, sophistication and confidence. The text will be treated in considerable detail.
C	Candidates will show clear, sustained understanding of the various aspects of the relationship supported by careful and relevant reference to the text.
E	Candidates will show understanding of the relationship between George and Lennie supported by some detail from the text.

Question 6

BAND	DESCRIPTOR
A	Candidates will use a comprehensive understanding of the text to write with great assurance in Curley's voice, revealing, to a high level, their understanding of the character's thoughts, opinions and feelings.
C	Candidates will have a good knowledge and understanding of Curley and be able to use this to produce writing expressed in a way that is fitting and authentic. Curley will be clearly recognisable through the voice assumed.
E	Candidates will show a basic understanding of what Curley does and thinks on this occasion. These ideas will show evidence of being expressed in an appropriate way.

Question 7

BAND	DESCRIPTOR
A	*Sustained and developed use of text* *Reflection on content/plot/character/motive/setting* Shows how Scout learns the importance of developing an open and unprejudiced mind through the influence and example of Atticus and how he allows her the space to be her boyish self and discover the value of placing herself in the other person's position. Precise comments on Atticus' role as a father with his standards of courtesy, honesty and good manners as well as his strong opinions and moral values and the kind of virtuous figure he represents to his children and in the community.
C	*More focused account, awareness shown of content/plot/character/motive/setting* Specific detail/incidents which reveal Atticus' qualities as a father and as a figure in the community who is prepared to stand up for justice and equality. And/or the growing maturity of Scout as she gradually realises the value of Atticus' strong beliefs in situations where people are prepared to ignore what is wrong.
E	*Predominantly narrative account, some developed comment on content/plot/character/motive/setting* Begins to use text to develop ideas. Comments on the relationship between Scout and Atticus with reference to Atticus's qualities. Makes some reference to Scout's development within the narrative and any of the various incidents that influence her to see Atticus as a man to admire.

Question 8

BAND	DESCRIPTOR
A	*Sustained and developed use of text* *Reflection on content/plot/character/motive/setting* Shows how it is possible to argue for the importance of the alternative themes in considerable detail, using appropriate and relevant, well selected examples to illustrate points of understanding. May refer (for example) to how the symbol of the mockingbird links themes like childhood and justice. Precise comments on how these themes are reflected in the behaviour and personality of the characters.
C	*More focused account, awareness shown of content/plot/character/motive/setting* Specific detail/incident(s) which illustrate understanding of any two alternative themes and offers some explanation as to why these themes are important. And/or indicates how these themes are represented through the narrative in the lives of the characters or in the events and situations of the plot.
E	*Predominantly narrative account, some developed comment on content/plot/character/motive/setting* Comments on any of the other themes such as courage, the family, justice or aspects of social history of Alabama in the mid 30s. Answer may focus on themes through character or offer a more general discussion of the themes. Makes some reference to why the selected themes are important.

Question 9

BAND	DESCRIPTOR
A	Candidates will explore the novel with sophistication, guided by Major's statement, and using the text in considerable detail to support their final judgement.
C	Candidates will show clear, sustained understanding of why man and pig are enemies to the 'lower animals' using the text carefully and relevantly in support.
E	Candidates will show some understanding of why man and pig are enemies of the 'lower animals', with some detail from the text to support this.

Question 10

BAND	DESCRIPTOR
A	Candidates will draw on a comprehensive understanding of the text to this point to write with great assurance in Snowball's voice, revealing a sophisticated understanding of his character.
C	Candidates will show clear, sustained understanding of Snowball at this point, expressing his reflections authentically and in a voice recognisable as Snowball's.
E	Candidates will show a basic understanding of what Snowball thinks at this point. These thoughts will show signs of being expressed in an appropriate way.

170

Question 11

BAND	DESCRIPTOR
A	•exploratory response to terms of the question •insight into writer's methods, purposes and characteristics •developed exploration of context/meaning/response •insight into structure and significance of patterns of detail •evaluative Answers are likely to include: •exploration of change, eg of how the episodes show a difference, or show him to be the same •measured/developed response to details of episodes relevant to change •measured/analytical comment on/response to writer's presentation of change, eg to what his words and actions show about him/his change •evaluative comment on change and/or presentation of change, eg the degree of change, and/or how Holden's language changes or stays the same in the 3 episodes, looking closely at the details of the episodes and drawing generalisations about Holden's presentation
C	•structured response to the question •sustained relevant knowledge •appropriate comment on meaning/style •understanding of how effects are achieved •effective use of details to support answer •sustained response to situations or ideas Answers are likely to include: •focus on change, eg on how the episodes show a difference, or show him to be the same •explained/sustained response to details of episodes relevant to change, eg to what his words and actions show about him/his change eg examining vocabulary, sentence structure, tone of voice •identification/explanation of writer's methods in presenting change, eg how Holden's language changes or stays the same in the 3 episodes eg characteristic phrases, significant utterances
E	•support points made •generalisation(s) about text/subject matter •some comment on specific details •some awareness of a writer at work •supported response to characters/situations/ideas Answers are likely to include: •selection of appropriate material about what Holden says and does, eg details of his words and actions from the 3 episodes •simple comment(s) on details of episodes relevant to change, eg on what his words and actions show about him/his change •some awareness of writer's methods in showing change, eg differences in Holden's language, or similarities, in the 3 episodes

Question 12

BAND	DESCRIPTOR
A	•exploratory response to terms of the question •insight into writer's methods, purposes and characteristics •developed exploration of context/meaning/response •insight into structure and significance of patterns of detail •evaluative Answers are likely to include: •exploration of teenage problems eg of a range of Holden's worries and difficulties, and how they are presented •measured/developed response to details of teenage problems, eg to details of Holden's relationships with people of different ages •measured/analytical comment on/response to the uses of language and/or structure in conveying Holden's mental state •evaluative comment on teenage problems and presentation,eg on the seriousness of the effects of the problems, and on the effectiveness of the presentation
C	•structured response to the question •sustained relevant knowledge •appropriate comment on meaning/style •understanding of how effects are achieved •effective use of details to support answer •sustained response to situations or ideas Answers are likely to include: •focus on teenage problems and presentation, eg on a range of Holden's worries and difficulties, and how they are presented •explained/sustained response to details of teenage problems, eg to details of Holden's thoughts and actions about girls and/or teachers •identification/explanation of writer's methods in presenting teenage problems, eg by the uses of language and/or structure in conveying Holden's troubles
E	•support points made •generalisation(s) about text/subject matter •some comment on specific details •some awareness of a writer at work •supported response to characters/situations/ideas •some comments on difference Answers are likely to include: •selection of appropriate material about teenage problems, eg details of Holden's worries and difficulties •simple comment(s) on details of teenage problems, eg about the pressure from his peers •some awareness of writer's methods in presenting teenage problems, eg by showing a range of different peers and girls

Question 13

BAND	DESCRIPTOR
A	•exploratory response to terms of the question •insight into writer's methods, purposes and characteristics •developed exploration of context/meaning/response •insight into structure and significance of patterns of detail •evaluative Answers are likely to include: •exploration of writer's presentation of character, speech and behaviour •measured/developed response to details of relationships •measured/analytical comment on/response to writer's presentation of Kingshaw and Hooper •evaluative comment on writer's purposes in presenting Kingshaw and Hooper
C	•structured response to the question •sustained relevant knowledge •appropriate comment on meaning/style •understanding of how effects are achieved •effective use of details to support answer •sustained response to situations or ideas Answers are likely to include: •focus on presentation of Kingshaw and Hooper •explained/sustained response to details of relationships •identification/explanation of writer's methods of presentation and writer's purpose
E	•support points made •generalisation(s) about text/subject matter •some comment on specific details •some awareness of a writer at work •supported response to characters/situations/ideas Answers are likely to include: •selection of appropriate material about Hooper and Kingshaw •simple comment(s) on details about their actions, thoughts and feelings •some awareness of writer's methods of presenting Hooper and Kingshaw

Question 14

BAND	DESCRIPTOR
A	•exploratory response to terms of the question •insight into writer's methods, purposes and characteristics •developed exploration of context/meaning/response •insight into structure and significance of patterns of detail •evaluative Answers are likely to include: •exploration of reasons for blame/degree of blame •measured/developed response to details of events •measured/analytical comment on/response to how the writer presents characters/situation •evaluative comment on who the writer wants the reader to blame most
C	•structured response to the question •sustained relevant knowledge •appropriate comment on meaning/style •understanding of how effects are achieved •effective use of details to support answer •sustained response to situations or ideas Answers are likely to include: •focus on who is to blame for Kingshaw's death •explained/sustained response to details of actions/events leading to Kingshaw's death •identification/explanation of writer's methods of presenting characters/suggesting blame
E	•support points made •generalisation(s) about text/subject matter •some comment on specific details •some awareness of a writer at work •supported response to characters/situations/ideas Answers are likely to include: •selection of appropriate material relevant to blame for death •simple comment(s) on details of events leading to Kingshaw's death •some awareness of writer's presentation of characters and writer's manipulation of readers' response

Question 15

BAND	DESCRIPTOR
A	•exploratory response to terms of the question •insight into writer's methods, purposes and characteristics •developed exploration of context/meaning/response •insight into structure and significance of patterns of detail •evaluative Answers are likely to include: •exploration of Billy's difficulties and achievement •measured/developed response to details of difficult situations and ways that Billy overcomes difficulties •measured/analytical comment on/response to how the author conveys ideas •evaluative comment on what the novel has to say about "achieving something in life".
C	•structured response to the question •sustained relevant knowledge •appropriate comment on meaning/style •understanding of how effects are achieved •effective use of details to support answer •sustained response to situations or ideas Answers are likely to include: •focus on Billy's difficulties and achievement •explained/sustained response to details of Billy's difficulties and achievement •identification/explanation of writer's ideas and purposes in presenting Billy's difficulties and achievement
E	•support points made •generalisation(s) about text/subject matter •some comment on specific details •some awareness of a writer at work •supported response to characters/situations/ideas Answers are likely to include: •selection of appropriate material relevant to Billy's difficulties and achievements •simple comment(s) on details of Billy's difficulties and achievements •some awareness of writer's ideas, purposes and/or presentation of achievements

Question 16

BAND	DESCRIPTOR
A	•exploratory response to terms of the question •insight into writer's methods, purposes and characteristics •developed exploration of context/meaning/response •insight into structure and significance of patterns of detail •evaluative Answers are likely to include: •exploration of ways in which Kes is important to Billy •measured/developed response to details of Billy's relationship with Kes •measured/analytical comment on/response to how the writer shows the importance of Kes to Billy •evaluative comment on writer's methods
C	•structured response to the question •sustained relevant knowledge •appropriate comment on meaning/style •understanding of how effects are achieved •effective use of details to support answer •sustained response to situations or ideas Answers are likely to include: •focus on the importance of Kes to Billy •explained/sustained response to details of Billy's relationship with Kes •identification/explanation of writer's methods of showing the importance of Kes to Billy
E	•support points made •generalisation(s) about text/subject matter •some comment on specific details •some awareness of a writer at work •supported response to characters/situations/ideas Answers are likely to include: •selection of appropriate material about Kes •simple comment(s) on details about Kes and Billy •some awareness of writer's methods and purposes in showing Billy's relationship with Kes

Question 17

BAND	DESCRIPTOR
A	•exploratory response to terms of the question •insight into writer's methods, purposes and characteristics •developed exploration of context/meaning/response •insight into structure and significance of patterns of detail •evaluative Answers are likely to include: •exploration of nature of heroism, eg how both Francis and Larry are heroes, but not heroes at all •measured/developed response to details of heroic actions and characters, eg to actions in war and actions at home •measured/analytical comment on/response to writer's methods and purposes in presenting heroism, eg to how the writer manipulates the reader's response by the use of structure •evaluative comment on nature of heroism and/or presentation, eg on degrees of heroism and how these are presented through language
C	•structured response to the question •sustained relevant knowledge •appropriate comment on meaning/style •understanding of how effects are achieved •effective use of details to support answer •sustained response to situations or ideas Answers are likely to include: •focus on nature of heroism and presentation, eg on how Francis is a hero and not a hero, and how this is gradually revealed •explained/sustained response to details of heroic actions and characters,eg to details about Larry's actions at different points in the novel •identification/explanation of writer's methods and purposes in presenting heroism, eg the ways he uses language and structure to gradually reveal the nature of the heroism of the central characters
E	•support points made •generalisation(s) about text/subject matter •some comment on specific details •some awareness of a writer at work •supported response to characters/situations/ideas Answers are likely to include: •selection of appropriate material about heroic actions and characters, eg details of the war episodes involving Francis •simple comment(s) on details of heroic actions and characters, eg on details of Francis playing table tennis •some awareness of writer's methods and purposes in presenting heroism, eg how nasty things are revealed about Larry to make the reader think about heroism

Question 18

BAND	DESCRIPTOR
A	• exploratory response to terms of the question • insight into writer's methods, purposes and characteristics • developed exploration of context/meaning/response • insight into structure and significance of patterns of detail • evaluative Answers are likely to include: • exploration of use of structure to shape reader's response, eg to the relationship between Francis and Larry • measured/developed response to details relevant to revelation of story and/or time changes, eg to details about the various injuries and deaths • measured/analytical comment on/response to writer's use of structure to shape reader's response, eg on how it makes the reader feel different about Larry at different points • evaluative comment on details relevant to revelation of story and/or time changes, and writer's use of structure to shape reader's response, eg on their importance in shaping the reader's final response to the novel
C	• structured response to the question • sustained relevant knowledge • appropriate comment on meaning/style • understanding of how effects are achieved • effective use of details to support answer • sustained response to situations or ideas Answers are likely to include: • focus on use of structure to shape reader's response, eg how the various revelations about war affect the reader • explained/sustained response to details relevant to revelation of story and/or time changes, eg to details about Larry's character, or how episodes are withheld • identification/explanation of writer's use of structure to shape reader's response, eg of the pattern of war/past/present, and how the writer uses this to make the reader respond to each phase, eg to the growing relationship between Francis and Nicole
E	• support points made • generalisation(s) about text/subject matter • some comment on specific details • some awareness of a writer at work • supported response to characters/situations/ideas Answers are likely to include: • selection of appropriate material about story relevant to structure, eg details from the war and details from the past at home • simple comment(s) on details relevant to revelation of story and/or time changes, eg how some information, eg Larry and Nicole, is held back • some awareness of writer's use of structure to shape reader's response, eg the way he interests the reader by revealing Francis's intention to kill Larry

Question 19

BAND	DESCRIPTOR
A	Candidates will show clear, sustained understanding of Mary Warren and of Miller's use of her to contribute to the impact of the play with some flair, showing imagination and originality, sophistication and confidence. They will show a strong awareness of Miller at work by examining the text in considerable detail and depth.
C	Candidates will show clear, sustained understanding of Mary Warren and of Miller's use of her to contribute to the impact of the play, with careful and relevant use of the text for support.
E	Candidates will begin to develop a response to Mary Warren, showing understanding of her contribution to the impact of the play, with some detail from the text.

Question 20

BAND	DESCRIPTOR
A	Candidates will use a comprehensive understanding of the text to write with great assurance in the voice of John Proctor, revealing, to a high level, their understanding of his thoughts, opinions and feelings.
C	Candidates will have a good knowledge and understanding of John Proctor and be able to use this to produce writing expressed in a way that is fitting and authentic. The character will be clearly recognisable through the voice assumed.
E	Candidates will show a basic understanding of what John Proctor does and thinks. These ideas will show some evidence of being expressed in an appropriate way.

Question 21

BAND	DESCRIPTOR
A	*Sustained and developed use of text* *Reflection on content/plot/character/motive/setting* Shows how despite his determination to be free, Winston is tricked by the state which lets him pursue his fantasy for just long enough to allow the state to deal with him in the most severe way and bring him back into line. Precise comments on Winston as a man with thought and courage enough to question the authority which so ruthlessly wipes out anyone who is out of step with what the state decrees.
C	*More focused account, awareness shown of content/plot/character/motive/setting* Specific detail/incident(s) which illustrates how Winston comes to understand the extent to which the Party manipulates the country and dictates policies – comments on the methods employed such as the encouragement to spy and betrayal of others as well as the complete manipulation of the truth and how the society is fed their thoughts in order to keep them subdued so that 'history' goes unchallenged, all of which is increasingly despised by Winston.
E	*Predominantly narrative account, some developed comment on content/plot/character/motive/setting* Comments generally on how Winston feels about conformity, the Party, Newspeak and the general way in which all individuality is obliterated – shows understanding of how individual thought and the freedom to think for oneself is what Winston values most. Makes some reference to the way Winston exercises caution and secrecy as he conforms to the patterns of the non-conformists.

Question 22

BAND	DESCRIPTOR
A	*Sustained and developed use of text* *Reflection on content/plot/character/motive/setting* Shows how the very language of 1984 is another method of state control from which it seems impossible to escape – comments on the way the basic human right of thought is denied and that values are twisted, such as making sure pride can be taken in a child who betrays her own father. Precise comments on the role of (for example) Newspeak to prevent alternative interpretations of the truth.
C	*More focused account, awareness shown of content/plot/character/motive/setting* Specific detail/incident(s) which help illustrate that in truth there are really no exceptions to those the state has under its control and that Winston and Julia's activites (for example) just provide the state with another opportunity to manipulate and bring the individual back in line. And/or indicates how the state manages to take over the very thought processes of every individual, directing the way people act and think.
E	*Predominantly narrative account, some developed comment on content/plot/character/motive/setting* Comments generally on the way characters in the novel cannot see a world with freedom because they have been brainwashed into accepting what the state provides for them. Makes some reference to examples of how the state controls the minds of individuals by the telecasts of Big Brother and the way in which hate is engendered against whoever the state decrees.

Question 23

BAND	DESCRIPTOR
A	Candidates will show clear, sustained understanding of the differences and how they are developed with some flair, and show imagination, originality, sophistication, confidence. They will treat the text in considerable detail.
C	Candidates will show clear, sustained understanding of the differences and how they are developed and make careful and relevant reference to the text.
E	Candidates will begin to develop a response to the differences and show understanding of how they are developed with some detail from the text.

Question 24

BAND	DESCRIPTOR
A	Candidates will use a comprehensive understanding of the text to write with great assurance in the voice of the two ladies, revealing, to a high level, their understanding of Mrs Bennet and Mrs Philips' thoughts, opinions and feelings.
C	Candidates will have a good knowledge and understanding of the two ladies and be able to use this to produce writing expressed in a way that is fitting and authentic. Mrs Bennet and Mrs Philips will be clearly recognisable through the voice assumed.
E	Candidates will show a basic understanding of what the two ladies do and think. These ideas will show some evidence of being expressed in an appropriate way.

Question 25

BAND	DESCRIPTOR
A	Candidates will handle the subject with sophistication, supporting their response to the characters with considerable textual detail.
C	Candidates will show clear, sustained understanding of why the opinions and traditions are important, making careful and relevant reference to the text in support.
E	Candidates will show some understanding of how Hardy uses the ordinary people, using some detail from the text in support.

Question 26

BAND	DESCRIPTOR
A	Candidates will use a full understanding of the novel to write with great assurance in Farfrae's voice, revealing their total understanding of his thoughts, opinions and feelings.
C	Candidates will have a good knowledge and understanding of Farfrae at this point and use this to reveal a fitting response. Farfrae will be clearly recognisable through the voice assumed.
E	Candidates will provide a basic understanding of what Farfrae thinks and feels about Lucetta's death. There will be some evidence of this being expressed in a way appropriate to Farfrae.

Question 27

BAND	DESCRIPTOR
A	Candidates will sustain a perceptive, convincing response to the portrayal of Ben and demonstrate a clear, analytical understanding of what this adds to the dramatic impact of the play, with well–selected references to the text.
C	Candidates will make a reasonably sustained response to the portrayal of Ben and show understanding of what this adds to the dramatic impact of the play, with some thoroughness in the use of detail from the text for support.
E	Candidates will make some relevant comment about Ben, and will show some understanding of what he adds to the dramatic impact of the play, with a little support from the text.

Question 28

BAND	DESCRIPTOR
A	Candidates will sustain a convincing, perceptive impression of Bernard's character, thoughts, feelings and 'voice' at this point in the play, based on a full, assured understanding of the text.
C	Candidates will have a sound working knowledge of Bernard's character and situation and will use many features of expression and thought which are suitable to him on this occasion.
E	Candidates will show some understanding of Bernard's character and situation at this point in the play through references made to the text. There will be some mention of feelings and ideas.

Question 29

BAND	DESCRIPTOR
A	Candidates will show clear, sustained understanding of the ways in which the English class structure is presented in the play, with some flair, showing imagination and originality, sophistication and confidence. They will treat the text in considerable detail.
C	Candidates will show clear, sustained understanding of the ways in which the English class structure is presented in the play. They will make careful and relevant reference to the text and respond with some thoroughness and detail to the way language works.
E	Candidates will show understanding of the way in which aspects of the English class structure are presented in the play, with some detail from the text.

Question 30

BAND	DESCRIPTOR
A	Candidates will show clear, sustained understanding of the ways in which their chosen characters are presented, supported by careful and relevant reference to the text, with some flair, showing imagination and originality, sophistication and confidence. The text will be treated in considerable detail.
C	Candidates will show clear, sustained understanding of the ways in which their chosen characters are presented, supported by careful and relevant reference to the text. They will respond with some thoroughness and detail to the way language works.
E	Candidates will begin to develop a response to their chosen characters, showing some understanding of the way in which they are presented, with some detail from the text.

THE ANSWERS

Question 31

BAND	DESCRIPTOR
A	*Sustained and developed use of text* *Reflection on content/plot/character/motive/setting* Shows how Birling's character is revealed and comments on his attitude towards others; his belief that wealth creates social position and that he can treat others as he pleases. How the use of language helps us to appreciate his attitudes towards others and life in general by the way he speaks to them.
C	*More focused account, awareness shown of content/plot/character/motive/setting* Specific detail about his behaviour; the way in which he treats people; his belief that wealth is all–important and creates his position in society. And/or indicates how his actions and the way he talks to others tells us a lot about him and what he believes e.g. that he is above the law or that poor people can be treated with disdain.
E	*Predominantly narrative account, some developed comment on content/plot/character/motive/setting* Comments on the way he behaves and what he says and how his upbringing has made him what he is. Makes some reference to him being a self made man, his position in society and where he thinks he's heading.

Question 32

BAND	DESCRIPTOR
A	*Sustained and developed use of text* *Reflection on content/plot/character/motive/setting* A full understanding of how the device, non–appearance, is used in the dramatic structure. For example, might explore with appropriate textual reference, the final scene of the play, when the Birlings and Gerald question her identity or existence.
C	*More focused account, awareness shown of content/plot/character/motive/setting* Uses specific detail chosen appropriately in order to discuss, for example, the concept of universality and the non–appearance of Eva Smith/Daisy Renton. May address "themes" and how the device aids the presentation of these.
E	*Predominantly narrative account, some developed comment on content/plot/character/motive/setting* Begins to use text to develop ideas, for example, comments on how the various members of the Birling household, and Gerald, relate to Eva/Daisy, and how the Inspector reveals these connections as the play progresses. Makes some reference to her non-appearance /Inspector's investigative method.

Question 33

BAND	DESCRIPTOR
A	*Sustained and developed use of text* *Reflection on content/plot/character/motive/setting* Shows how Eddie puts himself into a situation from which there is no real escape; he has antagonised all those around him and has no sympathy from anyone; his obsession for Catherine does not allow him to let anyone else have her. How the use of language reveals his desperate feelings and situation which can only be resolved if he can have Catherine.
C	*More focused account, awareness shown of content/plot/character/motive/setting* Specific details/incidents to show how Eddie was becoming more obsessed with Catherine so that he was beginning to lose all sense of reason and acceptable behaviour. And/or indicates how Eddie's feelings for Catherine affect his attitude towards others especially Rodolpho and Beatrice.
E	*Predominantly narrative account, some developed comment on content/plot/character/motive/setting* Begins to use text to develop ideas. Comments on what Eddie does and how he behaves towards others gradually cutting himself off from them. Makes some reference to his feelings for Catherine and how they are dominating the way he thinks and behaves.

Question 34

BAND	DESCRIPTOR
A	*Sustained and developed use of text* *Reflection on content/plot/character/motive/setting* Shows how the community sorts out its own problems outside the law of the country; how the immigrant situation has forced events onto Eddie which he cannot deal with. How the use of language demonstrates the feelings of the community and how the community should be one and not betray its members.
C	*More focused account, awareness shown of content/plot/character/motive/setting* Specific details/incidents to show how their community lives and some of its difficulties in mixing in a new country and trying to adopt different ideas. And/or indicates that the community does have its own laws and its own way of dealing with situations.
E	*Predominantly narrative account, some developed comment on content/plot/character/motive/setting* Comments on the Italian community and what they do and how they are a close knit but temperamental group. Makes some reference to the ways in which they support each other as a group of foreigners in another country.

Paper 3 — Section B

Question 35

BAND	DESCRIPTOR
A	•exploratory response to terms of the question •insight into poets' methods, purposes and characteristics •developed exploration of context/meaning/response •insight into structure and significance of patterns of detail •evaluative comparison and contrast **Answers are likely to include:** •exploration of response to time in the poems •measured/developed response to the importance of time in the poems and how it is conveyed •measured/analytical comment on/response to poets' methods/purposes in conveying time •evaluative comparison/contrast of the importance of time in the poems and how this is conveyed
C	•structured response to the question •sustained relevant knowledge •appropriate comment on meaning/style •understanding of how effects are achieved •effective use of details to support answer •sustained response to situations or ideas •sustained focus on similarity/difference **Answers are likely to include:** •focus on time in the poems •explained/sustained response to details of the importance of time in the poems •identification/explanation of poets' methods/purposes in conveying time. •structured/sustained comparison/contrast of the importance of time in the poems and how time is conveyed.
E	•support points made •generalisation(s) about text/subject matter •some comment on specific details •some awareness of poets at work •supported response to characters/situations/ideas •some comments on similarity/difference **Answers are likely to include:** •selection of appropriate material about time •simple comment(s) on details about time and/or importance •some awareness of poets' presentation of time •some linkage between time and/or importance and/or presentation

Question 36

BAND	DESCRIPTOR
A	•exploratory response to terms of the question •insight into poets' methods, purposes and characteristics •developed exploration of context/meaning/response •analysis of poets' use of language and effect(s) on readers •insight into structure and significance of patterns of detail •evaluative comparison and contrast Answers are likely to include: •exploration of nature of conflict between people in close relationships •measured/developed response to details of experience/situation/feelings/attitudes/revealing conflict •measured/analytical comment on/response to poets' use of language, form, structure •evaluative comparison/contrast of poets' purposes and methods
C	•structured response to the question •sustained relevant knowledge •appropriate comment on meaning/style •understanding of how effects are achieved •effective use of details to support answer •sustained response to situations or ideas •feature(s) of language interest explained •sustained focus on similarity/difference Answers are likely to include: •focus on conflicts in close relationships •explained/sustained response to details of experience/situation/feelings/attitudes •identification/explanation of how poets explore conflicts in relationships •structured/sustained comparison/contrast of conflicts/relationships/methods used to present them.
E	•support points made •generalisation(s) about text/subject matter •some comment on specific details •some awareness of poets at work •supported response to characters/situations/ideas •selection of quotation(s) to illustrate language interest •some comments on similarity/difference Answers are likely to include: •selection of appropriate material about experiences and situations •simple comment(s) on details of experiences and situations and/or feelings and attitudes •some awareness of poets' presentation of conflicts •some linkage between experiences and/or situations and/or feelings and/or attitudes and/or presentation and/or conflict

Question 37

BAND	DESCRIPTOR
A	• exploratory response to terms of the question • insight into poets' methods, purposes and characteristics • developed exploration of context/meaning/response • analysis of poets' use of language and effect(s) on readers • insight into structure and significance of patterns of detail • evaluative comparison and contrast Answers are likely to include: • exploration of response to statement(s) about poetry • measured/developed response to poems and reasons for agreement with one or both statements/disagreement with one • measured/analytical comment on/response to poets' methods and purposes • evaluative comparison/contrast of ideas about poetry, poems and response to them
C	• structured response to the question • sustained relevant knowledge • appropriate comment on meaning/style • understanding of how effects are achieved • effective use of details to support answer • sustained response to situations or ideas • feature(s) of language interest explained • sustained focus on similarity/difference Answers are likely to include: • focus on statement(s) about poetry • explained/sustained response to details of poems and reasons for agreement with one or both statements/disagreement with one • identification/explanation of poets' methods/purposes • structured/sustained comparison/contrast of ideas about poetry, poems and response to them
E	• support points made • generalisation(s) about text/subject matter • some comment on specific details • some awareness of poets at work • supported response to characters/situations/ideas • selection of quotation(s) to illustrate language interest • some comments on similarity/difference Answers are likely to include: • selection of appropriate material from chosen poems • simple comment(s) on details from poems relevant to quality or purpose(s) • some awareness of poets' methods and/or purpose(s) • some linkage between chosen poems in terms of qualities and/or purpose(s)

Question 38

BAND	DESCRIPTOR
A	•exploratory response to terms of the question •insight into poets' methods, purposes and characteristics •developed exploration of context/meaning/response •analysis of poets' use of language and effect(s) on readers •insight into structure and significance of patterns of detail •evaluative comparison and contrast Answers are likely to include: •exploration of events and experiences •measured/developed response to events/experiences and the extent to which children are affected by them •measured/analytical comment on/response to how language is used to convey events/experiences and effects •evaluative comparison/contrast of how children are affected and/or the extent to which they are affected/how language is used to convey events/experiences/effects
C	•structured response to the question •sustained relevant knowledge •appropriate comment on meaning/style •understanding of how effects are achieved •effective use of details to support answer •sustained response to situations or ideas •feature(s) of language interest explained •sustained focus on similarity/difference Answers are likely to include: •focus on events and experiences •explained/sustained response to details of events/experiences and effects •identification/explanation of how language conveys events/experiences and their effects •structured/sustained comparison/contrast of how language conveys events/experiences/effects
E	•support points made •generalisation(s) about text/subject matter •some comment on specific details •some awareness of poets at work •supported response to characters/situations/ideas •selection of quotation(s) to illustrate language interest •some comments on similarity/difference Answers are likely to include: •selection of appropriate material about events •simple comment(s) on details of events •some awareness of poets' methods in presenting events/experiences and/or effects •some linkage between events/experiences and/or effects and/or how written

Question 39

BAND	DESCRIPTOR
A	•exploratory response to terms of the question •insight into poets' methods, purposes and characteristics •developed exploration of context/meaning/response •insight into structure and significance of patterns of detail •evaluative comparison and contrast **Answers are likely to include:** •**exploration of** response to poets' presentations of experiences of war •**measured/developed response to** positive/negative experiences and situations, attitudes and feelings •**measured/analytical comment on/response to** poets' methods of presentation and their purposes •**evaluative comparison/contrast of** methods and purposes in presenting positive/negative attitudes to war
C	•structured response to the question •sustained relevant knowledge •appropriate comment on meaning/style •understanding of how effects are achieved •effective use of details to support answer •sustained response to situations or ideas •sustained focus on similarity/difference **Answers are likely to include:** •**focus on** experience of war •**explained/sustained response to details of** positive and negative experiences and situations, attitudes and feelings •**identification/explanation of** poets' methods of presentation and their purposes •**structured/sustained comparison/contrast of** poets' methods and purposes in presenting positive/negative attitudes to war
E	•support points made •generalisation(s) about text/subject matter •some comment on specific details •some awareness of poets at work •supported response to characters/situations/ideas •some comments on similarity or difference **Answers are likely to include:** •**selection of appropriate material** about the experiences of war •**simple comment(s) on details** of experiences •**some awareness of poets'** methods and/or purposes in presenting experiences of war •**some linkage between** experiences and situations/attitudes and feelings/methods and purposes

Question 40

BAND	DESCRIPTOR
A	•exploratory response to terms of the question •insight into poets' methods, purposes and characteristics •developed exploration of context/meaning/response •analysis of poets' use of language and effect(s) on readers •insight into structure and significance of patterns of detail •evaluative comparison and contrast **Answers are likely to include:** •**exploration of** what is unusual or striking about the poems •**measured/developed response to** the ways they are written •**measured/analytical comment on/response to** the poets' uses of form/language/structure •**evaluative comparison/contrast of** the ways the poems are written/what makes them unusual or striking
C	•structured response to the question •sustained relevant knowledge •appropriate comment on meaning/style •understanding of how effects are achieved •effective use of details to support answer •sustained response to situations or ideas •feature(s) of language interest explained •sustained focus on similarity/difference **Answers are likely to include:** •**focus on** what is unusual or striking about the poems •**explained/sustained response to details of** the ways they are written •**identification/explanation of** the poets' uses of form/language/structure •**structured/sustained comparison/contrast of** the ways the poems are written/what is unusual or striking about them
E	•support points made •generalisation(s) about text/subject matter •some comment on specific details •some awareness of poets at work •supported response to characters/situations/ideas •selection of quotation(s) to illustrate language interest •some comments on similarity/difference **Answers are likely to include:** •**selection of appropriate material** about form or language or structure •**simple comment(s) on details** about the way(s) they are written •**some awareness of poets'** uses of form/language/structure •**some linkage between** the ways the poems are written/what is unusual/striking about them

Question 41

BAND	DESCRIPTOR
A	• exploratory response to terms of the question • insight into poets' methods, purposes and characteristics • developed exploration of context/meaning/response • insight into structure and significance of patterns of detail • evaluative comparison and contrast Answers are likely to include: • exploration of what is interesting about the poems and what they have to say • measured/developed response to how understanding and appreciation is affected by the ways the poems are written • measured/analytical comment on/response to interesting aspects of language, or structure, or form • evaluative comparison/contrast of the ways the poems are written and what they have to say
C	• structured response to the question • sustained relevant knowledge • appropriate comment on meaning/style • understanding of how effects are achieved • effective use of details to support answer • sustained response to situations or ideas • sustained focus on similarity/difference Answers are likely to include: • focus on what is interesting about the poems and/or what they have to say • explained/sustained response to details of how understanding and/or appreciation is affected by the way the poems are written • identification/explanation of interesting aspects of language, or structure, or form • structured/sustained comparison/contrast of the ways the poems are written and what they have to say
E	• support points made • generalisation(s) about text/subject matter • some comment on specific details • some awareness of poets at work • supported response to characters/situations/ideas • some comments on similarity or difference Answers are likely to include: • selection of appropriate material from chosen poems relevant to interest • simple comment(s) on details about subject matter or how written • some awareness of poets' methods and/or purposes • some linkage between subject matter or how written

Acknowledgements

CGP would like to thank the following:

Page 94   'My child, the fire risk' *Dea Birkett, Friday April 4, 2003, The Guardian*

Page 96   'How to avoid teen tantrums' *Sarah Tucker, Saturday July 20, 2002, The Guardian*

Page 134   'Of Mice and Men' *John Steinbeck, Penguin 2000.*
                © John Steinbeck, 1937, 1965. Reproduced by permission of Penguin Books Ltd

Every effort has been made to locate copyright holders and obtain permission to reproduce sources.
For those sources where it has been difficult to trace the originator of the work, we would be grateful for information.
If any copyright holder would like us to make an amendment to the acknowledgements, please notify us and we will gladly update the book at the next reprint.

Index

Index

Index

Make sure you're not missing out on another superb
CGP revision book that might just save your life...

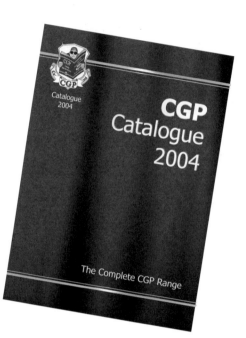

...order your **free** catalogue today.

CGP customer service is second to none

We work very hard to despatch all orders the **same day** we receive them, and our success rate
is currently 99.7%. We send all orders by **overnight courier** or **First Class** post.
If you ring us today you should get your catalogue or book tomorrow. Irresistible, surely?

- Phone: 0870 750 1252   (Mon-Fri, 8.30am to 5.30pm)
- Fax: 0870 750 1292
- e-mail: orders@cgpbooks.co.uk
- Post: CGP, Kirkby in Furness, Cumbria, LA17 7WZ
- Website: www.cgpbooks.co.uk

...or you can ask at any good bookshop.

EHS41